3 STEPS TO INVESTMENT SUCCESS

3 STEPS TO INVESTMENT SUCCESS

HOW TO OBTAIN THE RETURNS, WHILE CONTROLLING RISK

Rory Gillen

Published by OAK TREE PRESS
19 Rutland Street, Cork, Ireland
www.oaktreepress.com

© 2012 ILTB Ltd. (trading as GillenMarkets)

A catalogue record of this book is available from the British Library.

ISBN 978 1 78119 003 6 (Hardback)
ISBN 978 1 78119 004 3 (ePub)
ISBN 978 1 78119 005 0 (Kindle)

DISCLAIMER

Stock market investing carries risk and there is no guarantee that any of the approaches to investing outlined in this book will continue to work in the future. None of the approaches work all the time and there are several instances where individual approaches have lost money in particular periods.

Thus, neither the author nor the publisher assumes liability for any losses that may be sustained by use of the approaches outlined in this book, and any such liability is hereby disclaimed.

ACKNOWLEDGEMENTS

To Frances, for all her patience, and three great children, Darren, Aoife and Clodagh, who will soon be heading out into the real world.

I also must acknowledge contributions from several trusted colleagues, respected investors and successful authors in their own right. In particular, for reviewing early editions of this book and for providing essential feedback that was not only needed but of immense assistance, my thanks to Paul Callan, former Director, Global Equities, Zurich (Ireland), Jim Slater, author of *The Zulu Principle* (among several other investment books), Harry Sheridan, former Finance Director, CRH plc and John Shiel, business consultant. Thanks to Jack Schannep, editor of **thedowtheory.com** website and author of *Dow Theory for the 21st Century*, for the valuable contributions he made to **Chapter 22: Timing the Markets**, without which that particular chapter would carry much less weight.

In planning the book I commissioned a short story (*A Villa in the Sun*, which appears as **Chapter 26**) from Virginia Gilbert, a BAFTA-nominated, award-winning writer and director, in order to illustrate the very real dangers of speculating in markets (as opposed to investing). While having little previous experience of the workings of the financial markets, and after just three short meetings, Virginia has expertly captured the impulses that drive many would-be investors to take short cuts which, rather than improving returns, can lead to unnecessary losses, and sometimes worse.

Last, but by no means least, my thanks to Brian O'Kane of Oak Tree Press who didn't flinch when I had to do a complete revamp on the initial edition of the book.

CONTENTS

SECTION II: A TOUR OF THE ASSET CLASSES

SECTION III: IMPLEMENTING AN INVESTMENT PLAN

APPENDICES

INTRODUCTION

The aim of this book is to demonstrate that becoming a successful do-it-yourself (DIY) investor is within the reach of almost every person in society. The global credit crisis of 2007-2009 left most investors – even professional investors – with deep scars. It also provided would-be investors with reasons to remain on the sidelines. However, if our aim as investors is to increase our understanding, to take control of our own finances and investments, then the 2007-2009 years provided us with an important lesson: that an understanding of risk, and control of risk, is as important as our search for returns.

Stock markets can be a rollercoaster. Downturns bring volatility and uncertainty, which can impact on your confidence, judgement and desire to invest in a certain asset class. Bull markets do the opposite and bring over-confidence, tricking you into overlooking fundamental information. To maintain and grow your assets consistently, you need an approach that controls risk, reduces emotion, can be managed in a busy life and takes account of the significant volatility that is part and parcel of stock market investing.

Regardless of whether you are a novice investor and just getting started, someone who already invests in the stock markets, or someone working in the financial services industry, this book aims to improve your understanding of what is required to make a success of investing.

Saving or investing in the stock markets is for everyone – from parents with the children's allowance, to someone who has a lump sum to invest, to the person who has just started working but can save even €100 a month, to someone who is free to manage their own pension. Building an asset base from which you can earn income gives you choices later in life. My aim is that, when you close this book, you should be able to implement an easy-to-follow approach to investing in the stock markets, whilst minimising risk. No matter what level of experience you are starting from, this book is aimed at assisting you to obtain the returns on offer from the markets over time.

The advent of low-cost, online dealing has substantially lowered the cost of investing in markets. The Internet also has made it easier to access independent investment advice. If you wish to be a DIY investor, to reduce your reliance on product sellers, then the tools are now readily available to you.

APPROACHES TO INVESTING IN THE STOCK MARKET

Arming yourself with a proper strategy or plan, which dictates what you buy and when you sell, is the key to stock market investing, and developing one is a good deal easier than you may think. That plan might be simply to invest across the different asset classes where there appears to be clear value on offer; to concentrate on high yielding funds listed on stock markets as a method of generating income, while controlling risk; or to master some successful approach to stock selection similar to the one I outline in **Chapter 21, Value Investing in the FTSE 100.**

Most private investors underestimate the challenges of identifying suitable individual companies (shares) to buy and when to sell them. This book outlines why this is and offers an easy-to-follow mechanical approach to selecting a diversified portfolio of stocks from the UK FTSE 100 Index, an index that represents the 100 largest companies listed on the London Stock Exchange by market capitalisation.

Whichever approach you choose, you must realise that there is no silver bullet for investment success. You must have a plan, keep your emotions under control and have the discipline to adhere to your plan over time.

Over the years, the question that I have consistently tried to answer is: how can the ordinary private investor succeed with limited time, little understanding of company accounts and no access to management? For that is the true test as to whether stock market investing is for everybody or just the knowledgeable few.

Always bear in mind that it is the companies that produce the returns that the stock markets deliver, not the professional fund managers, not the speculators, not the media or individuals with inside information. It is the companies that generate the returns, and those returns reflect the growth in their profits, cash flows and dividends over time. You simply have to own a diversified list of them, either directly or through funds, to obtain those returns. Many private investors fail to do just that. For a variety of reasons, they get side-tracked.

You will learn also how to invest in the stock market indirectly through listed funds, such as exchange-traded funds and investment companies, which offer instant diversification, allowing you to more easily control risk.

Risk assets might be defined as those assets that do not offer a guarantee of your capital back but which have provided returns well above bank deposits to investors over the long-term. Equities (shares) are a risk asset, and have delivered returns of 9% to 10% *per annum* (before costs) over the past 100 years, or 5% to 6% annually above inflation. In contrast, short-term deposits with the banks have delivered *circa* 1% annually above inflation. Here lies the reason for investing in risk assets: the returns have been higher over the medium-to-long-term. They are not higher every year or indeed in every decade. For example, the 2000s have been miserable for investors in equities in the developed markets. But, as I will point out later in the book, this is because equities in the major developed markets simply were overvalued to start with in the late 1990s. We also will examine how that was relatively easy to see, even if the majority of investors ignored the signals at the time.

There are several factors that mitigate success in the stock markets. Our educational system does not even begin to equip us for what is one of the most important aspects of our lives – the management of our savings and pension monies. In many countries, the financial services industry serves the consumer poorly, often through the promotion of speculation rather than investment or by a focus on selling products as opposed to providing advice. Also, the menace of stock market volatility can all too easily play on our emotions and force errors, when none need be made. For these and other reasons, stock market investing needs to be learned.

We might ask ourselves what has driven progress over time in the developed, and now developing, economies and markets. The answer, of course, is the entrepreneurial spirit that is expressed through business – and the stock market is made up of a collection of publicly quoted businesses, as well as funds and financial instruments of one form or another. People trade with each other, from which businesses develop, and businesses drive the economy forward. Rising profits drive business values upwards over time. This, in turn, lifts incomes in society. Incomes underpin property prices, and higher incomes underpin rising property prices. So, property is secondary to business, for if we have no businesses we have no income to spend, or to invest in property.

It requires confidence in the future of the economy to believe that property and stock market values will rise in the years ahead. In democratic and pro-business economies, this confidence normally has been well-placed. In the past 10, 20, 50, 100 years or longer, developed economies such as the US, the UK, mainland Europe, and now many emerging economies, have made dramatic progress, despite the intermittent downturns. Wars aside, the probability that this will continue to be the case in the future is high. That said, Japan is a modern-day example of where it has simply not paid to invest in either the stock market or property over the past 20 years. Deflation gripped Japan and only non-risk assets, such as cash deposits and short- and long-dated government bonds have rewarded investors in Japan since early 1990.

Everyone can use the stock markets to invest for the future and to build wealth. And in the stock markets, you can start small – very small. You cannot do that when investing in physical property. In the stock markets, you can build an asset brick-by-brick, investing only when you can afford to and without any debt. My experience tells me that the majority of private investors feel that the stock markets are complex, and, consequently, are scared to get involved. This book hopefully will demonstrate to you that what you believe to be a complex subject can, in fact, be quite straightforward once you clear away the fog.

DEBUNKING SOME MYTHS

This book will de-bunk various stock market myths for you. Many private investors think that it is necessary to be an expert in stock market terminology; this is not the case. Some feel the stock markets are only for those with money; they are not. A great advantage of the stock markets is that anyone, with even a couple of hundred euros to invest each month, can build an asset from modest beginnings.

Many believe that the stock markets are just for gamblers. It is certainly true that the stock markets can fulfil the gambling instincts in human nature, but the stock markets are first and foremost an investment forum. As an owner of shares (directly or through funds), you are a part-owner of businesses and, if they prosper, so too should you. In other words, returns accrue naturally to the owners of assets, but not so easily to the traders of assets.

Finally, many are convinced that you have to predict which companies are the best to own, in order to make a success out of stock market investing. Nothing could be further from the truth. It should be a great relief to know that you do not have to predict anything to invest successfully *via* the stock markets.

COMMON INVESTING ERRORS

Many investors fail to plan their finances and to properly and honestly appraise their own risk tolerance. The balance to be achieved between investing in non-risk assets and risk assets is a personal one and must take several variables into account – like the sustainability of your income, the mortgage on your house and whether your pension is adequately provided for, among other issues. Many investors fail to adequately diversify either within an asset class or geographically. The herd instinct in human nature leads many to invest late in a popular asset class. More times than not, by that time the asset class is already overvalued, which leads to disappointing returns thereafter.

Without a proper plan, many end up speculating in markets rather than investing, and there is a world of difference between the two. Also, many investors fail to distinguish between a temporary loss and a permanent one. We will examine all these common investing errors at various stages throughout the book.

3 STEPS TO SUCCESSFUL STOCK MARKET INVESTING

I believe – and have been teaching for several years – that there are only three steps required to make a success out of investing.

The **first step** is to have the patience to let compounding work its magic over time. You cannot compound from zero, so you need to start somewhere and then have some patience. Generating a return of 8% *per annum* will turn a €250 monthly investment programme into €19,008 after five years. After 10 years, your capital will grow to €46,936; after 15 years, it will be worth €87,973; and after 20 years, €148,269.

If you can save a portion of your earnings each month, over time, you will build an asset for yourself with no debt attached. The size of that asset depends on several factors: what you put into it, how long you commit to it and the returns available from the asset class(es) you are investing in. If you can accumulate an asset base from which you can generate an annual income, then you are well on your way to achieving financial freedom.

The **second step** is to adopt a tried and tested approach to investing that has at its core an emphasis on value. For it is the value on offer in the asset you buy that largely determines the subsequent returns over the medium- to long-term.

I started out in the industry thinking that the more time and effort I put in, the better an investor I would be. Ten years later, I realised that a couple of hours a year spent selecting a portfolio of stocks or funds using certain simple but strict financial criteria to ensure value and diversification is more effective than all the hours of labour I used to put in.

In addition, any good approach to stock market investing must reduce the normal emotions of fear, greed and hope that lie within us all. Our emotions and a lack of understanding are the real enemies, but both are easily overcome with greater awareness and having a plan to follow.

The **third, and final, step** is to avoid letting volatility interrupt your savings or investment plan. The stock markets are volatile – sometimes violently so – and definitely more volatile than direct property investing. Investors must acknowledge this and have a plan that protects them from getting knocked off course by stock market volatility. This, in turn, will assist you to avoid turning a temporary loss into a permanent one.

You will come to understand that you have natural advantages over the institutional (professional) investor and that success accrues to the well-prepared investor but rarely to the speculator, who, too often, wants only quick results. The investor owns assets and benefits from the natural appreciation in the value of stock market and property asset values over time. The speculator trades assets in the search for short-term gains. But he is playing a zero sum game, as one trader's gain is another's loss. Many private investors become frustrated and mistrustful of the stock markets, and it is often because they have been speculating rather than investing, without understanding the difference.

There are not many people capable of learning in a vacuum, and nowhere is it more important to educate ourselves than when investing in the stock markets! We are not born with a natural understanding of investing, and it makes sense to take the time to learn, and to practise what we have learned. Few people on their first outing on a golf course hit a good drive down the fairway. Taking a few lessons, and putting what you have learned into practice, is the key to becoming a better golfer. You should have the same attitude to investing.

THE STRUCTURE OF THE BOOK

Section 1 of the book (**Chapters 1 to 8**) highlights the importance of personal financial and investment planning, outlines many of the common investing errors and provides an explanation as to why markets should rise over time. Also, this section highlights the power of compounding and explains how the phrase 'long-term' can vary depending on whether you are investing regularly (the regular investor) or at a point in time (the lump-sum investor). In addition, we will look at why the markets are often volatile, clarify the difference between investing and speculating and examine how stock market investing differs from investing in physical property. Lastly, this section finishes off by looking at the significant hurdles the private investor faces when attempting to select individual stocks.

Section II of the book (**Chapters 9 to 17**) provides a detailed tour of the various asset classes available, and examines the historical returns that each has delivered over time and where the value might lie today.

Section III of the book (**Chapters 18 to 24**) deals with the various ways of gaining exposure to markets, and includes a detailed look at the two fund types listed on the stock markets: exchange-traded funds (ETFs) and investment companies. Then it outlines specific investment strategies in risk assets:

- Investing across the various asset classes;
- Investing for income in funds;
- Value investing and direct stock selection in the UK FTSE 100 Index; and
- Approaches to timing the markets;

and deals with the practical implementation of each particular strategy.

Finally, in what is a break from the norm for an investment book of this type, I commissioned a short story, **A Villa in the Sun (Chapter 26)** from Virginia Gilbert, a BAFTA-nominated, award-winning writer and director, to drive home the often real consequences of speculating in markets rather than investing. Enjoy your reading.

Rory Gillen
Greystones, Co. Wicklow, Ireland
June 2012

SECTION I
SOME FUNDAMENTALS OF INVESTING

CHAPTER 1
PERSONAL FINANCIAL AND INVESTMENT PLANNING

Before you consider investing in markets or, indeed, in physical property you should carry out an analysis of your own financial position and how it might look a few years down the road. The following factors are all relevant:

- The sustainability of your income;
- How much you can save on a monthly or annual basis;
- The size of your mortgage;
- Your monthly and annual mortgage payments;
- Other assets you may have;
- Other debts you may have;
- Your pension arrangements.

The fact is that some jobs are more secure than others and the security of your employment and sustainability of your income is an important part of a decision to invest in risk assets. Clearly, the greater the confidence you have in your income, the lower the probability (and risk) that you will have to change tack and sell your investments due to changes in your employment circumstances.

Many people consider their house to be an asset but that is rarely the reality. With a mortgage attached, your house is actually a liability; even when you have paid off the mortgage, your house cannot be considered a free asset in the sense that you can dispose of it and release funds. Some people do decide to trade down when their children have grown up and have moved out or when they are coming to retirement, but this is not the case for most people.

PAYING DOWN YOUR MORTGAGE MAKES GOOD INVESTMENT SENSE

It makes sense to pay down your mortgage to a sensible level (to say 50% of your house value) before committing yourself to investing in the stock markets. To be carrying any other debt and investing in risk assets should be avoided altogether. As we will see in **Chapters 9** through **17**, equities have delivered annual returns of 9% to 10% (before costs) on average over the long-term. However, this is a pre-tax return.

If you are paying an interest rate of, say, 4% on your mortgage or debt, then by paying down your debt you are saving this 4%. This is equivalent to roughly an 8% pre-tax return (if you are paying tax at 50%) as you are paying down the debt from post-tax income. Hence, by paying down your mortgage early, in effect, you 'earn' a high gross return but without investment risk.

Investing in risk assets is best done with surplus savings and not with debt. Investors in physical property have a difficulty in this regard because an investment in a property is normally a significant one and often has to be partially financed with debt. Property investors still can lower the risk of taking on debt by ensuring that there is a secure and meaningful rental income available from the property.

Your pension arrangements are also a material consideration. It makes sense to ensure that you are contributing to your pension from an early age, as your obtain tax relief on your pension contributions up to specific limits dependent on where you are resident.

Many people will be investing through their company pension, while others have the flexibility to manage their own pensions through self-invested personal pensions (SIPPs) in the UK, 401(k)s in the US and personal retirement savings accounts (PRSAs) or self-administered pensions (SAPs) in Ireland. These pension vehicles also allow you to self-manage your pension monies through a stock broking account, including online, low-cost stockbroking accounts.

RISK ASSETS *VS* NON-RISK ASSETS

As we will see in **Chapter 9, Investment Choices and Returns,** risk assets, such as equities and property, have delivered the best returns over the long-term but that does not mean you should automatically commit all of your surplus savings to them. There is no one right choice as each of us is different and has different needs, desires and pressures to cope with. For one person, it might be entirely appropriate to have all their assets in risk assets; for another, this might be entirely inappropriate. Aside from financial issues, there are other factors that may influence your decision, ranging from your age, your temperament and your risk appetite to your understanding of investing.

Any likely commitment to risk assets also will be influenced significantly by whether you are:

♦ A lump-sum investor and not in a position to add further monies to your investment programme over time; or

♦ A regular investor and in a position to add monies to your investment programme over time.

The lump-sum investor does not get to take advantage of lower prices and better values should they arise, whereas the regular investor does. Hence, the risks in stock market investing are different for both investor types and we will examine this issue in more detail in **Chapter 5, Defining the Long-term**.

CHAPTER 2
COMMON INVESTING ERRORS

In the **Introduction**, I outlined a number of common mistakes that investors make, and we will now go through some of these errors individually:

♦ Inappropriate use of debt or leverage;

♦ A lack of diversification;

♦ Obtaining poor value;

♦ Speculating rather than investing;

♦ Mistaking a temporary loss for a permanent one; and, finally

♦ A haphazard approach to investing in individual stocks.

INAPPROPRIATE USE OF DEBT

Investing in risk assets should be mostly done with surplus savings. Risk assets, like equities (shares) and property, have delivered returns well in excess of cash deposits over the long-term but they do not come with a guarantee. As I mentioned in the **Introduction,** *investors seek returns but they must also control risk.* Unless you are particularly skilled at understanding value, then adding debt to your investment programme just increases the risk.

Investors in physical property traditionally have borrowed to enhance returns. As we will see in **Chapter 7, Stock Market and Direct Property Investing – Comparisons and Contrasts,** rental income from physical property is generally more stable than corporate earnings. For this reason, the risk of using debt to buy property can be controlled so long as the investor obtains value. But, as we saw in the developed world in the 2000s, most investors failed to understand this, and many were highly borrowed against overvalued property, and thus were exposed to risk they did not understand.

A LACK OF DIVERSIFICATION IN RISK ASSETS

For the majority of investors, it makes sense to diversify. If you are investing in individual companies, then diversifying into a selection of companies in different industries and perhaps even across different geographic regions reduces the specific risk of any individual company underperforming, or perhaps even of it going out of business.

Diversifying across different asset classes offers you the opportunity to obtain returns from asset classes that are not particularly dependent on, or correlated to, the economy or economic cycle. Returns from hedge and absolute return strategies, commodities, precious metals and government bonds often are unrelated to the general direction of the economy, and therefore can generate positive returns when equities and property, which are highly dependent on the performance of the general economy, are performing poorly. In this way, diversifying across different asset classes can reduce risk.

SPECULATING RATHER THAN INVESTING

Warren Buffett, the iconic Chairman of Berkshire Hathaway, made the following comment in his 2005 *Annual Report* to shareholders[1], and which I think neatly captures the difficulties faced by speculators in obtaining the returns on offer in stock markets:

> *Long ago, Sir Isaac Newton gave us three laws of motion, which were the work of genius. But Sir Isaac's talents didn't extend to investing: He lost a bundle in the South Sea Bubble, explaining later, "I can calculate the movement of the stars, but not the madness of men." If he had not been traumatized by this loss, Sir Isaac might well have gone on to discover the Fourth Law of Motion: For investors as a whole, returns decrease as motion increases.*

Buffett is referring to the fact that too much trading activity is likely to lower the returns one can reasonably expect to obtain from the stock markets over time. Constant activity is the hallmark of the speculator, and, while the primary role of stock markets is to match the financing

---

[1]   Buffett, W. (2005). *Warren Buffett's Annual Letter to Shareholders, 2005*, Omaha NE: Berkshire Hathaway.

needs of companies with the investment needs of savers, the markets also fulfil the gambling instincts in human nature.

For many would-be and even long-standing private investors, the distinction between investing and speculating may be foggy but an understanding of the differences is critical to ensuring long-term investment success in the stock markets. The investor and the speculator may occupy the same space, but they go about their business in very different ways.

To be an investor is to be an 'owner of assets'. By owning shares in businesses or properties, you are part-owner in them and should benefit from the returns on offer over time. All investors can make these returns, just as they can, and have done, with physical property.

In contrast, the trader or speculator is looking for gains over shorter time horizons and, therefore, does not have the time to benefit from the underlying asset growth in markets. For this reason, the trader/speculator is playing a 'zero sum game'. His gain must be someone else's loss. In fact, due to transaction costs (dealing costs, stamp duty, etc.), the trader or speculator is playing a negative sum game.

Figure 2.1: Speculating *vs* Investing

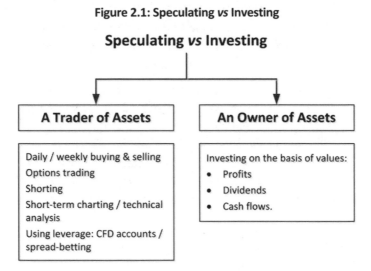

Figure 2.1 makes a distinction between the activities of the speculator and those of the investor. If you find that you have been trading too often, introducing charting, technical analysis and options trading, without having the necessary experience – and few private investors

have – the chances are high that you are engaged in speculative, rather than investment, activity. Most likely you are also getting a speculator's results, perhaps without fully understanding why.

OBTAINING POOR VALUE

In the US stock market, shares have been valued, on average, at 14 times historic earnings over the long-term. At this valuation level, the US stock market on average has delivered returns of 9% to 10% (before investors' transaction costs). If you pay substantially higher multiples of earnings for the US stock market, then you run the risk of much lower returns than the 9% to 10% that historically have been delivered. For example, in the late 1990s, investors were paying over 30 times the historic earnings of the S&P 500 Index. This fact goes a significant way to explaining why returns from the US stock market have been poor since. So value matters and the same argument applies to individual companies, property investing or, indeed, investing in any asset. Yet, investors often suffer from the herd instinct and buy into the most recent popular investment areas without realising that, as a result of this popularity, value is most likely to be absent.

MISTAKING A TEMPORARY LOSS FOR A PERMANENT LOSS

Without a strategy, it is all too easy to sell because markets are declining, the news flow is poor and you lose confidence. But declines in markets are normal and rarely lead to a permanent diminution of value. For example, the US equity market declined by over 50% in the 2007-2009 global credit crisis-driven bear market. During the same downturn, the share price of Coca Cola, one of the strongest companies globally, declined close to 40% from $64 in December 2007 to $39 in early March 2009. Yet, Coca Cola's earnings did not fall, it was never under financial strain and its shares were not overvalued at the start of the crisis (the Coca Cola example is discussed in greater detail in **Chapter 8, The Difficulties of Stock Picking**). The decline in Coca Cola's shares over this period was a temporary decline driven by market conditions and not by any signs of deterioration in Coca Cola's business.

Holders of Coca Cola shares who sold out during the 2007-2009 bear market mistook a temporary decline for a permanent one. In so doing, they converted a temporary loss into a permanent one.

A HAPHAZARD APPROACH TO INVESTING IN INDIVIDUAL STOCKS

Many investors start off in markets by buying a share, but without understanding why they are buying it and without examining what their long-term goals are. Without a plan, you will be prone to range of errors and the following are just a few examples that might resonate with you. The examples relate to buying and selling shares as opposed to funds but the same logic can be applied to fund investing.

Have you bought a share without knowing why?
The explosion of technology stocks in stock markets in the late 1990s saw many investors buying shares in businesses that had existed for only a limited time, about which they knew little and could not value.

Have you bought more of a share that you already owned, simply because it had dropped in price and you wanted to lower your average cost?
Again, this is not a strategy that is likely to work out in the medium-term for the majority of private investors. The danger with this approach is that you end up with a company that simply goes from bad to worse and never recovers. As we now know from the painful banking crash, this can happen. I show in **Table 7.3** in **Chapter 7, Stock Market and Direct Property Investing** that, of the companies that constituted the FT 30 Index in the UK in 1952, only four remain in that index today. While many were simply taken over or merged with other companies, some businesses did fail along the way. More recently, we can point to many banks in the developed world that will never recover fully from the problems they have encountered. Averaging down for the sake of it is not a sensible strategy for stock market investing. Of course, if you can distinguish between a temporary decline in price and the permanent loss of value, you may feel that you can average down in the shares you own. My experience, however, tells me that few private investors are equipped to make that distinction.

Have you bought a share, simply because you heard friends or colleagues talk glowingly about it?
In this instance, you probably had money burning a hole in your pocket and could not wait to get in. During the Internet boom that ended in early 2000, companies like Cisco, Intel, Vodafone and Yahoo! were vastly overvalued and subsequently lost an average of over 90% of their collective value during the 2000-2002 downturn, and not even Vodafone has recovered fully in price over the subsequent 12-year period. Again, reading about the 'flavour of the month' in newspapers and taking tips from others is not a strategy for stock market investing.

In **Chapter 21, Enhancing Returns: Value Investing in the FTSE 100 Index**, I outline a disciplined stock picking strategy for investing in, and most likely out-performing, the UK FTSE 100 Index that is easy-to-follow and implement and overcomes many of the problems investors encounter when faced with the decision as to what shares to buy and when to sell.

This chapter probably is worth re-reading when you have finished the book. Many of the other chapters address these common errors in a variety of ways, and the penny may drop for you following a revisit to this chapter.

CHAPTER 3
WHY MARKETS SHOULD RISE OVER TIME

In the main, the stock markets are made up of businesses, financial products and financial instruments quoted on regulated exchanges. A company can obtain a listing on any stock exchange but, as there are costs associated with each separate listing, only the larger companies tend to have multiple listings. For example, many of the larger UK companies are listed on the London Stock Exchange as well as on the New York Stock Exchange. Outside of companies, there are funds, government bonds and a variety of other financial instruments listed and traded on regulated exchanges across the world.

As the banking system is to savings and loans, so the stock market is to investment. People place their money on deposit (or in current accounts) with the banks, which then lend on those deposits to borrowers. In the stock markets, companies raise capital through initial public offerings (IPOs), aimed principally at institutional investors but often also including private investors, while simultaneously listing on to a stock exchange. The company's shares then are tradable by all investors in what is described as the 'secondary market'. These same companies can raise further monies from investors through rights issues, share placings and other means. Ultimately, institutional and private investors with capital to invest, and companies who need capital, meet in the marketplace (or the stock market).

A stockbroker is someone who is licensed to deal on the stock exchange, and private investors must deal through a stockbroker to buy and sell shares that are listed on the stock exchanges. It is a highly regulated industry. With the advent of the Internet, there are now low cost, execution-only online brokers as well as higher cost, full-service traditional brokers.

The developed stock markets always have made upward progress over time. It is important to understand why the markets have made this progress, in order to have the confidence that they will continue to do so in the future. Having this confidence is crucial to staying with your stock market assets when you encounter difficult economic conditions that will be reflected in weaker stock markets. Quite simply, we must believe that markets will recover after setbacks. If we doubt this, there is not much point in investing in risk assets of any variety, whether quoted on the stock markets or not.

RETURNS FROM RISK ASSETS MUST BE HIGHER THAN BANK DEPOSITS

People have always traded with each other. From trade, businesses develop, which leads to growth in the economy. It is not the other way around: the economy does not grow without businesses. Returns generated by businesses, in aggregate, always should be higher than bank deposit rates. If this was not so, then few, if any, businessmen would invest in their own businesses, because they would be better off leaving their capital sitting idle in the bank. If everyone did this, there would be no investing – only savings – and interest rates would decline to zero.

This is the reason why stock market returns, in the long-term, always should be higher than bank deposit rates. It is a simple law of economics.

Furthermore, in the stock markets, most companies retain a portion of their earnings to fund further growth. This could be to finance new products or services, or an entry into new markets. Overall, it is this reinvestment of earnings that propels the value of individual companies, and, in turn, the stock markets, higher over time.

BUSINESSES FIRST, THEN PROPERTY

This, then, is the simple explanation both as to why the stock markets generate higher returns than bank deposits over time, and why the markets make good upward progress over time. Indeed, it is also the reason why property markets move upwards over time. But it is business first, then property. For if we do not trade with each other, thus creating business (or businesses), then we will have nothing to invest in property. One might say that we build wealth through business and invest wealth in property.

Of course, the underlying assumption an investor makes is that he is dealing with a market where democracy is the order of the day, and where the government is pro-business. Markets in more politically unstable areas of the world have not necessarily delivered returns greater than risk-free cash deposits.

STOCK MARKET INDICES

The progress of the stock markets is tracked through stock market indices. Different indices have been developed to track different markets.

The oldest index in the world is the Dow Jones Industrial Average, otherwise known as the DOW, comprising 30 large US companies by market capitalisation from a broad selection of sectors across the US economy. The DOW Index tracks the average performance of these stocks. Similarly, the S&P 500 Index tracks the performance of the 500 leading companies in the US market.

In the UK, the most widely followed index is the FTSE 100 Index, which tracks the performance of the 100 largest companies by market capitalisation quoted on the UK stock market. In Ireland, we have the ISEQ Index, which tracks the average performance of all the companies listed on the Irish Stock Exchange.

And there are 'World Equity' indices, such as the MSCI World Index or the FTSE World Index, which track the performance of a large selection of companies from many different markets, in order to provide a guide on the progress of global markets.

Chart 3.1 displays the S&P 500 Index since early 1966. This index measures the progress of the top 500 US companies by market capitalisation across a wide spread of sectors or industries. The vertical left-hand scale represents the index, which started at 50 in 1957. The scale is a semi-log: the distance from 10 to 100 is the same as for 100 to 1,000 – each is a multiple of 10. Using a semi-log scale more accurately represents the percentage (or proportional) movements over time. This is not possible with traditional linear charts.

Chart 3.1: S&P 500 Index (1966-2011)

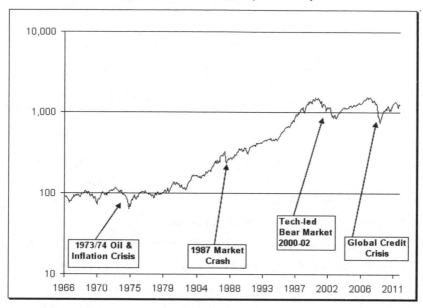

Source: GillenMarkets.

There are two main messages that can be taken from the chart. The first is that the returns from this basket of stocks have been 9.4% compound *per annum* since 1966, including dividends reinvested. The second is that the journey was volatile. From 1966 to 2011 inclusive, 11 years delivered a negative return, while 35 years generated a positive return, again including dividends.

The chart highlights that the US stock market went nowhere from 1966 to 1981. Substantial progress was made during the 1980s and 1990s. The US and most developed markets peaked in 1999, and have made no progress over the following 12-year period, a performance that is reminiscent of the 1966 to 1981 15-year period.

CHAPTER 4
THE POWER OF COMPOUNDING

You cannot compound from zero, so you need to start somewhere and then have some patience. Compounding takes time and success depends on a couple of key variables:

♦ The rate of return you can achieve on your assets;

♦ The length of time you give to your investment programme;

♦ The amount of money you commit to your investment programme.

We have choices in many areas of life and investing for the future is no different. As we will see in **Chapter 9, Investment Choices and Returns**, different asset classes have delivered different returns over the long-term. In the US, equities (shares) have delivered a 5% to 6% *per annum* compound return above inflation over the past 100 years. A return above inflation is referred to as a real return. Including inflation, returns on US equities averaged 9% to 10% per annum. In contrast, cash deposits have delivered a lower 1% *per annum* compound return after inflation over the same period, or 4% to 5% including inflation.

Today, inflation is running at circa 2.5% in the US. Hence, for the sake of keeping the argument simple, in the following examples we will assume that US equities deliver annual returns of 8% from here – made up of 2.5% inflation plus the long-term average real return of 5.5% (5% to 6%). Similarly, we will assume that cash deposits in the US deliver annual returns of 4% over the next 20 years. This 4% annual return is made up of inflation of 2.5% plus the long-term average real return of 1% (rounded up to 4%).

THE RATE OF RETURN MATTERS

Table 4.1 compares the value of a €2,000 annual investment programme at the end of a 25-year timeline. Investor A saved *via* cash deposits and generated an annual return on the monies invested of 4%. Investor B saved *via* equities and generated an annual return of 8%. As the investment programme is an annual one, it could be a pension investment just as easily as a savings programme. Taxes and exchange rates are ignored for the sake of simplicity.

Table 4.1: The Power of Compounding (Equities & Cash Deposits)

End of Year	Investor A 4% Return €	Investor B 8% Return €
1	2,080	2,160
2	4,243	4,493
3	6,493	7,012
4	8,833	9,733
5	11,266	12,672
6	13,797	15,846
7	16,428	19,273
8	19,166	22,975
9	22,012	26,973
10	24,973	31,291
11	28,052	35,954
12	31,254	40,991
13	34,584	46,430
14	38,047	52,304
15	41,649	58,649
16	45,395	65,500
17	49,291	72,900
18	53,342	80,893
19	57,556	89,524
20	61,938	98,846
21	66,496	108,914
22	71,236	119,787
23	76,165	131,530
24	81,292	144,212
25	86,623	157,909
Amount Invested	**€50,000**	**€50,000**
Investment Value	**€86,623**	**€157,909**

Table 4.1 shows that Investor A grew his €50,000 of savings to €86,623 while Investor B grew his €50,000 savings to €157,909. It is a theoretical and somewhat simplistic example but, nonetheless, it highlights why one might choose to invest in risk assets, like equities, over non-risk assets, like bank deposits. If the long-term returns have been higher in equities than in cash deposits, then, all others things equal, the historical evidence favours investing in equities, or other risk assets.

BUT TIME IS ALSO A POWERFUL FORCE IN COMPOUNDING

Table 4.2 highlights the situation of Investors C and D. It is a powerful example of compounding and demonstrates neatly why it is important to start a savings or investment programme as early in life as you can. In fact, the earlier you start, the less capital you will need to commit to your programme.

Investor C starts to save for retirement at age 25 and puts €2,000 into his investment programme each year until he is aged 34. That's 10 years of investing and a total investment of €20,000. He does not contribute anything further to his investment programme thereafter, but we'll assume he gets the long-term equity market return of 8% *per annum*. He continues with his investment programme until he retires at age 65. At that point, his €20,000 is worth €340,060. He has multiplied his monies 17 times.

In contrast, Investor D starts his investment plan later at the age of 35, just when Investor C has finished contributing to his plan. However, Investor D contributes €2,000 into his investment programme each year until he is aged 65 and gets the same annual return of 8% *per annum*. Over a period of 31 years, Investor D has put a total of €62,000 into his investment plan, representing over three times the amount Investor C committed. At 65, his €62,000 is worth €266,427. He has multiplied his monies just over four times.

So Investor C contributes a total of €20,000 to his investment programme over only 10 years, but starts earlier at age 25 and ends up with a substantially larger lump-sum of €340,060, whereas Investor D contributes a much larger €62,000 to his investment programme over a longer time period but started later at age 35, and ends up with the lower lump-sum of €266,427. Since Investor C only contributed a third of what

Investor D contributed (€20,000 compared to €62,000), how did he end up with a larger lump-sum at retirement?

Table 4.2: The Power of Compounding (Time Matters)

Age	Investor C		Investor D	
	Savings €	Value €	Savings €	Value €
25	2,000	2,160		
26	4,000	4,493		
27	6,000	7,012		
28	8,000	9,733		
29	10,000	12,672		
30	12,000	15,846		
31	14,000	19,273		
32	16,000	22,975		
33	18,000	26,973		
34	20,000	31,291		
35		33,794	2,000	2,160
36		36,498	4,000	4,493
37		39,418	6,000	7,012
38		42,571	8,000	9,733
39		45,977	10,000	12,672
60		231,439	52,000	172,702
61		249,954	54,000	188,678
62		269,951	56,000	205,932
63		291,547	58,000	224,566
64		314,870	60,000	244,692
65		340,060	62,000	266,427
Total Invested		**20,000**		**62,000**
Returns		**320,060**		**204,427**
Lump-sum at Retirement		**340,060**		**266,427**
Money Grew (x)		**17.0**		**4.3**

Note: An 8% annual return is assumed.

Figure 4.1 provides the answer to the puzzle: by the time Investor C has stopped contributing to his investment programme at age 35, he had already compounded his monies to €31,291. He adds nothing further to his investment plan at this stage, but he continues to generate an 8% *per annum* return which, in the following year, is €2,503 and already above the €2,000 that Investor D has just started to contribute to his investment programme. Investor D simply cannot catch up with Investor C in the time given.

Figure 4.1: The Answer to the Compounding Puzzle

Investor A	
Age 35:	€31,291
8% Return	€2,503
Investor B	
Age 35:	Starts to contribute €2,000 in that same year

This is a striking example of the power of compounding and why *time* is also a powerful force in compounding. After 10 years of saving and at the age of 35, Investor C had a lump-sum of €31,291. Of that €31,291 he had contributed €20,000, and the returns amounted to €11,291. Hence, in the first 10 years of his savings programme, it was more about what he put into it than the returns. However, over the subsequent 31 years, he contributed nothing further but generated returns of €308,769 (€340,060 *less* €31,291).

What this highlights quite clearly is that all the hard work is in the early years. But once he had an asset base built, compounding takes over and it builds momentum all on its own. No wonder Warren Buffett's biography was entitled *Snowball*.[2] Build a snowball and start it rolling downhill and, with momentum, it just keeps getting bigger and bigger all on its own. Likewise in **Table 4.2**, Investor C's capital kept growing without any new contributions from him after age 34.

Starting a financial savings or pension plan gives you choices later in life. You may start a savings plan simply to pay for school or college fees. You may wish to take a year off at some stage, and your savings plan may fund it. Or you may wish to have the option to retire early. Either way, with a savings programme in place, you give yourself choices later

---

[2]   Schroeder, A. (2008). *Snowball: Warren Buffett and the Business of Life*, New York: Bantam Books.

in life. And it is not nearly as onerous as you might have previously thought.

The key to financial freedom is to build an asset from which you can generate an annual income that covers your overheads or outgoings. If you achieve that, then you have choices. If your overheads or annual expenses are covered, you can pretty much do what you like without having to work.

If we assume Investor C retires at 65, then an 8% *per annum* return on his €340,060 lump-sum generates an annual income of €27,205 before taxes. If Investor C had contributed the slightly larger lump-sum of €5,000 *per annum* into his investment programme (starting at age 25) and obtained the same returns, at 65 his retirement lump-sum would have grown to €850,150, on which an 8% return would generate him an annual income of just over €68,000. Similarly, an annual commitment of €20,000 *per annum* into his investment programme would leave him with a lump-sum at retirement of €3.4 million and in a position to generate an annual income of €272,072, assuming a straight line 8% annual return (taxes ignored for the sake of simplicity).

Table 4.3: Retirement Income Scenarios

Annual Investment (starting age 25)	Value at age 65	8% Return at age 65
€2,000	€340,060	€27,205
€5,000	€850,150	€68,012
€20,000	€3,400,600	€272,048

In **Table 4.1**, both Investor A and Investor B compounded over 25 years. They ended up with different lump-sums at the end, as they chose to invest or save in different asset classes. Investor A chose equities and generated an annual 8% return. But there was no guarantee that he would achieve those returns, or indeed any returns at all. But he had history and the safety net of regular investing (dollar cost averaging) on his side. As we will see in **Chapter 5, Defining the Long-term**, regular investing hugely mitigates the risks of investing in equities or risk assets. Nonetheless, he still has the choice, as all investors have, to invest or save, and compound, *via* bank deposits.

In contrast to investing in physical property, which often necessitates a large upfront commitment of capital and most likely the use of considerable debt, a great advantage of starting a savings plan in the stock market is that you can start small. You can buy an asset in the stock market with as little as €800, if you deal through a low-cost online stockbroker (of which there are many), or nearer €1,200, if you are dealing through a traditional, full-service and higher cost stockbroker. If you can save even €250 a month, then every three or four months you will be in a position to add to your programme by buying another asset. Unlike the examples we looked at above, if you choose to invest in risk assets, the returns you obtain will not be straight line – they will vary considerably from year to year. However, on average, it should work out much as highlighted in these examples.

Compounding takes time, but it works phenomenally once momentum is achieved. Your goal should be to start an investment plan as early as you can, contribute as much to it each month (or annually) as you can, and to seek out the best returns. If you choose risk assets, you will have to put up with the volatility that the stock markets throw at you. But, as I repeat many times in this book and explain clearly in **Chapter 6, Understanding Stock Market Volatility**, volatility is not the same thing as risk – risk is using debt, buying poor quality assets, and not diversifying or buying overvalued assets.

CHAPTER 5
DEFINING THE LONG-TERM

Most investors will have heard that it is best to take a long-term view when investing in the stock markets. This is essentially correct, but what exactly defines the long-term? There is no standard definition, just as there is no standard investor. Indeed, investors have different priorities, different age profiles and different needs. At the one-day stock market training seminars that I have run since 2005, I make the point that what defines the long-term depends on whether you are:

♦ A lump-sum investor needing to protect capital; or
♦ Investing regularly to accumulate capital.

THE LUMP-SUM INVESTOR

I characterise a lump-sum investor as someone who has a single lump-sum of capital to invest. He or she may have saved for a lifetime in a pension fund or through personal savings, or perhaps has inherited some money or sold a business or some land. Whatever the background, the point is that the lump-sum investor is not in a position to add further monies to the investment programme.

This is a scenario faced by many people. The first choice such a person has is whether to invest in non-risk assets like cash deposits or government bonds, which have delivered *circa* 1% to 2% over inflation in the long-term. However, as we have already seen, returns from risk assets can be much higher, assuming that the asset in question is fairly valued at the time of purchase and that the investor can invest for a sufficient period that allows him to overcome the volatility inherent in the markets.

Rather than asking, 'what is the long-term?', perhaps we could turn the question around and ask, 'what is the probability of an investor making a profit or loss after five or 10 years with a single lump-sum investment in the stock markets at a point in time?'.

That is really what it's all about – the probability of getting a positive return over various timelines. There are no guarantees with risk asset investing and, as I outline in **Appendix 2, Guaranteed Structured Products**, guaranteed investment products certainly are not the answer. They exist to reward the seller, not the investor.

Chart 5.1: Barclays Capital US Equity Index: Annual Total Returns (1926-2011)

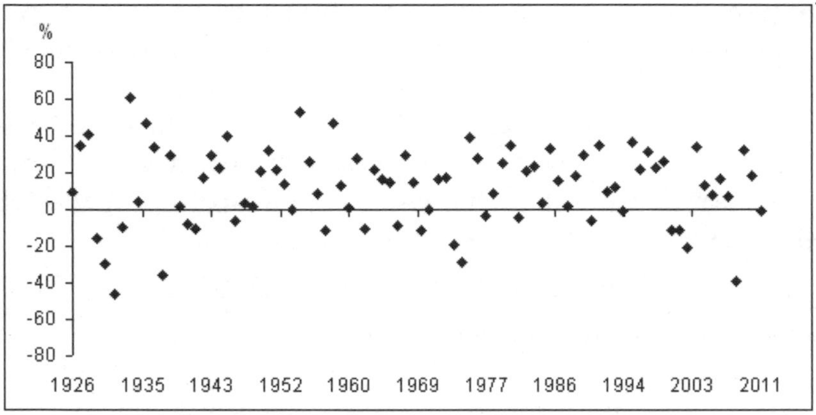

Source: Barclays Capital Annual Equity/Gilt Study 2012.

Chart 5.1 depicts the annual total returns on the US stock market from 1926 to 2011. A total return captures both the price return and the dividends earned. This 86-year period is more than enough for us to build a good picture of the rollercoaster ride investors have experienced over that time. We can observe from the chart that the vast majority of the annual returns lay between plus and minus 20%. There were a handful of years where the US stock market declined by greater than 20%, including the 1929-1932 period, the mid-1970s, 2002 and 2008. But there were far more years where the US stock market delivered returns in excess of 20%. That confirms the fact that returns are biased to the upside. That said, however, it is clear from this chart alone that returns are random, and that negative returns are not outlier events. In fact, they are quite normal.

Chart 5.2 depicts the rolling five-year compound *per annum* returns. The chart starts in 1930. The returns include the gains or losses on the US stock market each year, and include dividend income in the year. An investor who invested a lump-sum in the US stock market at the start of 1926 had completed a five-year investment period at the end of 1930. Likewise, someone investing a lump-sum in 2007 had completed a five-year investment period at the end of 2011.

Chart 5.2: Barclays Capital US Equity Index: Rolling 5-Year Total Returns *per annum* Compound (1926-2011)

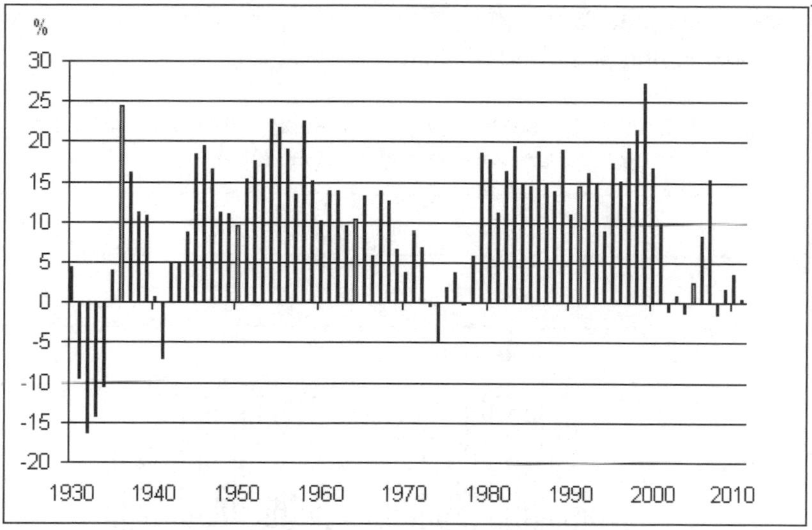

Source: Barclays Capital Annual Equity/Gilt Study 2012.

Successive negative five-year rolling returns from 1931 to 1934 reflected the Great Depression in the US and its impact on the US stock market. The outbreak of World War II in the late 1930s had an impact, and delivered a negative rolling five-year period by 1941. But it was not until the oil and inflation crises of the early-to-mid-1970s that investors experienced, once again, negative five-year rolling periods in 1973, 1974 and 1977. The bear market of the early 2000s had its impact, with negative five-year rolling returns in 2002 and 2004. The 2007-2009 global credit crisis ensured 2008 delivered a negative five-year rolling return for an investor who started with a lump-sum investment in the US market in 2004.

In all, from 1926 to 2011, there were 82 five-year rolling periods. Of those, 11 delivered negative returns, equivalent to 13% of the time frame covered. In other words, since 1926, there has been a one-in-eight chance of a negative return after five years. These figures do not include anything for costs – particularly costs within funds, which many investors use, as opposed to direct stock investing. Hence, my own estimate is that the probability of a loss in the markets after even a five-year period, when costs are taken into account, is somewhere around the 14% to 15% range, or one-in-seven.

Chart 5.3 depicts the rolling 10-year returns. The chart starts in 1935, covering the first full 10-year period from 1926 to 1935 inclusive. Thus, someone investing a lump-sum in 2002 had completed a 10-year investment period at the end of 2011.

Chart 5.3: Barclays Capital US Equity Index: Rolling 10-Year Total Returns *per annum* **Compound (1926-2011)**

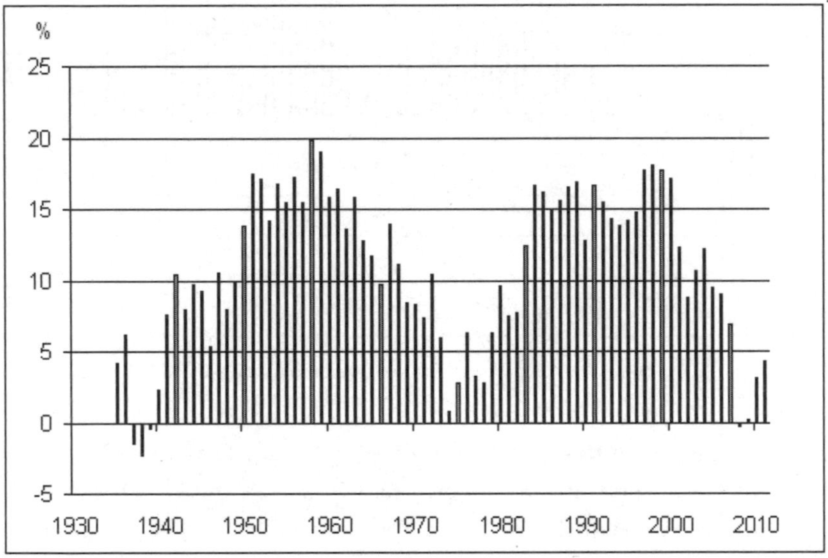

Source: Barclays Capital Annual Equity/Gilt Study 2012.

In all, from 1926 to 2011, there were 77 10-year rolling periods. Of those, only four 10-year rolling periods delivered negative returns, representing 5% of the time. In other words, since 1926, there has been a one-in-20 chance of a negative return after 10 years.

Again, these figures don't include anything for costs. Hence, my own estimate is that the probability of a loss in the markets after a 10-year period, when costs are taken into account, is probably somewhere around the 6% range (or 1 in 17).

How, then, do we define the long-term? Clearly, with the probability of a loss estimated at 14% to 15%, or one-in-seven, we can conclude that a five-year period is probably not sufficient to ensure a positive return. The probability of a loss reduces significantly to somewhere between 6%, or 1-in-17, if an investor takes a 10-year view.

An investor can increase his chances of positive returns over a five-year or 10-year period by buying equities when they are reasonably valued. **Chart 12.2** in **Chapter 12, Equities** compares the price an investor is paying to the 10-year average earnings when investing in the S&P 500 Index. As we show in **Table 12.5** in the same chapter, this value metric is reasonably good at predicting whether the subsequent 10-year returns are likely to be above or below average. It is overvaluation that is the enemy of investing. The US stock market was overvalued in 1929, the late 1960s and grossly overvalued by the late 1990s. It can be no surprise then that the negative five-year and 10-year returns outlined in **Charts 5.2** and **5.3** occurred subsequent to these periods of overvaluation. The corollary is that investing when the market is cheap, relative to historical valuation metrics, substantially increases the odds of a successful outcome for the investor after five to 10 years.

For the lump-sum investor, it appears that, if stock markets are reasonably valued (relative to historical valuation metrics), then a five-year to 10-year view is normally sufficient to ensure a positive outcome. In other words, five to 10 years can be considered to be the long-term for the lump-sum investor.

THE REGULAR INVESTOR

Investing regularly, as opposed to investing a lump-sum at one specific point in time, is a key tool in dealing with the natural volatility that exists in stock markets. As we have already seen, if the lump-sum investor invests at a time when markets are overvalued, then the probability of a disappointing outcome even on a five-year to 10-year period rises significantly. In contrast, the regular investor is investing in good times and bad: when markets are overvalued and undervalued. Hence, the regular investor ends up investing at average values, so that he or she is most likely to obtain the average long-term returns that markets have produced over the past 100 years of 9% to 10% (or 5% to 6% above inflation). Our goal here is to find out what a reasonable definition of the long-term is for a regular investor. We will examine two time periods, using live examples.

Regular investing is also described as 'dollar-cost-averaging' in the US, 'pound-cost-averaging' in the UK or 'euro-cost-averaging' in the Eurozone. Anyone who is investing in their pension either through their company scheme or through their own individual pension plan is, in effect, a regular investor.

Chart 5.4 represents the share price of a global equity exchange-traded fund (ETF)[3] that provides exposure to 100 companies across the global equity markets, spanning many different business sectors. This particular ETF (ticker code: IOO) was issued and listed by iShares (now part of the fund management group Blackrock) in December 2000. Like all ETFs, this tracker fund is quoted on the stock exchange in the same way as a share. The chart highlights the price of this ETF from December 2000 at just over $70, up to late August 2011 when the fund price was $54.83, and down 21% over this near 11-year period.

Chart 5.4: iShares S&P Global 100 ETF (2000-2011)

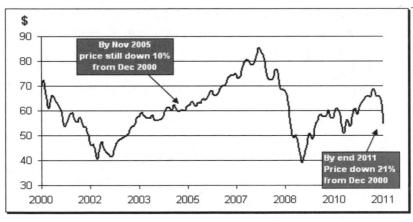

Source: GillenMarkets.

To explore the journey that a regular investor might have gone on, I have examined two five-year periods. The first five-year period highlights the journey of an investor who starts investing $500 monthly in December

---

3   Exchange-traded funds are funds that are quoted on a stock exchange and
     own all of the stocks in a particular index in order to replicate, and track the
     performance of, that index – in this case, the S&P Global 100 Index.

2000 and ceases investing at end-November 2005, as shown in **Chart 5.5**. The second five-year period highlights the journey of an investor investing $500 monthly starting in June 2006 and ending in May 2011, as shown in **Chart 5.6**.

Chart 5.5: iShares S&P Global 100 ETF: $500 Invested Monthly from December 2000 to November 2005

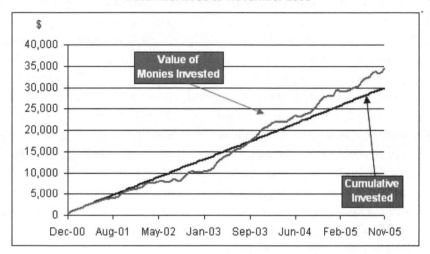

Chart 5.6: iShares S&P Global 100 ETF: $500 Invested Monthly from June 2006 to May 2011

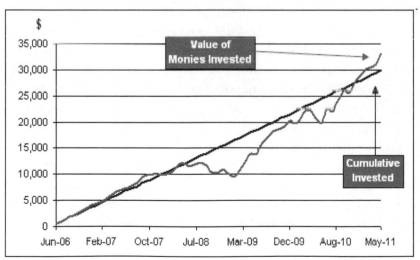

Both five-year periods were chosen because they straddled a serious bear market. With hindsight, we now know that many of the developed equity markets were grossly overvalued in 2000. While they were not as overvalued in 2006, valuations nonetheless were well above long-term norms. Hence, both five-year periods represent a robust test of what the regular investor might face when starting an investment programme when either equity markets are overvalued or when a subsequent bear market hits.

Over the initial five-year period (**Chart 5.4**), the price of the fund declined from near $70 to as low as $40 before starting a recovery to $63 by November 2005, representing a decline of 10% overall – mirroring global equity markets during that period. Over the five-year period, the regular investor invested a cumulative $30,000 (**Chart 5.5**). By end-November 2005, the investment was worth $34,543 for a 15% gain. I have not taken account of costs but neither have I included the dividend income that an investor received from the fund. Overall, I believe that the charts and figures are highly representative of the five-year period involved. The chart highlights that the regular investor, investing in a well-diversified equity fund, not only survived the first major equity bear market since the 1970s but generated a positive return, even though the underlying fund value was still down 10%, at $63 compared to the starting price of $70.

Over the second five-year period (**Chart 5.6**), the price of the fund declined from over $66.20 in June 2006 to as low as $40, before starting a recovery to $68.80 by end-May 2011, thus representing an overall gain of 4%. Over this second five-year period, which takes us through the global credit crisis, the regular investor again invested a cumulative $30,000. By end-May 2011, the investment was worth $33,090 for a 10% gain, even though the share price of the global equity ETF had risen only 4% over the starting price. Again, costs and dividends have been ignored, and should have partly offset each other.

So, you might ask, how did the investor make a better return in both five-year periods when the price of the fund (or ETF) was still well below the starting price (in the case of the first five-year period) and only modestly above the starting price (in the case of the second five-year period)?

A Hidden Benefit of Regular Investing (Dollar-Cost-Averaging)

Because a regular investor invests the same amount of money each month, he is able to buy more shares at lower prices. By investing the same amount of monies at lower prices, an investor obtains more 'bang for his buck'.

During the December 2000 to November 2005 period, the regular investor obtained a weighted-average buy-in price of $55. The recovery in the ETF price to $63.35 by end November 2005 explains why he showed a positive return over the five-year period even though the ETF was still 10% below its starting price. That is the power of dollar-cost-averaging. The same logic applies to the second five-year period from June 2006 to May 2011.

Clearly, the lump-sum investor who invested at the start of December 2000 or June 2006 would end up with a worse return after the five-year period. As the saying goes, you cannot make a silk purse out of a pig's ear. Similarly, regular investing in the stock markets is not a magical solution to severe and prolonged bear markets. Nonetheless, regular investing is effective at controlling risk, limiting the damage from a severe downturn in markets and ensuring that you are positioned to benefit when markets recover.

How Long To Breakeven?

In the first five-year period from December 2000 to November 2005, it took the investor 13 months from the bottom of the bear market in August 2002 to return to a breakeven position, and two years, nine months from the start of his investment programme in December 2000. In the second five-year period from June 2006 to May 2011, it took 22 months to get back to a breakeven position from the bear market bottom in February 2009 (unlike the US stock market, the global equity market bottomed in February 2009), and three years, six months from the start of his investment programme in June 2006. Hence, in two of the deepest bear markets investors have witnessed in the past 60 years, the regular investor was back to breakeven in under three to four years.

For the regular investor, then, it is reasonable to conclude that three to five years is a good proxy for the long-term under most market conditions. For it all to work out, we only need to assume that the market will recover at some stage. That may be a big assumption, but it is the crucial assumption all investors must make.

CHAPTER 6
UNDERSTANDING STOCK MARKET VOLATILITY

*It is neither possible nor necessary to understand the market;
the one essential is to come to terms with it.*
Brian Marber[4]

UNDERSTANDING THE MARKETS

You are driving home on a Friday and listening to the news on the radio, and it is all doom and gloom. On Saturday, you read your weekly diet from a couple of investment websites you subscribe to and there is a surprisingly negative tone to the commentary. You watch the news on the TV and the financial wizard being interviewed tells you, convincingly, that the Euro is doomed and the equity markets are in danger of falling off a precipice. You worry all weekend and are just about to sell a few shares or funds that you own on Monday when, to your surprise, the markets open up on the previous week's close, and you calm down.

So you go one step further over the following week. You listen to several programmes on the troubling Eurozone sovereign debt and fiscal crises, and read all you can on the issues. Having amassed both the positive and negative arguments, you feel better equipped to come to a conclusion – things are not quite as bad as those merchants of doom would have you believe. More relaxed, you stroll into work on the following Monday morning. However, this time, the markets open down 3%. What did you miss, you might ask yourself?

---

4   Marber, B. (2007). *Marber on Markets: How to Make Money from Charts*, Petersfield: Harriman House, p.162.

If these scenarios resonate with you, then rest assured that you are not alone. The markets are confusing and it is difficult to know at any particular time whether what is reported in the media is already discounted or understood by the markets and therefore already reflected in prices.

Take it to the extreme: if you tried to obtain everyone's view, positive and negative, think how long that would take and ask yourself whether it would help anyway?

A real-time example of markets doing the exact opposite to what the majority view was saying in the media or otherwise occurred in March 2009. Then, much of the media and general investment commentary was universally apocalyptic but the markets started rising for a very simple reason: the average investor was buying, not selling, as more and more fund managers believed the global economy would turn around, as it duly did. My point is that the market itself is our best guide as to the likely business and economic conditions ahead.

We have all experienced those times when we remained stubborn and tried to defy the markets, only to experience them running right over us. There is nothing so shocking to someone used to being right all their life as being totally wrong in markets. And it has nothing to do with intelligence. The fact is that your view will be wrong on many occasions in the markets. Get used to it!

The ability of stock markets to discount news – good or bad – ahead of time is the reason that the market is a discounting mechanism. Investors often make the mistake of trying to relate what the economy is doing today to what the market is doing. In early 2009, the news on the economy was still awful. But the market had discounted it fully, and, in March 2009, started to look forward to recovery, on the basis that central banks were providing liquidity to the banking system and that governments were spending heavily to offset the contraction in private spending. Markets started to anticipate recovery, a global stock market rally ensued, yet the business media was universally – and correctly – reporting negative news. The negative news was real, but investors, overall, had already discounted it. Hence, a recovery in share prices suggested that investors saw recovery – and they saw it right, as six months later the global economy started a recovery.

VOLATILITY IS NOT THE SAME AS RISK

The market's gyrations feel like risk. However, while volatility is part and parcel of stock market investing, it is not the same as risk.

Fear, greed and hope can undo the best laid plans and, if we lose control of our emotions due to a lack of understanding of volatility, then we may never reap the returns on offer in risk assets, despite our good intentions.

The volatility in stock markets adds to the confusion, but the investor's job is to understand why the markets can be so volatile and to ensure that your investment plan can deal with it. Understanding volatility in markets reduces the fear of it and the danger of you, an investor, acting irrationally in response to it. If you can deal effectively with the volatility, then you are well on your way to making a success of stock market investing. As I outlined in the **Introduction,** dealing with the volatility is one of the three steps to investment success.

The direction of the stock markets has always been erratic in the short- and even medium-term, while still having advanced by 9% to 10% *per annum* in the long-term.

The principle causes of volatility in the markets are:

♦ The economy is volatile and experiences periods of contraction as well as expansion;

♦ A contraction in the economy leads to lower revenues for business, and with fixed overheads this, in turn, amplifies the reduction in corporate earnings;

♦ Furthermore, stock markets are emotional and over-react relative to the likely change in these underlying business fundamentals.

ECONOMIC EXPANSION AND CONTRACTION

In the developed world, the normal order of events has been that economies have expanded over time. But a myriad of different factors, both internal and external, can knock an economy off course and lead to a contraction. Internal factors can include rising interest rates or credit contraction, either of which can lead to a reduction of investment. Social unrest or nationwide strikes can lead to lower output. External factors might include wars or energy price shocks. US real GDP growth (which excludes the impact of inflation) has grown at over 3% to 4% *per annum* compound since the early 1960s. As **Table 6.1** highlights however, growth was interrupted in 1982, 1991, 2001 and 2008.

Table 6.1: US Real GDP Growth and US Corporate Earnings[5]

Recessions	Real GDP Growth	US Corporate Earnings Growth
1981/82	-2.9%	-15.7%
1990/91	-1.4%	-6.2%
2001	-0.3%	-8.8%
2008/09	-5.1%	-49.8%

Source: www.bea.gov.

CORPORATE EARNINGS ARE VOLATILE

When the business cycle turns down and a recession occurs, corporate profits, which underpin share prices, can and do decline. As businesses have substantial fixed overheads, a decline in revenues for business will lead to a greater decline in earnings for business, in aggregate. **Table 6.1** highlights the greater decline in earnings for the US economy during the last four periods of contraction in the US economy in 1981/82, 1990/91, 2001 and 2008/09.

In 1981/82, while the economy contracted by 3% from peak to trough, earnings of corporate America declined by a greater 16%, in response to recession brought on by higher interest rates, as the Federal Reserve tightened monetary policy in its attempts to reduce inflation permanently. In each of the next three US recessions, the decline in corporate earnings was higher than the peak to trough contraction in the economy.

The value of stocks (companies) is underpinned first and foremost by their earnings. The uncertainty created by declining earnings is always unsettling for the markets, as investors attempt to gauge how far earnings will decline and how long it may take for earnings to recover.

---

5   While US GDP has been adjusted for US inflation, US corporate earnings have
     not been. But the impact of this in **Table 6.1** is marginal and does not detract
     from the overall message.

THE MARKETS ARE EMOTIONAL AND LIQUID

Fear, greed and hope play their part in the stock markets, and with share prices, in the short-term. As the old adage goes, stock markets have predicted seven out of the last four recessions. The point is that investors always are trying to predict what happens next, and often see things that simply are not there. In other words, emotions play a significant part in stock market volatility. The greater liquidity in markets means that investors' growing nervousness or bullishness can be acted on instantaneously by buying and selling.

There is no question that the stock markets are the best leading indicator of the likely business and economic conditions ahead, but this does not mean that the markets are always right. At times, investors look into the abyss, and, having sold off sharply in anticipation of recession or even a slow-down in economic activity, they then recover just as quickly when the reality is not as they first feared. Fears of recession in the US economy in mid-2010 and mid-2011 both led to sharp declines in the US stock markets. When it became clear that the economy was not in recession, the stock markets recovered quickly. **Table 6.2** highlights the occasions since 1987 that the US stock market declined by 7% or more when there was no corresponding decline in corporate earnings. The decline in earnings from April to October 1998 was barely noticeable.

Table 6.2: S&P 500 Index and US Corporate Earnings

Date	S&P 500 Index	US Corporate Earnings Growth
Aug-Nov 1987	-33.3%	9.0%
Apr-Oct 1998	-12.3%	-0.6%
Feb-Aug 2004	-7.1%	13.2%
Apr-Aug 2010	-12.5%	6.3%

Source: www.bea.gov and GillenMarkets.

CHAPTER 7
STOCK MARKET AND DIRECT PROPERTY INVESTING: COMPARISONS AND CONTRASTS

In this chapter, I look more closely at the factors that are common to both stock market and physical property investing, as well as highlighting several factors that set them apart.

THE COMPARISONS

The drivers behind stock market returns are pretty much the same as those that underpin returns from investing in physical property over the long-term. In the stock markets, the growth in corporate earnings is the fundamental driver of higher share prices over the long-term. The valuation of stock markets also is influenced by the level and direction of interest rates and sentiment is a silent, behind-the-scenes influence. Declining interest rates can make the earnings in the stock markets more valuable, which attracts money out of cash deposits and into the stock markets, pushing up prices. In contrast, rising interest rates can make those same earnings look less attractive, with the result that investors exit the stock markets in favour of leaving monies on cash deposit or in government bonds, and so share prices decline. Sentiment can push trends to extremes. If investors, overall, are jubilant or bullish, share prices can push up well ahead of the level that can be justified by either the earnings or interest rates at a particular time.

Table 7.1: The Key Drivers of Stock Market and Physical Property Returns

Stock Market Investing	Physical Property Investing
The growth in corporate earnings	The growth in rental income
The earnings yield versus interest rates	The rental yield versus interest rates
The direction of interest rates	The direction of interest rates
Investor sentiment	Investor sentiment

The Coca Cola Example

A quick example might help to make this analysis easier to follow. Let's take a look at Coca Cola, the US beverage giant. In 1998, Coca Cola earned $1.40 per share. In 2011, Coca Cola earned $3.85 per share. In other words, Coca Cola grew its earnings quite substantially between 1998 and 2011. Hence, in 2011, Coca Cola was backed by a higher level of earnings and was a more valuable company than it was in 1998.

Coca Cola's share price at the end of 2011 was close to $70. By comparing its 2011 earnings to the share price we can deduce that Coca Cola had an earnings yield of 5.5% at the end of 2011:

$3.85 / $70 * 100 = 5.5%

At the end of 2011, US short-term interest rates were 0.25% and long-term interest rates, as defined by the 10-year bond yield, were 1.88%. Hence, we can compare Coca Cola's earnings yield of 5.5% to the US 10-year bond yield of 1.88%. We also know that Coca Cola has a high probability of growing its earnings. It has done so consistently in the past and it seems reasonable to expect it to do so in the future. It would appear, then, that a starting earnings yield of 5.5% plus likely future growth in that yield is a far more attractive investment opportunity than buying the US 10-year bond which offers a yield of 1.88% and no opportunity for growth in that yield.

Coca Cola: Earnings yield = $3.85 / $70 * 100 = 5.5% (plus growth)

US 10-year Government Bond: Yield = 1.88% (no growth)

The difference in value between the two investment opportunities is described as the equity risk premium – the premium you are being offered to invest in a risk asset (Coca Cola). Supposedly, there is no risk in the US 10-year government bond whereas earnings at Coca Cola could fall in the future, so that the earnings yield of 5.5% today could be lower tomorrow. With long-term interest rates so low, and Coca Cola offering a much higher earnings yield, if investors believe that Coca Cola's earnings will remain stable and even grow, then they should sell the US 10-year bond and buy Coca Cola's shares.

Physical Property

In physical property investing, while investors are not necessarily as aware of the forces at play, the same factors essentially are driving prices upwards over time. As the rental income stream on a property grows over time, this underpins a higher value for that same property.

Declining interest rates mean that investors can no longer get the same return from bank deposits or government bonds, and money should exit bank accounts and bonds in search of the higher rental income (or rental yield) available from property, thus pushing up the price of property. Similarly, rising interest rates will make rental income (or the rental yield) on property less attractive, compared to what an investor can get from bank deposits or government bonds, which will force investors out of property and back into these non-risk assets.

That, of course, describes a rational world. In physical property investing, like the stock markets, sentiment can take over and the once-rational property investor can lose all sense of reason and buy or sell at any price. In these circumstances, property prices can rise well beyond, or fall far below, what can be justified by the rental yield and the prevailing level of interest rates.

This is exactly what occurred in many property markets in the developed world in the 2000s. For property buyers in the US and UK, for example, interest rates had come all the way down from between 12% to 14% in the early 1980s to *circa* 3% by 2003. This persistent decline in interest rates provided a strong tailwind for property prices over this near 20-year period in both these economies. By way of example, in 1982, UK long-term interest rates (20-year bond yield) ranged between 10% and 11%. The rental yield available from UK commercial property was 6% to 6.5% at that time. Investors were prepared to accept a lower rental yield on UK commercial property in 1982 as they expected that either rental growth would drive the rental yield up or UK long-term interest rates would decline, making the existing 6% to 6.5% rental yield more attractive.

As we now know, the rental yield on commercial property in many markets fell to unsustainable levels from 2003 to 2006, driven by the ease with which investors could access credit and the herd instinct, which saw investors anticipate only rising property prices despite the lack of rental yield and in the face of rising interest rates.

THE CONTRASTS

While there are significant similarities between the underlying drivers of returns in both stock market investing and physical property investing, **Table 7.2** outlines the major differences between these two asset classes.

Table 7.2: The Contrasts between Stock Market Investing and Physical Property Investing

Stock Market Investing	Physical Property Investing
A diversified portfolio is essential	Diversification is not as important
Markets are extremely liquid	Property can be an illiquid asset
Entry and ongoing costs are low	Entry and ongoing costs are higher
You can start small	Need a sizable lump-sum to start
Stock markets are not homogeneous	The property market is homogeneous
The risks of using debt are hard to control	Easier to borrow to enhance returns

Diversification

In the stock markets, investors should get used to the concept of buying a diversified portfolio of shares to reduce the risk of a particular share letting you down. The overall stock market can be making progress, while many individual companies lag well behind. Indeed, entire industries or sectors of the market can lag behind the returns of the overall market for a considerable period. In fact, some industries even disappear completely over time, while new ones emerge. The point is that the stock markets are dynamic and change shape over time to reflect the progress of businesses and the economy.

Table 7.3 shows the major companies that made up the UK FT 30 Index in 1952. Of the 30 companies that made up the FT 30 Index in 1952, just four remain as separately identified companies listed on the London Stock Exchange today. They are: GKN, Imperial Tobacco, Rolls-Royce and Tate & Lyle.

Table 7.3: Constituents of the UK FT 30 Index in 1952

Blue Circle	Harrods	Pinchin Johnson
British Motors	Hawker Siddeley	**Rolls-Royce**
Coats	ICI	Spillers
Courtaulds	**Imperial Tobacco**	Swan Hunter
Distillers	Lancaster Cotton	**Tate & Lyle**
Dunlop Rubber	Leyland	Tube Investments
EMI	London Brick	Turner & Newall
FW Woolworth	Murex	Vickers
GEC	Patons & Baldwins	Watney Combe Reid
GKN	Peninsular & Oriental	William Cory

Source: *The Financial Times.*

The Irish stock market has witnessed a similar level of change. Of the companies listed on the exchange in 1970, there are only three still trading on the Irish Stock Exchange today as separately identified business entities, or four if we include Smurfit in its restructured form.

Table 7.4: Major Companies on the Irish Stock Exchange in 1970

Allied Irish Banks	Silvermines	P.J. Carroll
Bank of Ireland	Guinness	**Cement Roadstone**
Ryan Tourist Holdings	United Distillers	Central Hotel
Alliance & Dublin Gas	Credit Finance	Gouldings
Clondalkin Paper	Bolands	Irish Dunlop
Heiton Holdings	Ferrier Pollock	Irish Ropes
Jefferson Smurfit	Arklow Pottery	Irish Shell
Freedex	Bralds	Metal Products (Cork)
May Roberts	Cahill	Williams (H)

Source: *The Irish Times.*

Of course, the changing shape of stock markets is not necessarily a negative. Many of the companies listed in the FT 30 Index in 1952 were simply taken over or merged with another company. A few companies no doubt went out of business but the vast majority still exist today in one form or another. The same points can be made in relation to the significant changes to the constituents of the Irish stock market in 1970.

My point is that **Tables 7.3** and **7.4** assist in making the case for diversification.

Diversification is not as important when investing in physical property (as opposed to property companies or funds). Unlike a company, a residential or commercial property can exist without the need for a management team, and it is often management that undermines an otherwise good company by over expanding. In addition, technological obsolescence is not a short-term concern for property investors. Granted, if you buy a house in a bog or on the side of a cliff where there is coastal erosion, you may not be guaranteed it will still be there in 10, 20 or 30 years. The major damage investors in physical property inflict on themselves occurs when they either buy when values are poor or add too much leverage to a property transaction.

Liquidity

The stock markets are extremely liquid. No matter what state the markets are in – depressed or euphoric – you can almost always buy or sell whenever you need to. Also, with advances in technology, the settlement time has narrowed to three days. This means that if you sell, you get your cash in three days. There are no administration or legal hurdles to overcome. You sell your shares in the marketplace and that's it, which is a great plus at times when you need cash quickly.

In terms of liquidity, physical property investing is far more cumbersome. Even in good times, it takes a long time and much legal form filling to complete a property transaction. In more difficult times, it can become almost impossible to sell a property. Liquidity seizes up. If you need cash – as property developers in particular have needed in this downturn – this is a major disadvantage and has lead to ruin for many who have debts to meet.

Costs

Online Brokers Have Transformed Stock Market Transaction Costs

There is a very low cost of entry to the stock markets. This is an important consideration for an investor, as you do not want costs to erode your returns. If annual stock market returns have been in the order of 9% to 10%, or 5% to 6% above inflation, over the long-term (in the developed stock markets anyhow), then your aim must be to minimise your costs in relation to those returns.

The only costs involved in stock market investing are the stockbroking commission, stamp duty (in the UK and Ireland) and the spread between the buy price and the sell price. Stockbroking commissions vary, but as a rough guide, the overall cost of buying a share in the stock market through a traditional full-service stockbroker is between 0.5% and 1.5% for the retail investor. Of course, if you use an online stockbroker, the costs are much lower, often as low as 0.25% and lower. In effect, the cost of buying into the stock market is low, particularly when you use online stockbrokers, and so long as you are not buying and selling regularly like a speculator, the costs don't significantly interfere with the eventual return.

Buying *via* funds is more costly but, for many, it is still the right option and, so long as you are buying and holding, the costs are still very manageable.

Exchange-Traded Funds Have Lowered Annual Fund Costs
The introduction of listed passive market tracking funds, referred to as exchange-traded funds (ETFs), enabled by the advances of technology, provides investors with the option of investing through funds where annual management charges are often well below 0.5%. ETFs are discussed in detail in **Chapter 18, Ways of Gaining Exposure to the Markets**.

The initial costs of investing in physical property are higher. Stamp duty is generally higher, legal costs must be paid and the intermediary's (estate agent's) costs are higher also. That said, investors in property normally hold their investment for several years and, again, the initial costs should be considered in relation to the number of years the property is held.

Minimum Investment Size

In the stock markets, an investor can start small. In fact, once you have your first job, you can start saving through the stock markets. With online dealing, all you need is *circa* €800 to be able to cost-effectively buy a share or fund. With traditional brokers, costs are higher and you probably need *circa* €1,200 to keep the overall cost of transacting from overly impacting on the likely returns.

With physical property investing, you have to commit to a sizable investment or none at all, unless you are prepared to invest *via* a syndicate.

Returns Evenly Spread in Property But Not in Stock Markets

Property returns are largely homogenous. By this I mean that, if you own a particular property and the property market rises in value, you can be fairly confident that your property will rise in value too. Granted, in property, they say that it is all about location, location, location. This probably refers to properties that attain premium prices. But overall, when property prices rise, all property prices rise.

However, returns are not evenly spread in the stock markets. Even when the markets are rising, some companies lag behind for considerable periods, while others simply go out of business. This is a further reason why diversification makes sense when investing in the stock markets.

Leverage

The big plus for investors in physical property is that it is easier to borrow to enhance the underlying returns. It simply is not anywhere near as easy to do that in stock market investing.

Let's take the example of an investor who buys a property for €500,000 in year one and borrows 80% of the money (€400,000) and adds the final 20% (€100,000) himself. For the sake of simplicity, we assume that the interest on the money borrowed is covered by the rental income.

If we then assume that the property rises in value by 5% *per annum* over the following 10 years, it will be worth €814,000 at the end of year 10. That represents a 63% rise in the value of the property over that time period. But on the investor's capital of €100,000, it represents a much higher return of 314%, or 15.3% *per annum* compound. In effect, the investor has boosted his return by the use of borrowings or leverage.

But Leverage Also Means More Risk

Of course, using leverage is a double-edged sword, as events in the property markets in many of the developed markets have shown since 2008. If property prices decline in value and the investor has borrowings attached, then it can be very painful indeed and, in some instances, can lead to insolvency. So, borrowing to buy physical property comes with the *caveat* that you buy at good value or – as they say in stock markets – buy with a good 'margin of safety'.

That said, when you buy your own home with a mortgage, you have all of your earnings and possibly your spouse/partner's earnings with which to cover the mortgage interest and capital repayments. That is an important safety net. So long as you buy a house at a price that makes sense relative to your income (or combined incomes) and allow for a rise in interest rates, you have most likely built in a margin of safety.

In the stock market, it is not as easy to use borrowings or leverage to boost your returns. Indeed, my experience leads me to conclude that the vast majority of private investors should avoid using leverage in the stock markets like the plague. The naturally higher level of volatility in stock markets can cause havoc with your nerves, and lead you to sell because you feel under financial stress. When prices are falling, your borrowings become an even larger part of the jigsaw. If an investor has invested €500,000 into the stock market using €100,000 of his own monies, and €400,000 of borrowings, and the market declines in value by say 15% (which is common), then the portfolio is worth €425,000. That's just €25,000 above the borrowings attached to that investment portfolio.

The bottom line is that borrowing to enhance stock market returns should be left to the professional investors or traders who can handle the gyrations in the stock markets without losing control.

CHAPTER 8
THE PITFALLS IN DIRECT STOCK PICKING

Most private investors underestimate the difficulties and dangers of selecting individual shares for their savings programme or pension fund. The subjective selection of shares is a minefield of risk, perhaps not in a bull market where the rising tide lifts all boats, but certainly over the normal stock market cycle, which includes both bull and bear market conditions. In this chapter, I will outline why the concept of a blue-chip stock is a dangerous one and why I feel that the majority of private investors should avoid selecting stocks subjectively.

RISK

In my view, most private investors are not well equipped to assemble a portfolio of shares for the simple reason that they cannot assess the three key risks involved in selecting and owning individual stocks:

♦ The business risks;

♦ The financial risks; and

♦ The valuation risks.

To examine these risks in more detail, I will outline a case study on Coca Cola, one of the world's best known and most successful companies.

The global credit crisis-driven bear market of 2007-2009 highlighted, better than at any other time, that:

♦ Business models change, and a good business model in one era does not guarantee that it will remain a good business model in all economic and business conditions. That being the case, the profits a company is making today could be lower in three to five years' time (the business risks);

♦ Management can add too much debt to the business, which can undermine an otherwise good business with catastrophic consequences for shareholders (the financial risks); and

♦ Good businesses, even conservatively financed ones, still have to be bought in the stock market at good value in order to secure decent returns (the valuation risks).

Business Risk

Many business models are undermined by ongoing advances in technology. Indeed, advances in technology will continue in the years ahead – and this is probably the only thing that is certain in the business world. The travel agency, the newspaper industry, the bookseller, film, DVD and music distributors, as well as traditional stockbroking businesses, to name but a few, have all felt the impact of fresh challenges and new competition from advances in technology.

Changes in fashion occur at regular intervals in all areas of life, altering consumer habits, tastes and demand. The retail industry is in a constant state of flux, and companies in the sector that fail to adapt simply disappear, while new companies take their place with new products to satisfy the demands of the marketplace.

The regulations and legislation that drive many industries also change the landscape by creating opportunities and threats for both existing players and new entrants. For example, pharmaceutical companies are under constant threat of product patent expiry, which significantly reduces the margin on existing products, as new entrants are free to compete with the introduction of generic alternatives. Indeed, approval of new drug discoveries by regulators has become ever more onerous, so that even well-established pharmaceutical companies have been finding it more difficult to bring new drugs to market than was the case 10 or 20 years ago. As we saw in **Table 7.3** and **7.4** in **Chapter 7, Stock Market and Direct Property Investing**, only a handful of the companies that existed in the UK FT 30 Index or on the Irish market still exist today. For these reasons, the concept of a blue-chip stock, one that can be held for the long-term, is probably a misleading one. The simple fact is that there are far fewer true blue-chip stocks in the global markets than most investors appreciate.

Financial Risk

Assessing the financial risk in companies is also a difficult, if not impossible, task for the majority of investors. Unless you have training that allows you to read and understand financial statements, and experience of businesses in different sectors, you cannot expect to be able to assess the financial risk in a company. You may be able to figure out the company's debt position, and even its cash flows, but how do you know how vulnerable those cash flows are if recession hits? After all, the stability or defensiveness of a company's cash flows varies enormously from one industry to another.

Valuation Risk

The valuation risk in a share is also a minefield. It is not simply today's earnings or dividend that determines the right value for a share but a myriad of different factors from the stability or defensiveness of its earnings to its growth prospects, the competitive landscape, its financing and the opportunity value that exists elsewhere. For example, a stable defensive company with an earnings yield of 7% and a dividend yield of 3% may offer good value when long-term interest rates are at 2% (as they are at present in the US, UK and Germany); yet that same value looks much less appealing if long-term interest rates are 6%. The majority of private investors can't expect to be able to judge valuation risk.

Avoiding the Permanent Loss

Any one of these three risks – business, financial or valuation – can expose the investor to a permanent loss. There is a world of difference between a permanent loss and the opportunity presented by temporary declines in prices. If you cannot tell the difference, then how do you know how to react to declining prices in a bear market and decide whether you need to:

♦ Cut a loss;

♦ Add to your position; or

♦ Stay as you are.

If you can't make these decisions in real-time, then you should give serious consideration to solely investing indirectly *via* funds rather than directly in shares of individual companies.

COCA COLA: CASE STUDY[6]

Coca Cola is one of the most successful companies in the world and it is also an easy company to understand. Despite its innumerable strengths as a business, **Chart 8.1** highlights that Coca Cola shares remain below where they were in late 1998. So, let us try and identify where the risk in Coca Cola's shares was all the way back in the late 1990s, had you been faced with the decision to buy the shares back then.

Chart 8.1 records Coca Cola's share price from 1989 to end 2011. The chart highlights that, while they are on the rise at the moment, Coca Cola's shares remain below the peak of $87 reached in late 1998.

Chart 8.1: Coca Cola's Share Price (1989 – 2011)

Source: GillenMarkets.

Chart 8.2 highlights the progress of Coca Cola's earnings per share, also from 1989 to 2011. Except for a brief dip during the 1998-99 period, the company's earnings progressed steadily upwards at a highly respectable 9% *per annum* compound since then. So, the world's largest manufacturer

---

6   For readers who may not have experience with stock market valuation terminology, there is a case study on CRH plc, the Irish-based global building materials group, in **Appendix 1**. You might find it useful to read over the CRH case study before progressing through the rest of this chapter.

of non-alcoholic drinks, which includes the iconic Coca Cola brand, continued to generate above-average growth in its earnings over the subsequent 13-year period from 1999 to 2011 inclusive. Clearly, investors would have been right in 1998 if they had concluded that there were few *business risks* in Coca Cola. However, this makes it even more puzzling as to why Coca Cola's shares remain below the 1998 peak of $87 some 13 years later.

Chart 8.2: Coca Cola's Earnings per Share (1989 – 2011)

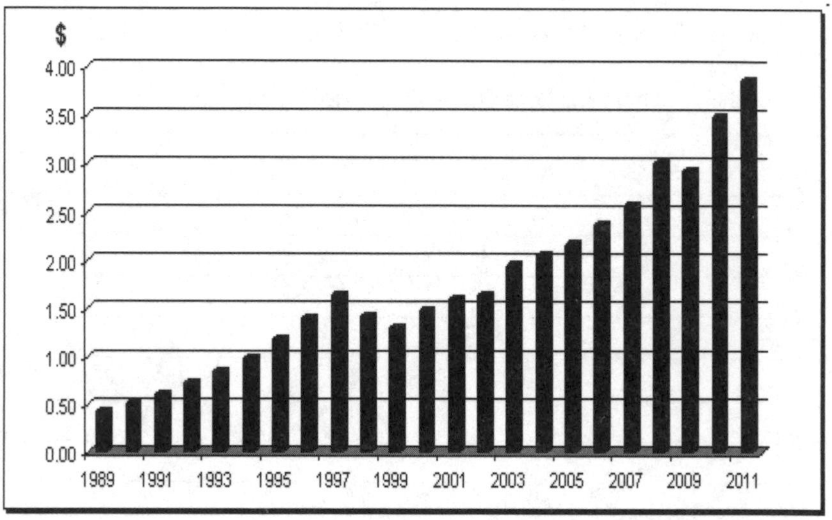

Source: Valueline Investment Survey.

Table 8.1 examines Coca Cola's financial position at 30 June 1998: the company was in excellent financial shape. Net debt was $2.5 billion but annual cash flows were running at $4.3 billion, which was more than sufficient to pay down the debt in a very short period as well as servicing a growing dividend. In short, there was minimal *financial risk* in Coca Cola in late 1998. With limited business and financial risk, it is left to us to identify the likely culprit – *valuation risk*.

Table 8.1: Coca Cola's Financial Position at 30 June 1998

	$ m
Cash	2,153
Short Term Debt	-3,971
Long Term Debt	-686
Net Debt	-2,504
Annual Cash flows	
Average of last 3 years	4,312
Annual Dividend Payment	1,470

Source: Valueline Investment Survey.

Indeed, the problem for investors in Coca Cola shares in the late 1990s was *valuation risk*. In 1998, Coca Cola earned $1.42 a share; with its shares trading at a peak of $87 in that year, investors at that time were paying 61.3 times the earnings of the company ($87 / $1.42 = 61.3). A price-to-earnings ratio of 61.3 equates to an earnings yield of 1.6%.

Chart 8.3 highlights how investors have valued Coca Cola's shares over the 23-year period from 1989 to 2011 inclusive. What we see is remarkable: even though there has been little change in the business, and earnings have grown in a steady and predictable manner, the price investors have been prepared to pay for the same business has been extremely volatile. Investor mood swings are often the primary reason why the valuation of a stock, or an entire stock market, can swing so widely over time.

Over this 23-year period, investors, on average, paid 27.4 times Coca Cola's historic earnings. That average included a period from 1996 to 2001 when investors were prepared to pay above 35 times Coca Cola's earnings (sometimes way above), and periods from 1989 to 1991, and from 2005 onwards, when investors were only prepared to pay a more modest 20 times earnings or less.

In late 1998, when Coca Cola's shares peaked at $87, an investor was paying 61.3 times earnings – equivalent to an earnings yield of 1.6%. This level of earnings yield was too small to support much of a dividend. In addition, a simple risk-free investment, like the US 10-Year government bond, was offering an annual yield of circa 5% for the next 10 years at

that same time. In the late 1990s, the value was in the US 10-year
government bond and Coca Cola shares were grossly overvalued.

Chart 8.3: Coca Cola's Price-to-earnings Ratio (1989-2011)

Source: GillenMarkets.

Roll forward: Coca Cola reported earnings of $3.85 per share for 2011
and its shares traded at circa $70 at end 2011. At that point in time, its
shares offered an earnings yield of 5.5%, which easily supported its
dividend yield of 2.8%, while the alternative, supposedly risk-free, US
10-year government bond offered a yield of below 2%. Today, the value
lies in Coca Cola's shares and the US government bond is most likely the
asset that is overvalued.

So, in the late 1990s, we had a world class business with a near-
impenetrable market position and whose financial position was secure,
but whose shares were overvalued to the extent that they remain below
the price then pertaining some 13 years later. Some might describe that
as a near permanent loss. It must be clear from this example that the
value you buy has a significant impact on the subsequent return.

The Coca Cola case study is a relatively straightforward one because
Coca Cola's business is easy to understand. Many businesses do not lend
themselves to such easy analysis. I would hope, then, that I have proved
a point – that assessing the risks in individual companies is a much more
difficult task than many private investors acknowledge or understand. A
strategy of buying a portfolio of stocks that is dependent on whims, tips

and other inconsistent sources is a flawed one. Yet, many private investors persist in taking such haphazard approaches to selecting stocks.

However, while all this might sound somewhat defeatist, the positive news is that **Chapter 21, Enhancing Returns: Value Investing in the FTSE 100 Index** contains a robust, easy-to-follow and successful approach to selecting stocks in the UK FTSE 100 Index that anyone reading this book can learn and implement. Of course, you will only appreciate the strength of the approach outlined in **Chapter 21** if you have already experienced the difficulties of trying to subjectively select stocks yourself in the past.

SECTION II
A TOUR OF THE
ASSET CLASSES

CHAPTER 9
INVESTMENT CHOICES AND RETURNS

INTRODUCTION

Section II of the book **(Chapters 9** to **17)** is aimed at providing you with an understanding of the investment merits of each asset class along with analysis of the returns each has delivered over the long-term.

This first chapter provides a summary review of the various asset classes, along with my own summary conclusions regarding the merits or otherwise of including particular asset classes in an investment portfolio at this point in time. Greater detail on each separate asset class is then provided in **Chapters 10** to **17**. However, I have purposely structured this section of the book so that less experienced investors simply can read this chapter which, in effect, is a summary tour of the assets classes and then move directly to **Chapter 18, Ways of Gaining Exposure to the Markets**. That said, I believe every reader will find **Chapter 15, Precious Metals – Gold** and **Chapter 17, Alternative Assets, Timberland (Forestry)** easy to follow and fascinating.

RISK ASSETS AND NON-RISK ASSETS

Investors have a wide choice of assets to invest in, and **Table 9.1** lists the major asset classes and categorises them into non-risk and risk assets.

We can define non-risk assets as those that guarantee the return of capital after a set period of time along with a rate of return on that capital, which, at the time of purchase, an investor expects to at least match inflation. Non-risk assets traditionally have included bank deposits and short-dated government bonds.

Risk assets, which do not provide a guarantee of capital, include equities, physical property, commodities, precious metals, hedge and absolute return strategies, corporate bonds and a range of alternative assets including timberland (forestry) and agricultural land, art and collectibles, diamonds, rare coins and stamps, fine wines and others.

Table 9.1: The Major Asset Classes

Non-Risk Assets
Bank Deposits
Short-dated Government Bonds
Risk Assets
Equities
Property
Medium- & Long-dated Government Bonds
Corporate Bonds
Commodities
Precious Metals
Hedge & Absolute Return Strategies
Alternative Assets (Timber, Diamonds, Rare Coins & Stamps etc)

Here, one might also categorise medium- and long-dated government bonds as risk assets for the following two reasons: firstly, as we can't predict what inflation will be beyond the short-term, medium- and long-dated government bonds, which provide a fixed income, are not particularly good at protecting against the risks of unexpected inflation; secondly, even the credit worthiness of some governments becomes unreliable over the duration of medium- and long-dated government bonds. It may be rare but, as the Eurozone sovereign debt crisis and other sovereign debt crises before it have shown, governments can, and do, default on bonds that they have issued. That said, many other commentators categorise medium- and long-dated government bonds as non-risk assets. It is a grey area of investing, I guess!

SUMMARY RETURNS FROM THE VARIOUS ASSET CLASSES

Table 9.2 provides a summary of the long-term returns from the various asset classes. A nominal return represents the actual return generated whereas a real return adjusts for inflation – a real return is the return above inflation – for example, if equities delivered a 10% return in a particular year and inflation was 4% in that year, the real return was 6%.

It is clear from this table that equities, property and timberland assets have produced the best returns after inflation over the long-term. Bank deposits, as one might expect, have provided only modest real returns. Medium- and long-dated government bonds, commodities and even the precious metals (as represented by gold) have provided surprisingly low real returns when measured over the long-term. Also, the hedge fund industry has delivered surprisingly low real returns as measured since the industry came of age in the mid-to-late-1990s.

Table 9.2: Long-Term Returns from the Major Asset Classes
(Compound *per annum*)

Asset Type	Market Covered	Nominal Returns	Real Returns	Period Covered
Commodities	TR/J CRB Index	3.1%	-0.9%	1960-2011
Gold		5.1%	1.3%	1935-2011
Hedge Funds	Global Market	5.5%	2.9%	1997-2011
Long-dated Government Bonds	US & UK Markets	6.0%	1.6%	1946-2011
Bank Deposits	Developed Markets	7.0%	1.8%	1970-2011
Index-linked Government Bonds	UK Market	7.5%	3.6%	1983-2011
Commercial Property	US & UK Markets	10.0%	4.3%	1971-2011
Equities	US, UK, European Markets	10.4%	5.1%	1970-2011
Timberland	US	13.0%	8.6%	1987-2011

In **Chapter 4, The Power of Compounding,** we examined the progress of two investors: Investor A, who saved through bank deposits and obtained an annual return of 4%; and Investor B, who saved through risk assets, in that case the US equity market, and obtained an annual return of 8%. After 20 years, the extra 4% *per annum* return made an enormous difference, not in any particular year but cumulatively over the 20-year period. The search for higher returns on a medium- to long-term horizon is the reason investors consider investing in risk assets.

Returns from some asset classes are uncorrelated to returns from other asset classes and, for this reason, diversifying across a number of different asset class can lower risk.

Uncorrelated Returns Explained

The term 'correlation' refers to a relationship between the movements in two asset prices. Positive correlation means that when one asset class is generating positive or negative returns the other asset class is performing similarly. For example, if the price of gold rises then, all other things being equal, returns from gold mining stocks should be positive.

Negative correlation describes the scenario where returns from two separate asset classes are correlated but they move in opposite directions. For example, rising interest rates on bank deposits is normally a headwind for equities and property as the rising cost of money makes the stock market earnings yield or property rental yield less attractive. Hence, other things being equal, rising interest rates should lead to negative returns from equities and property and *vice versa*.

The term 'uncorrelated return' is used to describe a scenario where there is no underlying relationship between the returns on two separate asset classes. An example of this is returns from equities and hedge funds. If returns from equities are positive or negative in a particular period, you still should not be able to determine what return the hedge fund industry is likely to have delivered in that same period, as there are no common factors driving returns in both asset classes.

For this reason, investors often diversify across a range of asset classes to try and generate inflation-beating returns from a variety of assets that are uncorrelated to each other.

BANK DEPOSITS

Bank deposits need little explaining. Data I have compiled from various sources over the years in a range of developed markets, as outlined in **Table 9.3**, highlight that returns after inflation averaged 1.8% *per annum* compound covering the period 1970 to 2011 inclusive. Several independent longer-term studies have concluded that bank deposits generated a return of *circa* 1% or less above inflation over the past 100 years. Looking forward, a 1% *per annum* return above inflation is probably a more realistic guide as to what investors should expect from this investment class on a long-term horizon.

Table 9.3: Bank Deposits: Returns *per annum* Compound (1970-2011)

Asset Type	Market Covered	Nominal Returns	Real Returns	Period Covered
Bank Deposits	US, UK, Ireland & Germany	7.0%	1.8%	1970-2011

Saving through bank deposits comes with a guarantee from the bank and, to some extent, from many governments through deposit guarantee schemes. The saver/investor who takes no risk can hardly expect to be rewarded much above inflation. That said, the saver is due a positive return over inflation for providing his capital to the banking system.

GOVERNMENT AND CORPORATE BONDS

A government bond is in effect a loan from the investor to a government. The government issues a bond and investors buy the bond, which provides funding to the government. The bond is issued at a certain price, offers a fixed rate of interest (or return) to the investor and the issuer guarantees that the capital will be repaid at a certain future date (the redemption or maturity date).

Once a bond is issued, it also can be listed on the stock markets, and investors can buy and sell these bonds on the secondary market. Hence, if you buy a government bond with a life of 10 years, you can still sell it on to another investor at any time in the market place, if you choose to. You are only guaranteed your capital back in full if you hold to the maturity date so that selling the bond before the maturity date can lead to either a capital gain or loss. Nonetheless, a secondary market exists in government bonds and you can buy and sell when it suits you.

Table 9.4 highlights that long-dated government bonds in the US and UK have averaged nominal returns of 6% *per annum* compound since World War II. When we deduct inflation, the real returns work out at a fairly low 1.6% return *per annum* compound. Given the length of time an investor has to hold a long-dated bond to ensure the return of his capital, this level of real return, after inflation is taken into account, hardly seems to have been worth chasing.

Table 9.4: 20-Year UK Government Bonds: Returns *per annum*
Compound (1946-2011)

Asset Type	Market Covered	Nominal Returns	Real Returns	Period Covered
Long-dated Govt. Bonds	US & UK Markets	6.0%	1.6%	1946-2011

At the time of writing, long-dated government bonds in the US, UK and Germany offer yields of below 2%. This rate of return does not even cover inflation, which is currently running at 2% to 3% in these three economies. Long-dated government bonds currently appear to offer poor value, which, in turn, suggests that, at this point in time, short-dated government bonds or cash deposits offer the better option for the conservative investor who wishes to take little risk.

Inflation-linked bonds provide an annual return that is linked to the rate of inflation. In this way, they protect the investor against an unexpected rise in inflation, which can erode the purchasing power of his money over longer timelines. Inflation-linked bonds were introduced in the UK in the early 1980s in response to investor demand following a period of rampant inflation in the 1970s. Many other governments also issue inflation-linked bonds – for example, Treasury Inflation-protected Securities (TIPS) in the US. Inflation-linked bonds generally form only a small part of the overall domestic government bond market.

Table 9.5: UK Inflation-linked Government Bonds: Returns *per annum*
Compound (1983-2011)

Asset Type	Market Covered	Nominal Returns	Real Returns	Period Covered
Inflation-linked Govt. Bonds	UK Market	7.5%	3.6%	1983-2011

As **Table 9.5** highlights, nominal returns from UK inflation-linked bonds have averaged 7.6% *per annum* compound since they were first issued in 1983 or 3.6% after inflation. Given that the only risk an investor is taking with UK inflation-linked bonds is the risk of default by the UK government, a 3.6% real return compares favourably with the longer-term real returns from equities. However, these returns are in the past and one cannot conclude from this that inflation-linked bonds are likely to deliver anything above inflation in the future.

As the time of writing in mid-2012, inflation-linked bonds in the UK and US are priced to deliver the investor a modestly negative return after inflation (in other words, they are priced for deflation). That said, if inflation does take off, inflation-linked bonds should still provide better protection and returns than traditional long-dated government bonds, which would perform poorly against such a backdrop.

Corporate bonds are similar in nature to government bonds and can be classified further as investment grade and non-investment grade corporate bonds. The yield on offer from investment grade corporate bonds has tended in the past to be 0.5% to 1.0% above the equivalent government bond. The yield on offer from non-investment grade corporate bonds, which carry higher risk, has tended in the past to be 3.5% to 4.0% above the equivalent government bond. That is a generalisation, of course. Higher yields from investment grade and non-investment grade corporate bonds are designed to deliver the investor higher returns for the higher level of risk taken.

EQUITIES (SHARES)

Equities are a catch-all category for businesses quoted on the global stock exchanges, and there are overlaps between some equity sectors and other asset classes – for example, commodity producing and mining companies obviously are dependent on the underlying commodity prices. For this reason, commodity producing and mining stocks provide indirect exposure to commodities and the commodity cycle.

As **Table 9.2** highlighted, outside of US timberland assets, equities in the developed markets have delivered the best returns over the long-term.

Over the 42-year period from 1970 to 2011, nominal returns were 10.4% *per annum* compound on average across the four economies I examined. The real return above inflation worked out at 5.1% *per annum* compound over this same period. As I highlight in **Chapter 12, Equities (Shares)**, returns over this 42-year period were skewed, with returns since 1999 having been more or less flat in nominal terms and negative in real terms (after inflation). This, however, reflects the fact that the developed equity markets in the US, UK and Eurozone were overvalued to start with in the late 1990s. A valuation framework for the key US equity market (also outlined in **Chapter 12**) highlights that, today, the US equity market is modestly above fair value compared to history. This suggests that nominal and real returns on a five- to 10-year view from here from the key US equity market may be lower than the long-term averages shown in **Table 9.6** below.

Table 9.6: Average of US, UK, European & Irish Equity Markets: Nominal and Real Returns *per annum* Compound (1970-2011)

Asset Type	Market Covered	Nominal Returns	Real Returns	Period Covered
Equities	US, UK, European Markets	10.4%	5.1%	1970-2011

COMMERCIAL PROPERTY

As we saw in **Chapter 7, Stock Market and Direct Property Investing**, returns generated by businesses (equities) and physical property are influenced by many of the same factors, and are quite dependent on the general economic backdrop and the level and direction of interest rates. For this reason, it should not be overly surprising that the returns from both asset classes have been similar over time. **Table 9.7** highlights that commercial property returns in the UK (from 1971 to 2011) and in the US (from 1978 to 2011) have averaged 10% *per annum* compound, or 4.3% *per annum* compound after inflation.

Table 9.7: US and UK Commercial Property: Returns *per annum* Compound

Asset Type	Market Covered	Nominal Returns	Real Returns	Period Covered
Commercial Property	US & UK Markets	10.0%	4.3%	1971-2011 (UK): 1978-2011 (US)

Rental income from commercial property is more stable than corporate earnings (as it is a fixed cost of business that is less likely to be cut even in recession). The greater stability of rental income from a property is a major reason why it is easier to borrow to finance the purchase of commercial property with debt. Borrowing at an appropriate rate of interest to part-finance the purchase of property can enhance the long-term returns to the investor from this asset class and suggests that investor returns for UK and US commercial property as outlined in **Table 9.7** may well be underestimating the returns generated by investors in commercial property in practice. Either way, it is clear that commercial property as an asset class generates decent real returns over the long-term, and provides additional diversification opportunities for the investor.

COMMODITIES AND PRECIOUS METALS

The asset class of commodities includes energy such as oil, gas and uranium; industrial metals such as copper, aluminium, lead, zinc and nickel; soft commodities, including soybeans, corn, wheat, sugar, coffee, cotton and others. The precious metals include gold, silver, platinum and palladium. Gold's primary use is for investment purposes where as demand for silver, platinum and palladium is principally driven by industrial applications.

Commodities generate no income in their own right. As **Table 9.8** highlights, general commodity prices have failed to keep up with inflation in the past 50 years.

Table 9.8: Commodity Returns *per annum* Compound (1960-2011)

Asset Type	Market Covered	Nominal Returns	Real Returns	Period Covered
Commodities	TR/J CRB Index	3.1%	-0.9%	1960-2011

Source: Thomson Reuters/Jefferies CRB Index.

Since 1960, commodities, as represented by the Thomson Reuters/Jefferies Commodity Research Bureau Index (TR/J CRB Index), have recorded a 3.1% *per annum* compound gain. However, after adjusting for inflation over the same timeline, a general basket of commodities has not even kept pace with inflation, recording a negative return of 0.9% *per annum* compound. A further complication is that investors cannot physically invest in energy, industrial or soft commodities either directly or through funds. After all, where would these commodities be stored? In practice, then, investing in most commodities is achieved by buying futures contracts. As these futures contracts have to be rolled over from one time period to the next, roll-over costs are incurred. Hence, it is likely that an investor would have done even worse from commodities than the negative 0.9% *per annum* return outlined in **Table 9.8**.

The practical issues of investing in commodities suggests that investors who wish to gain exposure to commodities (or the commodity cycle) might be better off investing in commodity production or mining companies listed on stock exchanges, which make up part of the overall equity markets. Investing in a fund containing a diversified list of such companies also is an option.

On the positive side, commodities, at times, have gone counter-trend to equities. For example, returns from commodities were particularly strong in the 1970s and again in the 2000s, as outlined in **Chapter 14, Commodities**. In both of these decades, equities performed poorly so that exposure to commodities during these periods added balance to a portfolio.

PRECIOUS METALS – GOLD

Gold is a fascinating metal and much more than a mere commodity; it is the oldest currency in the world and can rightfully claim its place as the only currency to have acted as a true store of value over the millennia. For this reason, it is worth examining in more detail to see whether it merits a place in an investment portfolio, and whether it offers value today following a rip-roaring bull run that has lasted for the past 11 years straight.

Paper currencies can be printed at will but new gold has to be found and then painstakingly mined from the ground. Due to limited supplies, and its rare physical attributes, gold has been the only currency to have protected capital over the millennia. An understanding of gold's remarkable physical attributes also helps us understand why gold came to be a currency in the first place thousands of years ago.

Gold is the heaviest metal (highest density). It is virtually indestructible, and its melting point is 1,064 degrees Celsius. It is the most stretchable pure metal known to man – a single gram can be crafted into a sheet one metre squared, which is so thin that the sun can shine through it. It does not oxidise (rust) in air or water; it has no taste in its purest form; and it is an excellent conductor of electricity. Its physical beauty has seen it used as jewellery for thousands of years and, more recently, its robustness and dependability has seen it in increasing demand in many new complex industrial applications, where price is less of a consideration.

In geological terms, gold-bearing rock is rare, and even when it is discovered an average tonne of gold ore currently yields only six grams of gold – that is six parts to a million – and even this figure has been declining over time. Its durability, rarity and divisibility make it valuable and tradable, and allow significant wealth to be stored or transported with relative ease. It is, therefore, easy to understand how gold has been an accepted form of money for thousands of years. Unlike commodities in general, gold can be stored and transported easily and at low cost, which means that it can be bought and held as an investment without fear that costs will overly interfere with returns, and it does not perish with time.

Table 9.9: Gold Returns *per annum* Compound (1935-2011)

Asset Type	Nominal Returns	Real Returns	Period Covered
Gold	5.1%	1.3%	1935-2011

Table 9.9 highlights the nominal and real returns from gold (in US dollar terms) since 1935. Over this 77-year period gold has returned 5.1% *per annum* compound or 1.3% *per annum* compound after inflation. Hence, gold has done no better than cash deposits after inflation over this timeline. In addition, returns from gold have been much more volatile and lumpy compared to simple cash deposits.

Of course, this comparison is against the world's reserve currency, the dollar. There have been many instances over the past 100 years where hyperinflation has savaged local currencies. Following World War II, the German currency became virtually worthless. The Zimbabwean dollar succumbed to hyperinflation as politics wrecked that country. More recently, the Icelandic Krona was heavily devalued following the global credit crisis. Gold is a universal currency and protects against the danger of currency devaluation whether through hyperinflation or otherwise.

HEDGE AND ABSOLUTE RETURN STRATEGIES

The global hedge fund industry really only came of age in the 1990s. Hedge and absolute return strategies (and funds that follow these strategies) exist to generate positive annual returns from equities and other assets or financial instruments listed on markets, regardless of the performance of the markets themselves.

Hedge and absolute return funds often use leverage with the aim of magnifying the underlying returns. The flexibility to sell stocks or financial instruments that they do not own (referred to as 'selling short') provides hedge and absolute return funds with the ability to generate returns irrespective of the overall direction of stock markets. For this reason, returns from hedge and absolute return strategies should be uncorrelated to returns from asset classes that are more sensitive to the economic cycle like equities and property. Hence, they offer further diversification options within an overall risk-asset investment portfolio.

As **Table 9.10** highlights, the HFRX Global Hedge Fund Index delivered a 5.5% *per annum* compound return from 1998 to 2011 inclusive, or 2.9% *per annum* compound in real terms (returns above inflation). These returns include the benefits of leverage within hedge funds but the returns also are after costs, which are particularly high in the industry.

Table 9.10: HFRX Global Hedge Fund Index: Returns *per annum* Compound (1998-2011)

Asset Type	Market Covered	Nominal Returns	Real Returns	Period Covered
Hedge Funds	Global Market	5.5%	2.9%	1998-2011

Most private investors probably associate hedge and absolute return funds with high returns. However, the evidence in **Table 9.10** highlights that, while the hedge fund industry has delivered positive annual returns after inflation, returns have been lower than one might have expected given the risks they take, the leverage (or gearing) they employ and their overall glamour image. In addition, an examination of the year by year returns from 1998 to 2011 (outlined in **Chapter 16, Hedge and Absolute Return Strategies)** highlights that the hedge fund industry generated negative returns in 2008 and 2011, at the same time as returns from equity markets were negative. Hence, in both of these years, the hedge fund industry failed to deliver on one of its stated aims and key attractions: to generate positive returns when equity markets are delivering negative returns. That said, hedge and absolute return strategies have generated real returns in the past, and provide additional diversification opportunities for the investor.

ALTERNATIVE ASSETS – TIMBERLAND (FORESTRY)

Alternative assets include a range of niche risk asset categories, including forestry (timberland) and agricultural land, fine wines, diamonds, rare stamps and coins and art and collectibles. It is beyond the scope of this book to examine the historical returns from all the alternative asset classes. Instead, I will focus solely on timberland as an asset class.

In any given year, the biological growth of timber in the ground is a significant contributor to overall timber returns. Irrespective of the economic conditions of the day, the timber grows and gains value during the year simply by virtue of the fact that there is more of it at the end of the year than there was at the start. Obviously, the eventual market price achieved for the timber can vary at the time it is harvested and sold. Weak economic conditions can, and do, lead to weak timber prices, just as with any other commodity. But any decent forestry company or timberland fund will own a variety of plantations with a staggered maturity profile that reduces the dependence on the market price at any specific time.

Table 9.11: NCREIF Timberland Index: Returns *per annum* Compound (1987-2011)

Asset Type	Market Covered	Nominal Returns	Real Returns	Period Covered
Timberland	US	13.0%	8.6%	1987-2011

As **Table 9.11** highlights, returns from US timberland assets have been higher even than equity returns over the 25-year period from 1987 to 2011 inclusive with returns of 13% *per annum* compound. When these returns are adjusted for inflation (the returns above inflation), they come in at 8.6% *per annum* compound. However, for reasons discussed in more detail in **Chapter 17 (Alternative Assets, Timberland),** it is not realistic to expect timberland or forestry assets to produce these types of returns into the future. Nonetheless, it is clear that timberland assets provide diversification opportunities and can add value to a portfolio of risk assets.

SUMMARY CONCLUSIONS

The conclusions I outline here on the merits or otherwise of including particular asset classes in an investment portfolio to a significant degree rely on the details provided in **Chapters 10** to **17**. For this reason, providing such opinions now could be viewed as 'putting the cart before the horse'. However, as I said at the outset of this chapter, I have structured this section of the book so that less experienced investors have the option of now skipping directly to **Chapter 18, Ways of Gaining Exposure to the Markets** once they have concluded this chapter. Hence, including my summary conclusions here is a compromise on my part that hopefully works satisfactorily.

Equities (Shares)

Equities, property and timberland assets, when fairly valued compared to history, have provided the best long-term returns to investors. Poor returns from the developed equity markets since 2000 initially reflected the overvaluation of equities at the outset in early 2000 and subsequently the varying impact of the global credit crisis on different markets.

In **Chapter 12, Equities**, the valuation framework for the key US equity market outlined in **Chart 12.2** suggests that US equities are currently priced to deliver returns of 6% to 7% *per annum* over the next five to 10 years, and somewhat below the long-term average. That said, using the same valuation framework, the equity markets of the Eurozone, Japanese and emerging markets offer the potential for above average returns over the next five to 10 years. The overhang of debt following the global credit crisis and the ongoing Eurozone sovereign and banking debt crises means the risks of deflation, which would erode values and returns, are above average.

Hedge and Absolute Return Strategies

The evidence to date suggests that the hedge fund industry, in aggregate, has flattered to deceive since the industry came of age in the mid-1990s. Returns from the industry have been lower than investors generally realise and they did not provide off-setting returns in the difficult years of 2008 and 2011 in equity markets. Hence, arguments for their automatic inclusion as part of balanced risk-asset portfolios are far from compelling. At a minimum, if you do include these fund types in your pension or investment portfolio, you should ensure you include several such funds as the manager-specific risk in hedge and absolute return funds is much higher than average.

Commodities and Gold

Commodities and gold generate no income in their own right and generally have only provided returns that match inflation over the long-term. Counterbalancing this, however, commodities and gold have tended to deliver positive returns when equities have been performing poorly, and therefore have offered off-setting returns to equities at certain times in the past. While investing in gold is straightforward, in practice, energy, industrial and soft commodities cannot be owned outright so that investors realistically can gain exposure to commodities only by buying commodity producing and mining companies listed on the global stock markets. On balance, and given the out-sized gains in commodity prices and gold since 2001, there seems no compelling reason why investors would look to gain exposure to these asset types beyond that which is naturally available through listed equities.

Medium And Long-dated Government Bonds

At the time of writing, long-dated government bonds in the developed economies offer poor value relative to history, and expose investors to potentially significant declines in bond prices if inflation takes off and/or interest rates globally reverse trend and start to rise. In addition, long-dated bonds in the same regions offer no meaningful income. More conservative investors looking for a non-risk asset would be better off staying in short-dated government bonds or bank deposits. The conundrum for investors at this time is that risk-free short-dated government bonds and bank deposits in the developed world offer no income either and no protection against inflation.

Inflation-linked Government Bonds

Inflation-linked bonds have merit as a hedge against future inflation, as their returns are directly linked to the prevailing rate of inflation. However, as they are currently priced, returns are likely simply to match inflation from here. That said, in a world that still faces deflationary threats, inflation-linked bonds continue to offer diversification options in an investment portfolio.

Guaranteed Structured Products – Serving the Sellers, Not Investors

Guaranteed structured products are not a separate asset class. These investment products are structured by banks, insurance companies and other product sellers to provide a guarantee of capital and to deliver some of the upside from risk assets. However, the costs of assembling and selling these products are onerous, and more times than not they simply serve to pander to investors' fears. In addition, the charging structure is not transparent and there has been no proper monitoring of returns delivered to investors over time from guaranteed structured products. The pros and cons of these products are outlined in more detail in **Appendix 2** but it is clear to me that there is little merit in including these products as part of a diversified investment portfolio.

OVERALL CONCLUSIONS

In conclusion, at the time of writing, the value and income lies in equities and property but risks are unusually high against the backdrop of a debt overhang in the developed economies, an absence of a full solution to the Eurozone crisis and low GDP growth generally. Of course, to invest in short-dated government bonds or to stay in bank deposits runs the risk of falling behind inflation and losing purchasing power. The conundrum for today's investor who wishes to take little risk is that there is unlikely to be any return for several years.

CHAPTER 10
BANK DEPOSITS

Several long-term studies have shown that returns from bank deposits have averaged about 1% above inflation over the past 100 years and more. **Table 10.1** highlights the returns from 3-month bank deposits in the UK, US, Germany and Ireland over a 42-year period from 1970 to 2011 inclusive, a period of time that serves as a reasonable proxy for the long-term.

Table 10.1: Bank Deposits: Nominal Returns *per annum* Compound (1970-2011)

Year	Ireland	UK	US	Germany	Average
1970s	9.7%	9.7%	8.1%	6.8%	8.6%
1980s	12.5%	13.0%	10.4%	6.7%	10.7%
1990s	7.7%	7.7%	5.4%	5.7%	6.6%
2000s	3.3%	4.3%	3.4%	3.3%	3.6%
2010s	3.0%	0.5%	0.2%	1.0%	1.2%
1970 - 2011	8.0%	8.1%	6.4%	5.4%	7.0%

Source: GillenMarkets.[7]

Note: Assumes three-month bank deposits and the reinvestment of income.

In isolation, **Table 10.1** tells us very little other than that interest rates varied over the period from an average of 5.4% in Germany to an average of 8.1% in the UK, and that high interest rates were a feature in most developed markets in the 1970s and 1980s, and are now as low as they have been in recorded history.

---

[7] The data has been compiled from a variety of sources over the years, using historical data from newspapers, and more recently from government and central bank websites.

Table 10.2 highlights the three-month bank deposit returns after inflation (referred to as real returns) in the UK, the US, Germany and Ireland over the same 42-year period.

Table 10.2: Bank Deposits: Real Returns *per annum* Compound (1970-2011)

Year	Ireland	UK	US	Germany	Average
1970s	-3.5%	-2.0%	0.5%	1.8%	-0.8%
1980s	4.5%	4.9%	5.1%	3.9%	4.6%
1990s	5.1%	3.6%	2.5%	3.1%	3.6%
2000s	0.3%	1.1%	0.4%	1.2%	0.7%
2010s	2.2%	-4.1%	-2.0%	-1.3%	-1.3%
1970 - 2011	1.6%	1.6%	1.9%	2.3%	1.8%

Source: GillenMarkets.

Note: Assumes three-month bank deposits and the reinvestment of income.

The real returns on bank deposits are detailed for each decade, and show that, even on cash deposits, returns are not always above inflation. If we average out the returns from 1970 to 2011, bank deposits across the four regions delivered compound *per annum* returns of *circa* 1.8% after inflation. This real return, compiled from my own records, is somewhat higher than suggested by several other longer-term studies in the past. Nonetheless, the figures in **Table 10.2** still provide us with comfort that bank deposits generally deliver positive returns after inflation over the long-term.

The logic of why bank deposits will only ever provide a modest return over inflation in the long-term is that the depositors' monies are guaranteed. The investor who takes no risk cannot expect to be rewarded much above inflation. That said, the saver is due a positive return over inflation for providing his capital to the banking system. The bank lends on this capital and the borrower should pay the saver a real return for access to this capital.

CHAPTER 11
GOVERNMENT AND
CORPORATE BONDS

Governments finance their spending by issuing bonds that are bought by both institutional and private investors. A traditional government bond offers a fixed rate of interest and your money back at the maturity date – a guarantee of your capital back at an agreed future date.

Governments issue short-, medium- and long-dated bonds. Short-dated bonds typically have maturity or redemption dates of three years or less at the time they are issued. Medium-term bonds generally are issued with three to seven years to maturity and long-dated bonds typically mature beyond an 8-year horizon.

Table 11.1: Government Bonds: Maturity Profiles

Category	Maturity Date
Short-term Bonds	3 years or less
Medium-term Bonds	4-7 years
Long-term Bonds	8 years or longer

Of course, the price of the bond may vary in the marketplace, in reaction to changes in interest rate expectations, but each particular bond should revert back towards its redemption price the closer it gets to the maturity date. So long as the investor holds to maturity, the price volatility in between is largely irrelevant, as the investor gets his money back, having earned a predetermined fixed level of interest income.

Like equities, government bonds are listed and traded on the exchanges, so that even though you may buy a 10-year bond, you can still sell it on to another investor in the marketplace at any time. But if you sell it before the official maturity date, you cannot be sure you will get all your capital back along with the agreed interest income stream.

The rate of interest offered on medium- and long-term government bonds is normally dictated by the marketplace, and influenced by both the level of short-term interest rates and inflationary expectations over the medium- to long-term.

Normally, the further out the maturity date of a government bond, the higher the rate of interest an investor should obtain. In effect, the investor has to be compensated for the longer period that he is lending his money to the government.

Government bonds traditionally have been considered a non-risk asset because governments provide a guarantee of the return of investors' capital. But, like companies, governments can come unstuck and get into financial difficulties, at which stage previous guarantees may not be delivered on.

Government bond prices and the yields they offer move inversely to one another. Take the example of a government bond that is issued at €100 and offers a coupon (or yield) of 3%: if the bond price moves upwards due to demand to, say, €110, the yield will have declined to 2.73%. Conversely, if the bond price falls to €80, the yield will rise to 3.75%. Hence, investors often describe a weak bond market as one where prices are falling or yields are rising. Equally, a strong bond market is characterised by rising bond prices and declining bond yields.

Table 11.2: Government Bond Prices and Yield

	Price	Yield
Initial bond price	€100	3.00%
Bond price rises	€110	2.73%
Bond price declines	€80	3.75%

NO INCOME FROM DEVELOPED MARKET GOVERNMENT BONDS

Chart 11.1 highlights the trend of US government bond yields since 1979. The 1970s were characterised by rampant inflation but, by the early 1980s, inflation had peaked, and investors became more confident that inflation was on a sustainable downward trend. With inflation beaten, US government bond yields (long-term interest rates), which had been rising since the late 1960s, began a long decline from the early 1980s onwards to early 2012. As shown in **Table 11.2**, declining bond yields reflects rising bond prices. In other words, since the early 1980s, there has been an ongoing bull market in the US government bond market where bond prices have been rising consistently (and bond yields declining). The same trend has been in existence in most of the other developed economies of the UK and continental Europe.

Chart 11.1: US 10-Year Government Bond Yield (1979-2011)

Source: GillenMarkets.

Like any other asset, government bonds, and particularly long-dated government bonds, normally deliver a real return (a positive return post-inflation), at least over long term horizons. But, as we don't know the future when we buy a bond, sometimes this works out and at other times it does not. Hence, there is a greater risk with long-dated government bonds (compared to short-dated bonds) that inflation exceeds the return (or coupon) you receive on your capital.

Table 11.3 highlights the *per annum* compound returns before and after inflation (real returns) on 20-year US government bonds and 20-year UK government bonds since 1946, providing 66 years of data.

The late 1940s, the 1950s, 1960s and 1970s all produced negative returns after inflation (negative real returns) for buyers of long-dated bonds in the US and UK. However, inflation was finally subdued in the early 1980s and three-plus decades of positive bond returns after inflation were ushered in. For the whole 66-year period, the real return above inflation averaged out at 2.1% *per annum* compound on US 20-year government bonds and 1.1% on UK 20-year government bonds. Seen in that context, the last three decades have delivered extraordinarily high real returns on US and UK long-dated government bonds.

Table 11.3: US & UK 20-Year Bonds: Nominal & Real Returns *per annum* Compound (1946-2011)

Period	US Bonds		UK Bonds	
	Nominal Return	Real Return	Nominal Return	Real Return
1946-1949	1.6%	-4.7%	-3.4%	-6.2%
1950s	0%	-2.0%	0.9%	-3.2%
1960s	0.8%	-1.1%	1.6%	-1.9%
1970s	5.4%	-1.7%	8.3%	-4.1%
1980s	11.9%	7.3%	14.5%	6.9%
1990s	7.7%	5.5%	11.9%	8.3%
2000s	6.9%	4.4%	5.2%	2.6%
2010-2011	17.3%	14.8%	14.9%	10.0%
1946-2011	5.5%	2.1%	6.5%	1.1%

Source: Barclays Capital Annual Equity/Gilt Study 2012.

With the current yield on 10-year government bonds in the US and UK at below 2.0% (at the time of writing), it would appear that very little is currently being priced in for future inflation – in other words, inflationary expectations for the next 10 years are currently exceptionally low. For example, if inflation averages 2.5% over the next 10 years, then buying 10-year bonds today will provide a negative return after inflation annually for the next 10 years. At the time of writing in mid-2012 however, economic growth in the developed world is being constrained by the debt overhang following the global credit crisis of 2008. Investors appear to have concluded that inflation, and short-term interest rates, in the developed world will stay low for a long time.

The prospect of lower short-term interest rates for a longer period in the developed economies is fuelling demand for the yield on offer in longer-dated bonds. In addition, increased regulatory pressure on banks and insurance companies to hold a higher level of capital following the global credit crisis, and to hold that capital in the form of 'guaranteed' capital (in other words, bonds), also is fuelling demand for long-dated bonds.

The supply of government (sovereign) bonds also has increased significantly in the past decade, particularly since the onset of the global credit crisis in 2008. Most governments in the developed world are running huge fiscal deficits and are issuing record quantities of new bonds to finance those deficits. But as the *Barclays Capital Annual Gilt/Equity Study 2012* points out, a significant portion of developed market sovereign bonds has to be excluded from the supply pool on the basis that they are now considered a credit risk (for example, Italian and Spanish government bonds and US mortgage-backed bonds in particular). Hence, despite the huge increase in triple A-rated bond issuance globally, demand for the highest quality government bonds is outstripping the supply, for the time being at least.

So, are we looking at a bubble in the valuation of long-dated government bonds in the developed markets? My own personal view is that a 30-year plus bull market in government bonds where yields are now below inflation, demand is artificially inflated and supply temporarily depressed, together with the likelihood that governments in the UK and US will continue to print money in response to ongoing deflationary forces, suggests that the risks of a substantial decline in bond prices is high in the years ahead.

It appears to me then that, even if inflation stays extraordinarily low over the medium-term from here on, buying or owning long-dated government bonds in the developed markets is a high risk investment at this time. At the very least, we might conclude that long-dated government bonds offer no protection against inflation and little by way of income.

Inflation-linked Government Bonds

Inflation-linked bonds also can be referred to as inflation-protected or indexed-linked bonds. They are designed to protect the investor against inflation. Some inflation-linked bonds accomplish that by varying the interest rate coupon to reflect the rise in inflation and others do it by varying the principal repayment. Many countries issue inflation-linked bonds, although the asset class remains a smaller part of the overall global government bond markets. Inflation-linked bonds are traded on the stock markets and can be bought individually or *via* funds.

Table 11.4: Barclays Capital UK Index-linked Bond Fund: Nominal and Real Returns *per annum* Compound (1983-2011)

Period	Nominal Returns	Real Returns
1983-1989	6.8%	1.4%
1990s	9.4%	5.7%
2000s	4.6%	1.9%
2010s	15.1%	9.7%
1983-2011	7.5%	3.6%

Source: Barclays Capital Annual Equity/Gilt Study 2012.

Table 11.4 highlights the returns from a Barclays Capital Index-linked Government Bond Fund, containing a representative list of long-dated UK index-linked government bonds starting in 1983. The returns above inflation, or the real returns, work out at 3.6% *per annum* compound over this 29-year period. Clearly, UK index-linked bonds did their job and provided a decent return when adjusted for inflation over the last three decades.

As we stand in mid-2012, with UK and US interest rates likely to stay low for an extended period (due to the debt overhang) but with inflation a constant threat from commodity price inflation and quantitative easing programmes, index-linked government bonds remain a non-risk asset offering protection against inflation. However, the real yield on index-linked government bonds in the UK and US is currently negative, which means that the best investors are likely to achieve from these bonds from here on is to match inflation (less a bit) over the medium-term. The same point most likely can be said about Eurozone index-linked government bonds.

Corporate Bonds

A corporate bond is similar to a government bond, in that it is issued with a fixed rate of interest and a guarantee of repayment at an agreed date in the future. But most companies are not considered to be as financially secure as governments, and so the guarantee attached to corporate bonds is not considered as strong. That, of course, is a general rule. Corporate bonds also are traded on the stock markets and investors can buy them directly or *via* corporate bond funds.

Corporate bonds can be categorised further into investment grade and non-investment grade bonds. In short, investment grade corporate bonds carry a lower risk of default than non-investment grade. For that reason, investment grade corporate bonds offer lower interest coupons than the non-investment grade variety. As a general rule, top quality corporate bonds have had to offer interest coupons of *circa* 0.5% to 1% over the equivalent government bond, over the long-term. For example, if the US government can issue a five-year bond with a 3% coupon, then an investment grade company on average will be able to issue a five-year bond with a 3.5% to 4% coupon.

As you would expect, given the added risk implicit in non-investment grade companies they have to offer a more substantial interest rate premium on any corporate bonds (debt) they issue for funding purposes. Again, as a general rule, non-investment grade corporate bonds tend to offer yields of *circa* 3% to 4% in excess of the equivalent government bond (or 2% to 3% above top quality investment grade corporate bonds). At the time of writing, for example, non-investment grade corporate bond ETFs (exchange-traded funds), which contain a good spread of such bonds, offer annual yields of 6% to 7%, which is currently some 4% to 5% ahead of inflation.

It follows, then, that if one believes long-dated government bonds are overvalued, one is likely also to conclude that long-dated investment grade corporate bonds are similarly overvalued. However, non-investment grade corporate bonds, with annual yields of 6% to 7% appear to be more rationally priced for the risks of default. In a corporate bond fund (or ETF), which should be well diversified and typically can contain up to 100 separate non-investment grade corporate bonds, the risk of default is well spread and the annual yield of 6% to 7% would appears to justify the risk. Hence, I feel that non-investment grade corporate bond funds offer the prospect of reasonable returns along with added diversification in a risk asset portfolio.

CHAPTER 12
EQUITIES (SHARES)

Several studies have shown that the long-term returns from equities have averaged *circa* 9% to 10% *per annum* compound, or 5% to 6% *per annum* compound above inflation, over the long-term. We will now see whether we can gather the relevant data to prove that for ourselves.

Shares or equities refer to individual companies listed on the stock markets, including companies operating in a wide range of industries such as the food, beverage, building, property, mining, healthcare, transport, financial, telecoms, technology and many other industries.

Table 12.1: Equities: Nominal Returns *per annum* Compound (1970-2011)

Year	Ireland	UK	US	Europe	Average
1970s	13.4%	10.3%	5.9%	3.2%	8.2%
1980s	24.8%	22.2%	17.6%	19.7%	21.1%
1990s	16.6%	14.0%	18.0%	16.4%	16.3%
2000s	-3.0%	1.7%	-1.1%	-0.4%	-0.7%
2010s	1.2%	5.4%	8.6%	-8.1%	1.8%
1970 - 2011	11.9%	11.5%	9.8%	8.5%	10.4%

Source: GillenMarkets.[8]

Note: Returns represent capital returns plus dividend income reinvested.

Table 12.1 highlights the returns from the equity markets of the UK, US, continental Europe and Ireland over the same 42-year period from 1970 to 2011. Again, the returns across these four equity regions are detailed for each decade. The table highlights that returns averaged just over 10% *per annum* compound across the four regions. Returns were particularly high in the 1980s and 1990s but were mostly negative in the 2000s. We will see further on in this section that the negative returns from US

---

[8]   Data assembled from a variety of sources over the years, including government databases, newspapers and third party reports.

equities, for example, in the 2000s can be explained largely by significant overvaluation in this major equity market in the late 1990s. But, again, in isolation, the returns outlined in **Table 12.1** don't tell us how investors in equities (shares) fared relative to recorded inflation.

Table 12.2 provides us with the equity returns above inflation, or the real equity returns, from these four markets over the same timeline from 1970 to 2011 inclusive. If we average out the returns from 1970 to 2011, equity returns across the four regions were 5.1% *per annum* compound above inflation.

Table 12.2: Equities: Real Returns *per annum* Compound (1970-2011)

Year	Ireland	UK	US	Europe	Average
1970s	-0.2%	-1.5%	-1.5%	-1.7%	-1.2%
1980s	15.9%	13.4%	12.0%	16.5%	14.4%
1990s	13.8%	9.8%	14.7%	13.5%	12.9%
2000s	-5.8%	-1.1%	-3.6%	-2.3%	-3.2%
2010s	0.4%	0.6%	6.2%	-10.3%	-0.7%
1970 - 2011	5.2%	4.7%	5.1%	5.3%	5.1%

Source: GillenMarkets.

Note: Returns represent capital returns plus dividend income reinvested.

The message is clear. The inflation-adjusted returns from equities across these four regions worked out fairly close to the 5% to 6% long-term average quoted in several longer-term studies.

Again, the 2000s delivered negative real returns across the four regions of -3.2% *per annum* compound, and the most recent two years of 2010 and 2011 combined have not been any better (with the exception of the US). Is it any wonder retail investors have practically given up on equities!

Equities are volatile and there is the ever-present risk that the value of shares may decline – sometimes significantly – in the short-term. But over the medium- to long-term, the returns have justified investors taking the added risk.

A VALUATION FRAMEWORK FOR THE KEY US EQUITY MARKET

A critical piece in the investment jigsaw for investors is that the value on offer in any asset class at the point of purchase has a significant bearing on the subsequent returns. As equity markets and property assets produce a stream of income (or earnings), they can be valued in the context of history and relative to the income available from competing asset classes.

We now will examine a framework that provides a reasonable guide regarding:

♦ The valuation of the key US equity market at any point in time over the past 100 years;

♦ The likely returns an investor could have expected over any subsequent 10-year period; and,

♦ A guide as to the expected returns from the key US equity market on a five- to 10-year view from here.

In the past, when this particular valuation framework highlighted that the US stock market was undervalued relative to history, the returns to investors were above average over the subsequent 10 years. Likewise, when the model highlighted that the US equity market was overvalued, the returns to investors were below average over the subsequent 10 years. In this regard, the strength of the valuation framework outlined here is that it has proved in the past to be reasonably *predictive* of the subsequent returns on a five- to 10-year view. That is important, as our ability to compound our savings or pension monies is dependent on the likely returns available. If the evidence suggests that equities, as an asset class, are overvalued, then we always have the option of investing where there is better value on offer or in simple, risk-free bank deposits.

The US equity market has the most easily accessible long-term valuation and return statistics, so it is the obvious market on which to examine this valuation model. At the end of 2011, the 500 companies making up the US benchmark equity index, or the S&P 500 Index, had reported earnings of $89.50 per share for the previous 12 months.[9]

---

[9]   **Appendix I** outlines some basic stock market terminology and valuation
       metrics, and some readers may wish to read the appendix before reading
       further into this chapter.

At the end of 2011, the S&P 500 Index was trading at 1,258. Hence, if we bought an exchange-traded fund, or ETF (ETFs are explained in detail in **Chapter 18**), which replicates the S&P 500 Index for an investor, we could say that we were paying $1,258 for $89.50 of earnings. At the end of 2011, then, the value on offer in the S&P 500 Index could have been expressed in two ways:

- We were paying an average of 14.1 times the earnings of these companies (1,258 / 89.5 = 14.1); or

- We were buying an earnings yield of 7.1% when we bought the S&P 500 Index at $1,258 (89.5 / 1,258*100 = 7.1%).

The price-to-earnings (P/E) ratio of 14.1 is the same as the earnings yield of 7.1%. One is simply the inverse of the other. As a measure of value, the earnings yield has two advantages. Firstly, it is easier to relate to and, secondly, it can be directly compared to returns on offer from other assets. For example, at the end of December 2011, European Central Bank overnight interest rates were 1% and the yield to redemption (maturity) available on a 10-year German government bond was 1.83%. Expressing the earnings on the S&P 500 Index as a percentage of the price paid gives us the earnings yield, and allows us to do a quick comparison across other asset classes.

But that is as far as the usefulness of the comparison goes. The comparison also begs the question: why hold cash deposits or bonds if the earnings yield from the stock market is higher?

There are a number of understandable reasons. Companies, and their shares, are risky, and the earnings they are generating today may be lower tomorrow or in six or 12 months' time. So, for the stock market, the earnings yield is indicative of value only if the earnings are stable. Even for an entire market, owned through an exchange-traded fund, the earnings are subject to the business or economic cycle. Over time, corporate earnings have tended to rise to reflect the growth of business in the economy, but there have been the inevitable recessions that impact on corporate earnings along the way.

Chart 12.1 highlights the growth in earnings on the S&P 500 Index from 1970 to 2011 inclusive. Over this 42-year period, the average earnings (per share) of the 500 companies making up the S&P 500 Index grew from $5.80 per share at the end of 1969 to $89.50 by end-2011. That represents growth of 6.7% *per annum* compound. Of course, recessions in the 1970s, 1980s, 1990s and 2000s all interrupted the growth in earnings from time to time (marked in **Chart 12.1** with an arrow), but corporate earnings always recovered and went to new peaks. The declines in earnings during the recessions of the early and late 2000s were particularly steep.

Chart 12.1: S&P 500 Index: Earnings per Share (1969-2011)

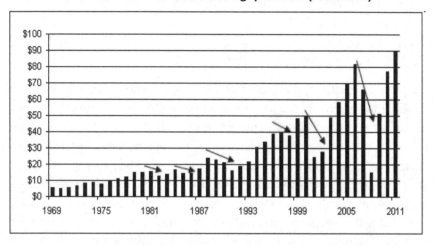

Source: Robert Shiller (http://www.econ.yale.edu/~shiller/data.htm).

The volatility in corporate earnings, in large part due to the ups and downs in the business cycle, makes it hard to say at any particular point in time, with any degree of confidence, that the earnings you see are the earnings you get. Hence, the earnings yield (or P/E ratio) at any particular point in time can be misleading as a measure of value.

Ben Graham, author of *The Intelligent Investor* (first edition published in 1949, and considered the all-time investment classic), used to take the average of the past 10 years' earnings, and compare that figure to the current price, in order to compute the earnings yield or the P/E ratio. This, of course, was a useful way of ironing out the ups and downs in earnings due to the business cycle. By comparing the average of the last 10 years' earnings to the current price being paid for an index like the S&P 500, an investor could avoid having to judge the value in the overall market using a point-in-time earnings figure, when earnings could easily be either temporarily inflated or depressed.

As an example, **Table 12.3** provides the calculation of the price-to-10-year-average earnings ratio on the S&P 500 Index at the end December

2011. The S&P 500 Index's earnings per share for the past 10 years works out at an average of $58.50, and when compared to the S&P 500 Index level of 1,258 indicates a price-to-10-year average earnings ratio (P/E ratio) of 21.5. In other words, investors buying the S&P 500 Index at the end of 2011 at 1,258 were paying 21.5 times the average of the last 10 years' earnings.

Table 12.3: S&P 500 Index: Earnings Per Share (2002-2011) and Price-to-10-Year Average Earnings Ratio (at 31 December 2011)

Year	S&P 500 EPS $
2002	27.6
2003	48.7
2004	58.6
2005	69.9
2006	81.5
2007	66.2
2008	14.9
2009	51.0
2010	77.4
2011	89.5
10-Year Average EPS	$58.5
S&P 500 Index @ 31 Dec 2011	1,258
P/E Ratio @ 31 Dec 2011	21.5

Source: S&P 500 earnings data - www.standardandpoors.com.

Next, we need to see how the US equity market was priced relative to this 10-year average earnings measure for as far back in time as we can go. This will show us the valuation cycles in the key US equity market, and highlight times when the US equity market was either overvalued or undervalued compared to long-term norms.

Chart 12.2 compares the 10-year average earnings to the S&P 500 Index price level back to 1900, providing a useful value guide over time. What is clear is that there have been significant swings in valuation. Only a sense of history can provide a guide as to when the US stock market appears to have been fairly valued, overvalued or undervalued.

Chart 12.2: S&P 500 Index: Price-to-10-Year-Average Earnings Ratio (1900-2011)

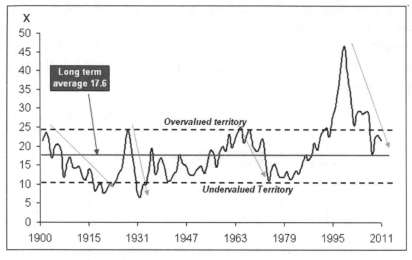

Source: Robert Shiller (http://www.econ.yale.edu/~shiller/data.htm).

For example, in the early 1900s, investors buying the US stock market were paying over 20 times the average of the last 10 years' earnings. But between then and 1920, investors were paying less and less for each dollar of earnings, and by end 1920 they were paying only eight times the average of the previous 10 years' earnings. From there, investors became increasingly optimistic and, by 1929, once again, were paying nearly 25 times the average of the last 10 years' earnings. This same valuation cycle has played itself out several times since then.

In the early 1980s, using this measure, the US stock market was undervalued relative to history. Corporate earnings were growing and interest rates had started to decline. The triple drivers of stock market returns were perfectly aligned, and one of the longest and strongest bull markets of the past 100 years was born in mid-1982.

By the mid-1990s, however, although corporate earnings had been rising and long-term interest rates remained low and declining, the US stock market was valued at levels not seen in the past century. Once the market peaked in late 1999 or early 2000, returns since then have been miserable even though US corporate earnings kept growing – albeit interrupted by two severe recessions – and interest rates remained low and declining. The simple fact is that the US stock market has made no progress since the late 1990s as it has had to work off the previous overvaluation. The parallels with the Coca-Cola case study in **Chapter 8, The Pitfalls in Direct Stock Pricing**, are striking.

Predicting Returns

Table 12.4 highlights the 10-year returns *per annum* compound from the S&P 500 Index after it hits a trough valuation of 10 times earnings or a peak valuation of *circa* 25 times earnings, based on the price-to-10-year-average earnings ratio. The five occasions where the index hit trough valuations can be identified easily on **Chart 12.2** as 1920, early 1932, 1941, late 1974 and late 1981. Hence, when the S&P 500 Index hit a trough valuation of 10 times earnings in the past (based on the average of the last 10 years' earnings), the S&P 500 Index went on to deliver double-digit returns *per annum* compound over the following decade.

Table 12.4: S&P 500 Index: Returns *per annum* Compound following extremes of undervaluation and overvaluation

Market Undervalued	
1921-1930*	11.60%
1932-1941	10.4%
1942-1951	17.4%
1975-1984	16.7%
1982-1991	16.7%
Market Overvalued	
1928-1937	-2.30%
1965-1974	2.80%
1969-1978	2.70%
1996-2005	9.50%
2000-2009	0.20%

Source: Barclays Capital Annual Gilt/Equity Studies.

* Returns for the 10-year period 1921-1930 were estimated from a number of sources.

In contrast, **Table 12.4** also highlights that when the S&P 500 Index hit a peak valuation of 25 times earnings (based on the average of the past 10 years' earnings) – as it did in early 1928, early 1965, late 1968, late 1995 and early 2000 (see **Chart 12.2**) – the US stock market went on to deliver well below average returns over the next decade. The exception was the decade from 1996 to 2005. As **Chart 12.2** highlights, by end 1995 the S&P

500 Index was once again trading on a price-to-10-year-average earnings ratio of over 25. Yet, despite this apparent overvaluation, the returns over the next decade were 9.5% *per annum* compound, and equal to the long-term average. Clearly, it was taking a lot longer than normal for the S&P 500 Index to correct its previous overvaluation relative to history.

In hindsight, we can point to two particular issues that delayed the correction in the valuation of the US equity market from the mid-to-late-1990s. Firstly, investor optimism regarding the long-term demand for technology following the advent of the Internet and a once-off replacement cycle around the year 2000 was misplaced and the S&P 500 Index got even more overvalued by early 2000 than it had been in 1995. Secondly, the US Federal Reserve (Central Bank) lowered interest rates in the 2001 to 2003 economic downturn to support business and consumer confidence, and this most likely also contributed to the delay in the correction of valuations.

In conclusion, the subsequent higher than expected returns from the US equity market after 1995, given the overvaluation of the market at that time probably can be put down as an aberration. Investors are better off working on the basis that when the US equity market is overvalued relative to history, the subsequent returns over the following five to 10 years are likely to be below average.

At the end of 2011, **Chart 12.2** suggests that the US stock market, as represented by the S&P 500 Index, remains somewhat overvalued relative to the past. While we can't know the future with certainty, the evidence suggests that the annual returns from the US stock market over the next five to 10 years are likely to be below the long-term averages of 9% to 10%. My own estimate is that US equities are currently priced for annual returns of 6% to 7% on a five- to 10-year timeline from here.

On the positive side, although space did not permit me to outline similar valuation statistics here, at the end of 2011, the Eurozone and Japanese equities markets offered exceptionally good value using this valuation framework. The emerging markets also offered above average value on this measure of value at end 2011. Hence, at end 2011, many equity markets appeared reasonably well positioned to deliver the average long-term returns of the past over the next decade. We shall see!

CHAPTER 13
COMMERCIAL PROPERTY

While investors can invest indirectly in property *via* property companies and property funds listed on the stock markets, they also can choose to own physical property outright. Many large institutional investors, like insurance companies and pension funds, invest directly in physical property.

Tables **13.1** and **13.2** provides the *per annum* compound returns and real returns (the returns above inflation) on the UK commercial property market over the 41-year period from 1971 to 2011 inclusive and on the US commercial property market over the 34-year period from 1978 to 2011 inclusive. Both returns series offer a reasonably good proxy of the long-term returns that have been available from the commercial property markets in two major developed economies.

Table 13.1: UK Commercial Property Market: Returns *per annum* Compound (1971-2011)

	Total Returns	Real Returns
1971-79	16.2%	2.2%
1980s	14.5%	7.0%
1990s	7.2%	3.6%
2000s	6.4%	3.6%
2010s	11.4%	6.3%
1971 - 2011	10.9%	4.2%

Source: Property returns – Investment Property Databank (www.ipd.com); Inflation data – Barclays Capital Annual Gilt/Equity Studies.

Table **13.1** highlights that, since 1971, the UK commercial property market has delivered returns of 10.9% *per annum* compound or 4.2% after inflation. Table **13.2** highlights that, since 1978, the US commercial property market has delivered returns of 9.0% *per annum* compound or

4.4% after inflation. These returns include both capital appreciation and rental income reinvested.

**Table 13.2: US Commercial Property Market: Returns *per annum*
Compound (1978-2011)**

	Total Returns	Real Returns
1978-1979	18.3%	1.5%
1980s	11.6%	5.9%
1990s	5.5%	2.2%
2000s	7.3%	4.6%
2010s	13.7%	11.2%
1987 - 2011	9.0%	4.4%

Source: Property returns – NCREIF Property Index (http://www.ncreif.org/property-index-returns.aspx); Inflation data – Barclays Capital Annual Gilt/Equity Studies.

Hence, we can conclude that commercial property returns also have delivered real returns well above cash deposits and government bonds over the long-term, even if the data series I have do not match exactly the same timelines.

Same Drivers of Property Returns as Equities

As we first saw in **Chapter 7, Stock Market and Direct Property Investing**, returns from equities and commercial property are not straight line, and the prices investors are prepared to pay for property are influenced by many of the same factors driving equities.

If we buy a commercial property generating rent of, say, €25,000 *per annum*, and pay €500,000 for it, we obtain a 5% rental yield. So the rental yield is a measure of value in property. Rent, of course, is a fixed cost to business and, in general, it is far more stable than corporate earnings. After all, a business must pay its rent if it wants to remain in its premises, and few businesses want the disruption of relocating. For that reason, rents, which are a fundamental determinant of property prices, tend to be far more stable than corporate earnings.

But rental income is not entirely immune to declines and a good example of this can be seen in the decline in commercial rents in Ireland following that country's banking and fiscal crises. According to CBRE (Ireland), prime commercial property rents in Ireland's capital, Dublin, have declined by *circa* 50% since the onset of the global credit crisis in 2008 to the end of 2011 (**Chart 13.1**).

Hence, both corporate earnings and rental income can vary with the business or economic cycle. The growth in corporate earnings is a fundamental driver of stock markets in the medium- to long-term. Likewise, the growth in rental income is a fundamental driver of the value of commercial property.

Chart 13.1: Dublin: Prime Office Rent (1989-2011) (per sq. mtr. p.a.)

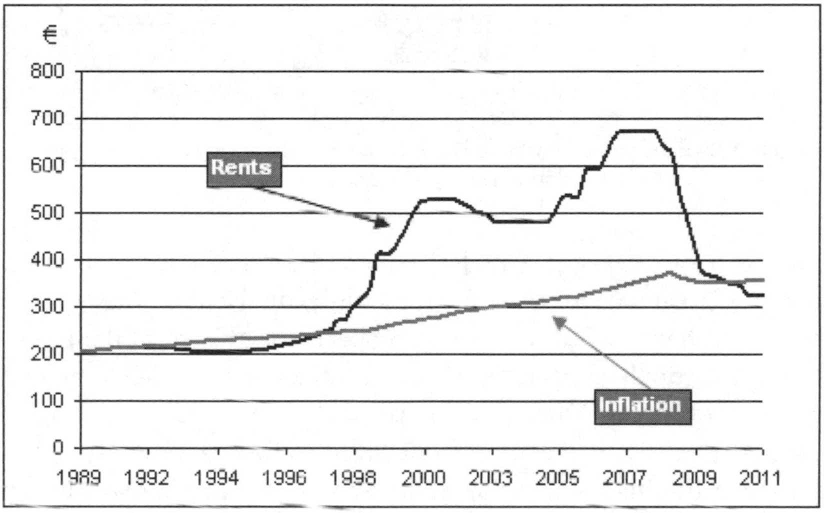

Source: Rents data – CBRE, Dublin; Inflation data – GillenMarkets.

Switching back to the UK commercial property market, **Chart 13.2** highlights the rental yield on the UK commercial property market, and compares that rental yield with the yield available on long-dated UK government bonds from 1982 to 2011 inclusive.

Chart 13.2: UK Commercial Property Market Rental Yield *vs* UK 20-Year Government Bond Yield (1982-2011)

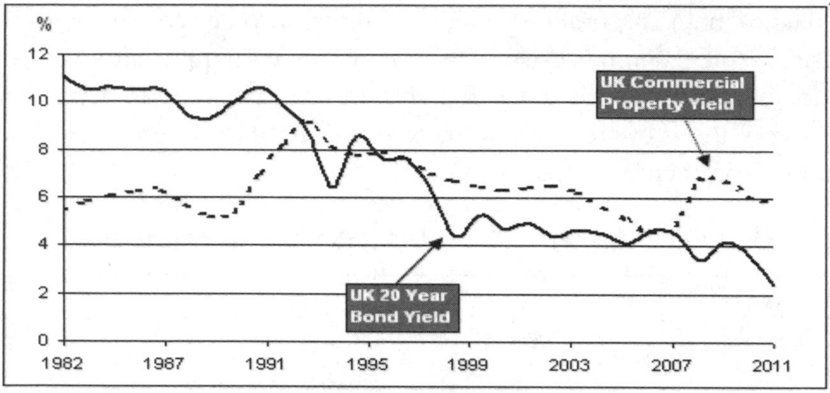

Source: Rental yield – International Property Databank (www.ipd.com); Bond yield data – Barclays Annual Gilt/Equity Study 2012.

At the end of 2011, the rental yield on the overall UK commercial property market was 5.8%. At the same date, the yield on a 20-year UK government bond, which offers no prospects for growth in the income, was 2.4%. Growth in rents and capital values in the UK commercial property market may be weak at present, hampered by a stagnant economy. Returns in the future on UK commercial property will be determined by this initial rental yield, any subsequent growth in rents and the direction of UK long-term interest rates from here. As we stand, and assuming long-term interest rates don't shoot upwards to offer investors' high single-digit yields, the UK commercial property market appears to be sensibly valued and likely to deliver decent returns above inflation going forward.

CHAPTER 14
COMMODITIES

The asset class of commodities includes energy such as oil, gas and uranium; industrial metals such as copper, aluminium, lead, zinc and nickel and soft commodities, including soybeans, corn, wheat, sugar, coffee and cotton. Gold is often classed as a commodity but it is a currency. The precious metals also include silver, platinum and palladium. Some commodities are perishable, while others are simply too bulky to be stored for investment purposes.

Investors can only buy commodities indirectly either by buying commodity futures, exchange-traded funds (ETFs) or exchange-traded notes (ETNs) that contain commodities futures (all dealt with in **Chapter 18, Ways of Gaining Exposure to the Markets**). Commodity producing and mining companies listed on the stock markets offer indirect and leveraged exposure to underlying commodity prices.

CAN COMMODITIES BE VALUED?

A basic commodity is not a business and generates no income in its own right. Its value is determined solely by the forces of demand and supply in the market place. Different factors drive commodity prices at different times and commodities, as an asset class, have tended to generate returns at different stages than equities and property. In that regard, at times, commodities can act as a diversifier in a portfolio of risk assets.

That said, commodities have a difficulty in justifying their place as a separate asset class in a risk-asset portfolio as, over the long-term, their collective value has only just about matched inflation. Even cash deposits in banks have delivered returns of *circa* 1% to 2% over inflation annually over the long-term.

We saw in **Table 9.8 in Chapter 9, Investment Choices and Returns,** that commodities, as represented by the TR/J CRB Index, failed to match inflation since 1960. GMO, a US fund management group, has tracked the price performance of a wider basket of commodities all the way back to 1900. **Chart 14.1** highlights the progress of the GMO Commodity Real Price Index[10] over the past 112 years – it is a commodity price index adjusted for inflation. It also shows that commodities have been a poor investment over the past century, as commodities, in aggregate, lagged inflation by 1.2% *per annum* up until 2002. Even now, after a nine-year bull market in commodity prices, the GMO Commodity Real Price Index has only risen back to where it was in January 1900 (adjusted for inflation).

The horizontal line in the middle part of **Chart 14.1** represents the price level that the basket of commodities would have had to attain to match inflation. Hence, when the GMO Commodity Real Price Index is below this middle horizontal line, commodity prices have lagged the rate of inflation. Since 1900, returns from commodities have simply matched inflation and have significantly lagged the returns from equities and commercial property over the same 112-year period.

Chart 14.1: GMO Commodity Real Price Index (1900-2010)

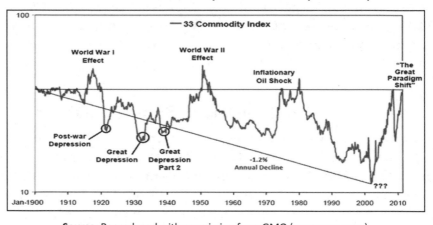

Source: Reproduced with permission from GMO (www.gmo.com).

The bull market in commodities since the early 2000s has been unparalleled and it is possible that, as GMO's Jeremy Grantham

---

10   The GMO Commodity Real Price Index comprises 33 commodities, equally weighted at initiation, including: aluminium, coal, coconut oil, coffee, copper, corn, cotton, diammonium phosphate, flaxseed, gold, iron ore, jute, lard, lead, natural gas, nickel, oil, palladium, palm oil, pepper, platinum, plywood, rubber, silver, sorghum, soybeans, sugar, tin, tobacco, uranium, wheat, wool and zinc.

describes it, a paradigm shift has occurred and the global economy may well now be in the midst of a 'commodity super-cycle', driven by several structural factors that, while unpredictable, are unlikely to reverse anytime soon.

Of course, when dealing with the future, there are divided views. As Grantham argues, a secular shift has occurred and a scarcity of supply of these finite resources is most likely to eventually lead to permanently higher prices. This time, he argues, is different. Others, such as Neils Jensen[11] of Absolute Return Partners in London, believe that human ingenuity should never be underestimated and that solutions to commodity supply shortages have always been found. This time, he argues, is no different. As investors, we would like certainty but, as ever, it is not on offer.

There is the additional practical difficulty of investing in commodities. The costs involved in using futures contracts, which have a defined timeline and need to be constantly rolled from one period to the next, are high and these roll-over costs further erode returns.

Investors, then, have two difficulties when considering whether to include commodities as part of a risk asset portfolio. Returns from commodities over the past century have just about matched inflation and have been even more volatile than equities with big bull markets tending to be followed by prolonged and sometimes deep bear markets. And there are the added costs and uncertainty of having to invest through futures contracts. For most private investors, then, it is impractical to obtain direct exposure to commodities with the only realistic way to gain exposure being indirectly through commodity producing and mining companies, which are normally already covered as part of an equity portfolio.

---

[11] Jensen, N. (2011). 'Note 2 – The Case for Human Ingenuity', *The Absolute Return Letter*, May, Absolute Return Partners LLP (**www.arpllp.com**).

CHAPTER 15
PRECIOUS METALS – GOLD

Gold is a fascinating metal and, for that reason, it gains more coverage in this book than perhaps it warrants. Gold is more than a mere commodity; it is the oldest currency in the world and can rightfully claim its place as the only currency to have acted as a true store of value over the millennia. For that reason, it is worth examining in more detail to see if it merits a place in an investment portfolio, and whether it offers value today following a rip-roaring bull run that has lasted for the past 11 years straight.

Gold can be bought directly or, more recently, *via* exchange-traded commodities (ETCs) listed and traded on the stock exchanges. Gold mining companies listed on the stock exchanges offer indirect and leveraged exposure to the gold price.

Gold is a real asset and not someone else's liability. In comparison, all paper currencies are IOUs from governments, and, in that regard, each paper currency reflects money a government owes the investor. In addition, of course, there is nothing to stop governments printing new monies and degrading the value of existing monies in circulation. In comparison, new gold cannot be printed (mined) at will. Gold, therefore, is the currency of choice and the ultimate protector of capital.

The current gold bull market, which started in 2001, is all about gold's superior monetary attributes, compared to paper currencies. But first, a reminder of gold's remarkable physical attributes can help us understand why gold came to be a currency in the first place thousands of years ago.

THE PHYSICAL ATTRIBUTES OF GOLD

Gold is the heaviest metal (highest density). It is virtually indestructible, and its melting point is 1,064 degrees Celsius. It is the most stretchable pure metal known to man – a single gram can be crafted into a sheet one metre squared, which is so thin that the sun can shine through it. It does not oxidise (rust) in air or water; it has no taste in its purest form; and it is an excellent conductor of electricity. Its physical beauty has seen it used as jewellery for thousands of years and, more recently, its robustness and dependability has seen it in increasing demand in many new complex industrial applications, where price is less of a consideration.

In geological terms, gold-bearing rock is rare, and even when it is discovered an average tonne of gold ore currently yields only six grams of gold – that is six parts to a million – and even this figure has been declining over time. Its durability, rarity and divisibility make it valuable and tradable, and allow significant wealth to be stored or transported with relative ease. It is, therefore, easy to understand how gold has been an accepted form of money for thousands of years. Unlike commodities in general, gold can be stored and transported easily and at low cost, which means that it can be bought and held as an investment without fear that costs will interfere overly with returns, and it does not perish with time.

RETURNS FROM GOLD

When looked at from this angle, if you were told that you were going to Mars for 30 years, which asset would you prefer to hold your savings in: a bank deposit (paper currency) or gold bullion? At least you can say that your gold will be there in 30 years: you can't say that for definite with bank deposits. For even if your deposits are still there, the government may have printed lots more money and degraded the value of your purchasing power by the time you return (inflation). It was said that an ounce of gold could buy you a good quality suit in New York in the early 20th century – and it still can. Unlike paper currencies, where the supply can be increased at will by governments to cover their excess spending, gold supplies cannot be increased at will. As a direct result of limited supplies, gold protects, or adjusts, for inflation.

Table 15.1 highlights the nominal and real returns from gold (in US dollar terms) since 1935. Over this 77-year period gold has returned 5.1% *per annum* compound or 1.3% *per annum* compound after inflation. Hence, gold has done no better than cash deposits after inflation. In addition, returns from gold have been much more volatile and lumpy compared to simple cash deposits.

**Table 15.1: Nominal and Real Gold Returns *per annum*
Compound (1935-2011)**

	Nominal Returns	Real Returns
1935-1970	0.1%	-2.9%
1970s	32.8%	24.3%
1980s	-4.6%	-9.4%
1990s	-3.1%	-6.1%
2000s	14.7%	11.9%
2010-2011	19.1%	16.5%
1935 - 2011	**5.1%**	**1.3%**

Source: GillenMarkets and www.bea.gov.

Chart 15.1: The Gold Price *vs* the Inflation-adjusted Gold Price (1935-2011)

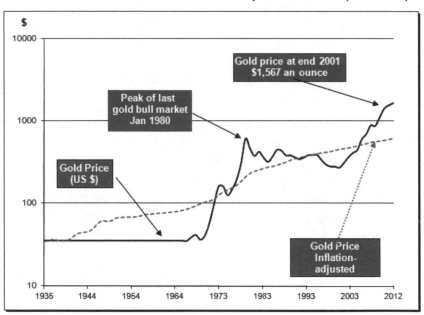

Source: GillenMarkets.

Chart 15.1 plots two prices for gold. It is a semi-log graph – the distance between gold at $10 an ounce and $100 an ounce is the same distance between $100 and $1,000 an ounce. A semi-log graph is much better at displaying the percentage (or proportional) movements over long timelines.

The dark solid line in **Chart 15.1** is the actual traded price of gold in dollars from 1935 to 2011. The lighter dotted line represents what the gold price would have been had it simply increased in value in line with recorded US consumer price inflation. I chose to begin the chart in 1935, as the US devalued the dollar against gold at that time, so 1935 provides us with a reasonable starting point where central bank and government forces most likely provided a somewhat realistic price for gold against the dollar at that time. The dollar has been falling in value against gold ever since, and at the end of 2011 it took $1,567 to buy an ounce of gold.

But just as equities or property prices can become unhinged from their anchors of value (earnings, rental income and interest rates), so too can gold become unhinged from its fundamental driver: inflation. From 1935 to 1967, the official price of gold was fixed against the dollar at the $35 level that had been stipulated in the mid-1930s. But from the mid-1960s, the US government had been printing so many dollars to finance the Vietnam War and other activities that it could no longer afford to give investors back an ounce of gold for only $35 dollars. There were so many new dollars in circulation that the US gold reserves would have been quickly depleted if even a fraction of those holding US dollars requested an ounce of gold back for every $35 of paper currency (or deposits) to their name. In 1971, President Nixon officially authorised the closing of the gold/dollar exchange window, effectively reneging on the US government's previous commitment to deliver an ounce of gold for $35. In other words, the US officially devalued the dollar against gold in 1971. Thus, the 1970s gold bull market was born, and gold shot upwards. But, as **Chart 15.1** highlights, by early 1980, gold had overshot relative to reported inflation.

The 1970s gold bull market ended in January 1980 at over $800 an ounce. By the early 1990s, the market price of gold was back in line with the long-term average inflation-adjusted price. But just as an asset can get overvalued relative to its fundamental value, so too can it become undervalued. By the late 1990s, gold had become grossly undervalued relative to reported US inflation. There is nothing like a bull market that starts from a position of significant undervaluation. Just as the US stock market was obviously undervalued relative to corporate earnings and interest rate trends in the early 1980s (see **Chart 12.2**), so too was gold substantially undervalued relative to US inflation by the late 1990s. Roll forward to 2011 however, and we can no longer say that gold is a cheap asset, as the gold price of $1,567 at end 2011 (solid line) was significantly ahead of the price that could be justified by reported US inflation (dotted line).

Of course, **Chart 15.1** is not perfect and I should point out some potential flaws. First, the end point is dependent on the starting point, and starting in 1935 is subjective on my part. Starting earlier or later would result in a different theoretical inflation-adjusted gold price today. Secondly, some argue that US inflation is under-reported and I have sympathy with that view. But, in the absence of any better inflation source, the above serves as a reasonable guide and highlights, albeit crudely, that gold is no longer a cheap asset – far from it, in fact. That, of course, does not signal the end of this current gold bull market.

Gold is an asset that generates returns that are uncorrelated to other risk assets and can also be a good diversifier in an investment portfolio. Like commodities, the *caveat* is that gold can contribute better diversification and possibly better overall returns in a portfolio when it is undervalued relative to recorded inflation. But it is likely to be less useful in this role when it is overvalued relative to recorded inflation, as **Chart 15.1** suggests. My personal view is that the gold price is going higher before this gold bull market is over. But I find it hard to argue that we won't revisit the current price at some stage in the future. Hence, I see no compelling reason why investors should currently add gold to a risk asset portfolio. I feel that the current predicament facing gold investors is somewhat similar to that which faced investors in the Irish property market in 2003: already overvalued, but likely to get more overvalued before the bull market is over.

CHAPTER 16
HEDGE AND ABSOLUTE
RETURN STRATEGIES

Hedge and absolute return strategies (and funds that follow these strategies) exist to generate positive returns from the stock markets, and other assets or financial instruments of one form or another that are quoted on the stock exchanges. Hedge and absolute return funds often use leverage with the aim of magnifying the underlying gains. The flexibility to sell stocks or financial instruments that they do not own (referred to as 'selling short') provides hedge and absolute return strategies with the flexibility to generate returns irrespective of the market direction. For this reason, returns from hedge and absolute return strategies can be uncorrelated to returns from asset classes that are more sensitive to the economic cycle, like equities and property. Hence, hedge and absolute return strategies and funds offer further diversification options within a risk asset portfolio.

Following the implementation of European-wide UCITS[12] III legislation in the mid-2000s, UCITS (European retail investor funds) can now facilitate many of these alternative investment strategies which were not previously available to the retail investor. Of course, not all absolute return funds adopt strategies that include 'selling short' markets or financial instruments. Some simply use derivative contracts to protect the downside. Hence, for several years now retail investors have been able to access hedge and absolute return strategies *via* funds sold directly by fund managers or insurance companies or *via* funds separately listed on the stock exchanges.

Like equities, which are generally priced to provide a return to the investor for the risk taken, hedge and absolute return strategies attempt to capture the returns offered for taking exposure to alternative sources of risk in markets and financial instruments. Examples include currency

---

[12] Undertakings for Collective Investments in Transferable Securities.

carry-trades, where the investor buys a higher yielding currency and sells a lower yielding currency to try and capture the income differential. A further example is trend investing, where the investor buys the best performing stocks or currencies and sells the weakest performing ones in an attempt to generate returns from defined trends while having no net exposure to the market or asset in question. As these strategies (and funds) take risks to generate returns, and don't come with a guarantee, they are rightly classed as risk assets. The key question for an investor is how this asset class has performed in the past, and in particular over the last decade when equity returns from the major developed markets have been poor.

Table 16.1: HFRX Global Hedge Fund Index: Annual Returns (1998-2011)

	Nominal Returns	Real Returns
1998	12.9%	10.8%
1999	26.7%	22.6%
2000	14.3%	11.2%
2001	8.7%	7.2%
2002	4.7%	2.9%
2003	13.4%	10.7%
2004	2.7%	-0.7%
2005	2.7%	-0.8%
2006	9.3%	6.3%
2007	4.2%	0.0%
2008	-23.3%	-23.3%
2009	13.4%	9.7%
2010	5.2%	3.4%
2011	-8.9%	-11.3%
1998-2002 c.p.a.	13.2%	10.7%
2003-2011 c.p.a.	1.4%	-1.2%
1998-2011 c.p.a.	5.5%	2.9%

Source: Hedge Fund Research, Inc. (www.hedgefundresearch.com).

Table 16.1 provides us with the annual returns of the HFRX Global Hedge Fund Index[13] from 1998 to 2011 inclusive. This is an asset-weighted index – that is, the larger the hedge fund, the more weight that is attributed to its return in the index. As **Table 16.1** highlights, over the 14-year period from 1998 to 2011 inclusive, the HFRX Global Fund Index gained 5.5% *per annum* compound or 2.9% *per annum* compound above inflation. These returns are after all costs. The majority of hedge funds have higher than average annual management fees of 2% *per annum* as well as performance fees of *circa* 20%, which normally kicks in after some hurdle rate of return has been earned.

We can make two relevant observations on the returns delivered by the hedge fund industry over this 14-year period. The first observation is that the industry generated negative returns in 2008 and 2011 along with equity markets in both those years. Hence, the hedge fund industry did not deliver uncorrelated (or off-setting) returns in either of these years. The ability of the hedge fund industry to deliver off-setting returns is the major attraction of these strategies (or funds) to investors – positive returns in all years but particularly when equity markets are declining. The second observation is that the returns were stronger and less correlated to equity returns in the years 1998 to 2002 inclusive. Thereafter, the returns were much less attractive and more correlated to equity markets. **Table 16.1** highlights that, from 2003 to 2011, for example, the HFRX Global Hedge Fund Index recorded returns of only 1.4% *per annum* compound. In fact, the index generated a negative return of -1.2% *per annum* compound after inflation over this 9-year period.

The HFRX Global Hedge Fund Index also has come in for criticism. In *The Hedge Fund Mirage*,[11] author Simon Lack argues, fairly convincingly, that the hedge fund industry is unregulated and hedge funds provide returns data voluntarily. As poorly performing hedge funds are less likely to provide returns data or are more likely to cease to provide such data if returns deteriorate, there is likely to be what is referred to as

---

[13]   The HFRX Global Hedge Fund Index is designed to be representative of the overall composition of the hedge fund universe. It comprises all eligible hedge fund strategies; including but not limited to convertible arbitrage, distressed securities, equity hedge, equity market neutral, event-driven, macro, merger arbitrage, and relative value arbitrage. The strategies are asset weighted based on the distribution of assets in the hedge fund industry.

[14]   Lack, S. (2012). *The Hedge Fund Mirage*, New Jersey: John Wiley & Sons.

'survivorship bias' in the HFRX Index returns data – that is, the returns may be overstated due to the absence of returns data from poorly performing funds.

Table 16.2: HFRX Global Hedge Fund Index *vs* FTSE World Index:
Annual Returns *per annum* compound (1998-2011)

	HFRX	FTSE World	Out / Under Performance
1998	12.9%	23.1%	-10.2%
1999	26.7%	25.4%	1.3%
2000	14.3%	-10.3%	24.6%
2001	8.7%	-16.3%	25.0%
2002	4.7%	-19.2%	23.9%
2003	13.4%	33.4%	-20.0%
2004	2.7%	16.1%	-13.4%
2005	2.7%	12.4%	-9.7%
2006	9.3%	21.9%	-12.6%
2007	4.2%	12.5%	-8.3%
2008	-23.3%	-43.2%	19.9%
2009	13.4%	39.2%	-25.8%
2010	5.2%	11.5%	-6.3%
2011	-8.9%	-6.4%	-2.5%
1998-2011 c.p.a.	5.5%	4.5%	1.0%
2003-2011 c.p.a.	1.4%	7.8%	-6.4%

Source: HFRX returns – Hedge Fund Research, Inc. (www.hedgefundresearch.com);
FTSE World Index – price data from *The Financial Times* (annual dividends added in to
provide an estimate of annual total returns data).

Table 16.2 highlights that from 2003 to 2011 inclusive the HFRX Global Hedge Fund Index delivered a nominal (before inflation) 1.4% *per annum* compound return while the FTSE World Index delivered a nominal 7.8% *per annum* compound return over the same period. In *The Hedge Fund Mirage,* Lack suggests that the higher correlation of returns with equities and more lacklustre returns since the early 2000s reflects the growth in assets under management in the global hedge fund industry. Poor performance from equities since 2000 no doubt has provided a strong incentive for pension funds among other investors to seek returns elsewhere, and the hedge fund industry has been one of the biggest beneficiaries. However, Mr. Lack's contention is that hedge funds as an asset class may not be able to replicate the returns of the past.

As he puts it:

> The steady deterioration in relative returns of hedge funds, compared with equities, is surely the most compelling evidence that size hurts returns.[15]

There are other pitfalls with hedge and absolute return funds that would-be investors should be mindful of. In the same way as there is success and failure in all areas of the investment markets, investors should expect variations in performance and disappointments among hedge and absolute return funds. When investors buy an equity fund that tracks the global equity markets, like a global equity exchange-traded fund (a global ETF), they are fairly sure that they will end up with the returns on offer, positive or negative. It is not particularly important which global equity ETF an investor buys; the returns should be more or less the same. We cannot say this within the hedge and absolute return funds category. Different investment strategies, different levels of leverage (debt) and a myriad of other factors can lead to significant variations in returns from one hedge or absolute return fund to another. For this reason, it is probably best to own a selection of hedge or absolute return funds.

Traditionally, the charging structure within hedge funds has been a 2% annual management fee plus a 20% performance fee above a certain benchmark return level. This greater cost structure within the hedge fund industry also largely explains why, in aggregate, their returns after costs must be less than the long run 9% to 10% returns from equity funds (which have substantially less costs). Some will argue that hedge funds can employ gearing (borrowings) to enhance returns. Indeed they can – but the use of gearing means a higher level of risk.

In summary, the disappointing performance of the hedge fund industry since 2003, its substantially higher cost structure along with the likely variable returns among individual hedge and absolute return funds call into question whether investors gain any real advantage by including this asset-type in portfolios. At the very least, investors should ensure they invest across a selection of such funds. Ideally, this should be

---

[15]   Lack, S. (2012). *The Hedge Fund Mirage*, New Jersey: John Wiley & Sons, p. 162.

done by selecting several individual funds rather than through a fund of funds, which often comes with double costs.

CHAPTER 17
ALTERNATIVE ASSETS:
TIMBERLAND (FORESTRY)

Alternative assets include a range of niche risk asset categories, including forestry (timberland) and agricultural land, fine wines, diamonds, rare stamps and coins and art and collectibles. It is beyond the scope of this book to examine the historical returns from all the alternative asset classes. Instead, I will focus solely on timberland as an asset class.

In any given year, the biological growth of timber in the ground is a significant contributor to overall timber returns. Irrespective of the economic conditions of the day, the timber grows and gains value during the year simply by virtue of the fact that there is more of it at the end of the year than there was at the start. Obviously, the eventual market price achieved for the timber can vary at the time it is harvested and sold. Weak economic conditions can, and do, lead to weak timber prices, just like any other commodity. But any decent forestry company or timberland fund will own a variety of plantations with a staggered maturity profile that reduces the dependence on the market price at any specific time. Due to high transportation costs, timber can be a local product, and weakness in timber prices in one region does not always lead to weakness in prices in other geographic regions.

Table 17.1 outlines the returns from the US-focused NCREIF Timberland Index[16] since 1987.

As **Table 17.1** highlights, returns from US timberland assets have been higher even than equity returns over the 25-year period from 1987 to 2011 inclusive with returns of 13% *per annum* compound. When these returns are adjusted for inflation (the returns above inflation), they come in at 8.6% *per annum* compound.

---

[16] The NCREIF Timberland Index is a quarterly time series composite return measure of investment performance of a large pool of individual US timber properties acquired in the private market for investment purposes only.

Table 17.1: NCREIF Timberland Index: Returns *per annum* Compound (1987-2011)

	Total Returns	Real Returns
1987-1989	31.3%	25.2%
1990s	16.4%	12.8%
2000s	7.3%	4.6%
2010-2011	0.7%	-1.5%
1987 - 2011	13.0%	8.6%

Source: NCREIF Timberland Index (www.ncreif.org/timberland-returns.aspx).

However, similar to the HFRX Global Hedge Fund Index, the NCREIF Timberland Index is operated on a voluntary basis – so transaction values are reported on a voluntary basis. Hence, when returns are negative, data providers can be less likely to submit data. The result may be that NCREIF Timberland Index returns are somewhat overstating reality.

In addition, the high returns recorded in the late 1980s and early 1990s need to be put into context. Traditionally, timberland in the US was held on the balance sheets of big paper producing companies at cost. A trend away from holding timberland directly on balance sheets, which got underway in the late 1980s, most likely resulted in attractively priced timberland being transferred into investment vehicles, enabling them to record outsized returns in the initial years. After a number of years, with a greater amount of money available for investing in timberland, the market became more competitive and transaction prices became more realistic. This most likely explains a lowering of subsequent returns after the late 1990s. Looking forward, it is sensible to expect that returns from US timberland assets will more closely approximate equity and property returns.

Nonetheless, timberland returns are not as sensitive to the economic cycle by virtue of the fact that a major part of the return is created by annual biological growth.

Returns from US timberland assets over the past five years have been negative after inflation, most likely reflecting the impact of the housing and general construction downturn in the US economy, which has been particularly severe in this cycle. Timber prices are unlikely to be as subdued globally but in my search for statistics in this area I have been restricted to data on the US market. That said, it is fairly clear that timber is a producing asset likely to deliver decent real returns over the long-term at least equal to both equities and commercial property. Hence, timberland or forestry assets appear to have the potential for decent long-term returns, and offer further diversification options for risk asset portfolios.

Exposure to timberland or forestry assets can be obtained through funds (both investment companies and ETFs) or indirectly by investing in companies listed on the stock exchanges whose business it is to grow, harvest and sell timber products.

FINAL NOTE

If you have made it through the detailed analysis of the various asset classes, you might find it beneficial to revisit the Summary Conclusions at the end of **Chapter 9** before progressing to **Chapter 18, Ways of Gaining Exposure to the Markets.**

SECTION III
IMPLEMENTING AN INVESTMENT PLAN

CHAPTER 18
WAYS OF GAINING EXPOSURE TO THE MARKETS

You can gain direct exposure to several, but not all, asset classes by buying shares directly on the stock market. Shares, or equities, cover a wide range of business sectors as well as property companies and mining companies. You also can buy government and corporate bonds directly on the markets and, more recently, precious metals through exchange-traded commodities (ETCs). Exposure to private equity, hedge and absolute return strategies and many alternative assets can only be obtained indirectly through funds. Funds, however, provide exposure to every asset class. Funds that are quoted on the stock exchanges include exchange-traded funds (ETFs) and investment companies (investment trusts or closed-end funds).

INVESTING THROUGH FUNDS

Investing *via* funds, or 'collective investment vehicles' as they are more accurately referred to, can be labelled as indirect investing. The major distinction I would highlight is between:

♦ Unlisted funds. Funds that are not quoted on a stock exchange; and

♦ Listed funds: Funds that are quoted and traded on a stock exchange

Funds not Quoted on Stock Exchange(s) – Unlisted Funds

In the major markets of the US, UK and continental Europe, products such as mutual funds (US), unit trusts (UK), OEICs[17] and SICAVs[18] (Europe) are examples of fund types not quoted on regulated stock exchanges. Different countries or regions have different regulatory bodies that regulate unlisted funds. Such funds are sold to private

---

[17] Open-Ended Investment Companies.
[18] *Société d'investissement à capital variable.*

investors through investment intermediaries. In Ireland, unit-linked funds dominate the non-bank retail savings and pension markets, and are offered mainly by life assurance companies, including Irish Life, Zurich, Canada Life, New Ireland and Aviva among others. In Ireland, these products are similarly sold to the public through investment intermediaries (investment advisors / insurance brokers).

As these fund types are not listed on any stock exchange, an investor has to buy into or sell out of them *via* an investment intermediary, or directly through the fund management company. As your monies are invested into these funds or redeemed from them, new units in the fund either are created or redeemed as part of that process. For this reason, the fund always reflects the value of the underlying portfolio of investments. The creation and redemption of units in these fund types means that they are constantly expanding and contracting in size depending on investor demand.

Funds Quoted on Stock Exchange(s) – Listed Funds

Funds quoted on stock exchanges are bought and sold through a stockbroker, be that a traditional full-service stockbroker or a low-cost, online stockbroker. The two main types of funds quoted on the stock exchanges are:

♦ Exchange-traded funds (ETFs);

♦ Investment companies or closed-end funds.

When private investors buy funds that are listed on a stock exchange through a stockbroker, they buy them in the same way as they buy a share – by transacting with another investor in the marketplace. The distinction here is that you do not deal with the fund management company that manages the fund either directly or indirectly *via* an investment intermediary.

The main reasons why you might consider buying ETFs or investment companies through a stockbroker, rather than mutual funds, unit trusts or unit-linked funds through an investment intermediary, is that they carry lower costs, offer better transparency and can be bought and sold without the continuous administrative hassle associated with buying into and selling out of unquoted funds. As an advisor in Ireland once said to me, "unit-linked funds are like the old black-and-white TV and exchange-traded funds and investment companies are the colour TV versions".

Stocks and funds quoted on stock exchanges, to a greater or lesser degree, are cheaper for the investor in the long run, as the stock market is a more efficient vehicle through which to invest. Unquoted funds are handicapped with higher costs reflecting their lack of scale compared to the stock markets, or their need to 'sell' the products through investment intermediaries.

EXCHANGE-TRADED FUNDS

Advances in Technology Have Been a Catalyst

Advances in technology undoubtedly have fuelled the phenomenal growth in exchange-traded funds since the early 1990s. Costs of dealing and administering funds have been reduced significantly, the introduction of fund platforms has been made possible and transparency and investor confidence in listed funds has improved. The growth in the internet probably captures this theme as well as any and **Chart 18.1** highlights how the growth of Internet usage has correlated well with the explosion of the exchange-traded funds market.

Chart 18.1: The Growth of ETFs and Internet Use

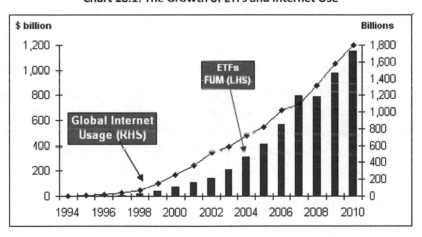

Source: Funds under management (FUM) data from iShares's quarterly reviews.

ETFs remain the world's fastest-growing investment product. The retail investor is the winner, and it can be no surprise that currently 50% of all new monies invested in ETFs in the US market are from private investors. Outside the US, the take-up of ETFs by private investors is less pronounced, but they are sure to follow the US trend in time. The equivalent statistic for Ireland is not currently available but I suspect that perhaps under 5% of the investing public use ETFs.

DO-IT-YOURSELF (DIY) INVESTING

ETFs are a low-cost investment product. Due to the fact that they simply replicate an existing index, no fund manager is required and only minimal marketing or distribution costs are incurred.

ETFs have several advantages over non-listed funds (like mutual funds, unit trusts or unit-linked funds), including lower annual management fees, minimal entry costs, better transparency and liquidity, as well as being less administratively onerous to transact. ETFs are designed as index trackers, and, as such, they effectively replicate the relevant market return.

While an investor does no better than the market with an ETF, he does no worse either. For investors, ETFs are a flexible and efficient way to manage personal savings or pension monies across the major asset classes. The instant diversification on offer through ETFs reduces, if not eliminates, the stock-specific risk inherent in managing a portfolio of shares.

THE KEY CHARACTERISTICS OF ETFs

Following the introduction of the first exchange-traded fund in 1993 in the US, the market in ETFs has grown substantially. Today, there are over 2,000 ETFs worldwide, with the majority listed on the major stock exchanges in New York and London as well as on the European, Asian, Australasian and Japanese exchanges.

Simple and Efficient Products
The defining characteristics of ETFs are that they are open-ended funds that passively replicate the performance of a particular index, commodity or currency, and are listed on a recognised stock exchange. As such, ETFs can be bought and sold in the same way as shares. They also are regulated products.

Index Tracking

ETFs simply aim to track an index or market – referred to as 'passive funds management'. For example, by buying an ETF that tracks the FTSE 100 Index in the UK, an investor obtains the returns that the FTSE 100 Index delivers: no more, but, equally, no less. The ETF owns all the stocks that are in the FTSE 100 Index, and in the exact proportion to their index weighting. For example, if GlaxoSmithKline shares make up 2.5% of the FTSE 100 Index, then GlaxoSmithKline shares represent 2.5% of a FTSE 100 ETF portfolio.

ETFs Cater for all Asset Classes

ETFs cover all the major asset classes. Within equities, there are ETFs to provide exposure to the global market, major regions of the world, individual country markets and individual sectors. Within the government bonds category, there are ETFs that provide exposure to short-, medium- and long-dated government bonds, inflation-protected bonds and investment grade and non-investment grade corporate bonds, covering the US, UK, Eurozone and Asian bond markets.

In the property category, it is possible to gain broad exposure to global, US, European, Eastern European and Asian property markets, and some other single country property markets through ETFs quoted on the major exchanges. In the more specialised private equity and hedge fund sectors, there is an increasing range of listed ETFs available, providing diversified exposure to these areas. All the major commodities from precious metals like gold, silver and platinum; to soft commodities like wheat and grain; to base metals like copper, zinc and lead, and to energy commodities like oil and gas are covered by ETFs and exchange-traded commodities (ETCs). Currency ETFs have become more widely available in the past couple of years.

Investors can buy exposure to the S&P 500 Index through an ETF listed on several different exchanges. However, from an investor's viewpoint, it is irrelevant where and in what currency an ETF is listed. If an investor buys an iShares S&P 500 ETF in London in sterling, he or she still has dollar exposure and not sterling exposure. The currency exposure (risk) is determined by what securities make up the ETF portfolio.

Avoid Short And Leveraged ETFs

As ETFs are bought and sold in the same way as shares, they also can be sold short (an investor can sell an ETF he does not own). Indeed, traders can buy an ETF that itself is 'short' stocks. If markets decline, then the 'short' ETF will rise in value. In addition, traders can buy leveraged ETFs that magnify the returns in both directions. Thus, if the market falls, then a leveraged ETF will decline by a greater amount and *vice versa*. Leveraged ETFs in particular carry hidden dangers, as they only guarantee magnified returns over daily timelines. In summary, short and leveraged ETFs are more suited to traders and, as this book is about investing, I do not go into any further detail on them. Suffice it to say that I feel most private investors should avoid them.

Passive Index Tracking Has its Pitfalls

ETFs track traditional stock market indices, which are weighted by market capitalisation. For example, the fact that Microsoft had a substantially greater market capitalisation than, say, Kellogg in the S&P 500 Index in early 2000 meant that any ETF designed to track this index would have had a substantially bigger holding in Microsoft than Kellogg at that time, irrespective of which company offered better value. In hindsight, we now know that the majority of technology stocks were overvalued in early 2000 and the subsequent substantial decline in the price of the majority of technology stocks over the next few years weighted heavily on the S&P 500 Index, and any ETFs tracking the index.

Table 18.1 highlights that, from 1996 to 2005, an equal-weighted S&P 500 Index outperformed the standard S&P 500 market capitalisation-weighted index by a wide margin. The equal-weighted S&P 500 Index, through constant rebalancing, had a smaller exposure to the tech sector from 1996 to 2005 inclusive and suffered less in the aftermath of the tech burst.

Table 18.1: S&P 500 Index: Market Value-weighted and Equal-weighted Returns

S&P 500 Index	Market Value -weighted	Equal-weighted
1996 to 2000	132%	120%
2001 to 2005	1%	51%
Total (1996 to 2005)	133%	171%

Source: www.rydexfunds.com/etf/.

Fundamental or Intelligent Funds Provide a Solution

A newer breed of ETFs, described as fundamental or intelligent ETFs, take the advantages that are so obvious in equal-weighted ETFs one step further. Fundamental ETFs weight an index by a fundamental value factor such as the dividend yield or earnings or cash flows, or some combination of these factors. In this way, fundamental indices avoid having to take a higher weighting in a stock simply because it is bigger in size, which may reflect solely the fact that its share have become too popular and expensive.

Research by RAFI (Research Affiliates Fundamental Indices) has shown that fundamental indices can add *circa* 1% to 2% per annum to the returns generated by traditional market capitalisation-weighted indices. In the context of long-term returns of 9% to 10% from equity markets, an extra 1% to 2% *per annum* is significant.

PowerShares and WisdomTree are two US specialist ETF providers that specialise in fundamental or intelligent ETFs. They are both included in **Table 18.2** further on in this chapter. On the GillenMarkets website, I tend to recommend fundamental ETFs where I have the choice to for subscribers.

THE KEY PROMOTERS / SPONSORS OF ETFs

The major issuers of ETFs include Blackrock, following its purchase of the iShares ETF brand and business from Barclays in 2009, State Street Global Advisors (SPDRs or S&P Depository Receipts), Vanguard, Lyxor Asset Management, HSBC, Deutsche Bank (db x-trackers series) and Nomura Asset Management, among others.

Boutique ETF issuers concentrating on alternative investment strategies include PowerShares, ProShares, WisdomTree, Guggenheim, Rydex and Van Eck Associates among others. ETF Securities specialises in commodity ETCs and ETFs.

Having a track record in the funds industry and a demonstrated ability to distribute the product (that is, to raise money for an ETF launch) largely determines who can sponsor and launch a new ETF successfully. Blackrock, the largest fund management company in the world, is now the largest issuer of ETFs, with the iShares series.

An institution that sponsors an ETF can list it on multiple stock exchanges. Indeed, different institutions can launch an ETF that covers the same underlying index on different exchanges. For example, State Street Global Advisors sponsored the first ETF – which tracks the S&P 500 Index in the US (ticker code: SPY) – and listed that ETF on the US stock exchange in 1993. Since then, other iShares ETFs were launched to track the S&P 500 Index, and they are listed on both the London (ticker code: IUSA-L) and US (ticker code: IVV) stock exchanges.

Table 18.2 provides a list of the main ETF/ETC providers globally along with relevant website addresses.

Table 18.2: Key ETF/ETC Providers

General ETF Sponsors	Specialised ETF Sponsors
iShares (Blackrock) http://us.ishares.com/home.htm http://uk.ishares.com/index **SSgA** (State Street Global Advisors) www.spdretfs.com **Vanguard** www.vanguard.com **DB X-Trackers** (Deutsche Bank) www.dbtrackers.com **Lyxor Asset Management** (Société Générale) www.lyxoretf.co.uk	**PowerShares** (Fundamental ETFs) www.invescopowershares.com www.invescopowershares.co.uk **WisdomTree Investments** (Fundamental ETFs) www.wisdomtree.com **Rydex** www.rydexfunds.com/etf **Van Eck Associates** (Mining ETFs) www.vaneck.com **Guggenheim Funds** www.guggenheimfunds.com **ProShares** (Short and leveraged ETFs) www.proshares.com **ETF Securities** (Commodities ETFs and ETCs) www.etfsecurities.com

THE STRUCTURE OF ETFs

The creation of an ETF is relatively straightforward. A sponsor, like an investment bank or fund management company, promotes a certain fund strategy and markets it to an institutional investor base. Institutions then deposit the assets in question (shares, bonds, commodities, etc) into the fund, in exchange for units in the fund. Once the ETF is listed on the exchanges, private investors can buy and sell shares in them on the secondary market.

ETFs are regulated products and must comply with the relevant regulations that allow them to be marketed in a particular jurisdiction. In the US, ETFs are regulated under the *1933 Securities Act* and the *1940 Mutual Funds Act*, while in Europe ETFs must comply with UCITS regulations.

Prospectus Required for Stock Exchange Listing

To obtain a listing for a fund on a recognised stock exchange, a prospectus must be prepared and made available for viewing. Once listed on an exchange, the fund is then an exchange-traded fund (ETF) or, more simply, a fund that is traded on the exchange. The European UCITS regulations place certain shareholding and counterparty limits on funds, although there are exceptions. In short, by complying with UCITS regulations, the sponsor in effect obtains approval for the distribution and marketing of the fund across the various European jurisdictions.

While institutional investors can purchase or redeem units in an ETF (minimum size 50,000 shares) by dealing directly with market specialists (appointed by the fund sponsor) even after the fund has been listed, retail investors do not have this option. Rather, retail or private investors must buy and sell units or shares in the ETF from other investors in the marketplace through a stockbroker.

The process for the creation and redemption of units in an ETF – where institutions can swap a basket of the underlying assets held in the ETF for units in the ETF (or swap units for shares held in the ETF) – helps ensure that the share price of an ETF closely reflects the value of the underlying portfolio of assets held in the fund.

Physical and Derivative-Based ETFs

The basic ETF comes in two forms. The first is a fund that uses its cash to buy the physical assets outright. The fund then has the flexibility to engage in stock lending to generate extra income, or to employ dividend enhancement activities, as most ETFs do. These activities, of course, expose the fund to modest counterparty risk. The second form of ETF does not buy the underlying assets of the index it is tracking but, instead, buys a swap-based product (or derivative contract) from a third party (counterparty), which is designed to replicate the index returns for the fund. Swap-based products or derivative contracts involve counterparty risk. Given the calamity in financial markets in 2007-2009, where the survival of many financial institutions was in doubt, this risk reared its head, where previously counterparty risk was not considered an issue when dealing with the major investment banks worldwide. In spite of that, I would not overplay the risk. Under European UCITS regulations, the exposure to any particular counterparty is limited to 10% of the fund value. Also, sponsors can offset counterparty risk in a variety of ways.

Exchange-Traded Commodities

Exchange-traded commodities (ETCs) are open-ended securities that trade on regulated exchanges.[19] They are designed to accurately track the underlying performance of the commodity index or individual commodity.

In the case of physically-backed ETCs, the structure is probably even more robust than many ETFs, which often have counterparty risk through their stock lending activities or dividend-enhancing strategies.

ETCs enable investors to gain exposure to commodities without trading futures or taking physical delivery. Similar to ETFs, there are two types of ETCs. The first is an asset-backed ETC that is fully backed by the relevant commodity. For example, several of the gold ETCs are securities backed by the equivalent amount of gold bullion, with the bullion being deposited and stored in a bank vault. The second, and more common type, is a swap-based ETC which is a security backed by a swap-based (or derivative) contract.

The most comprehensive site covering ETCs is the London-based ETF Securities (**www.etfsecurities.com**). The majority of ETF Securities' swap-based ETCs are backed by 100% collateral held by the Bank of New York Mellon. This eliminates counterparty risk attached to any particular swap-based ETC sponsored by ETF Securities.

Thus, key questions for the ETF/ETC investor include:

♦ What index or asset is the product tracking?

♦ How does the ETF/ETC replicate the performance of the asset/index?

◊ Does the ETF/ETC own the underlying assets?

◊ Does the ETF/ETC use derivative contracts?

♦ What is the counterparty risk?

♦ What is the annual total expense ratio (TER)?

♦ Is the dividend income paid out? If so, how often?

♦ What are the taxation implications of selling a particular ETF/ETC?

---

[19]   In technical terms, they are secured, undated, zero coupon guaranteed notes issued by special purpose vehicles with segregated liabilities, and are generally protected by a trustee structure.

Exchange-Traded Notes

Exchange-traded notes (ETNs) are a separate product tradable on markets but I do not cover them in detail in this book. Nonetheless, I referred to them previously and, for that reason, provide a short explanation of what they are here.

In simple terms, ETNs are securities issued by an investment bank or financial institution guaranteeing to replicate the return of a certain index return. They normally have a defined timeline, and mature and are redeemed at the end of that timeline. ETNs have no underlying portfolio and use derivatives (futures and options) to achieve their aims. ETNs are part of the financial institution's balance sheet and, when investors buy an ETN, they take on the credit risk of that financial institution. They can be sold short and leveraged through margin (CFD) accounts. The ETN structure allows investors to gain exposure to some sectors or strategies previously difficult to access.

INVESTMENT COMPANIES (INVESTMENT TRUSTS OR CLOSED-END FUNDS)

Just as ETFs offer an easy, low-cost and risk-controlled method of managing your savings and pension monies, so too do investment companies – known in the UK as investment trusts and in the US as closed-end funds (US). Investment companies similarly cover all the asset classes.

Investment companies are the oldest fund-type in the world, having been first used in London in the 19th century to finance the development of railroads in Latin and North America. Since then, they have grown to provide access to every asset class and most of the world's markets.

Like other fund-types, an investment company owns a portfolio of investments. By owning shares in an investment company, an investor in effect has part ownership of the underlying portfolio of investments owned by the fund. Whereas unlisted funds are generally governed by the financial regulator or some similar regulatory body in separate countries or regions, investment companies are governed by the Companies Act, in whatever country the company incorporates. Apart from this regulatory difference, the major practical difference is that investment companies, like ETFs, are quoted on recognised stock exchanges. Hence, investors can buy listed investment companies through a stockbroker to provide indirect exposure to most asset classes of choice and most markets of choice.

CHARACTERISTICS

Let's look at some of the characteristics of investment companies in more detail.

Investment Companies – Active Funds Management

Investment companies tend to be actively managed by professional fund managers. In essence, an investment company acts like a fund, but trades like a share, and can make an excellent vehicle through which an investor can gain exposure to a wide spread of shares or assets (and achieve diversification, which is essential to controlling risk). It can be difficult for individuals with limited resources to achieve diversification on their own. Because it trades just like a share, an investment company can be held in a stockbroking account, like any other share. This improves the visibility of your investments (keeping them all in the one account) and lessens the administration involved in investing in the stock markets.

Instant Diversification

Investment companies are another flexible and efficient way to manage personal savings or pension monies across the major asset classes. The instant diversification on offer through investment companies reduces, if not eliminates, the stock-specific risk inherent in managing a portfolio of shares.

Fixed Amount of Capital

Most collective investment vehicles, including unit trusts, mutual funds, unit-linked funds and ETFs, are said to be 'open-ended', as they issue new units to new investors and redeem units when investors wish to sell. In essence, the number of units in existence is constantly expanding and contracting, which provides less certainty for the fund manager, who is never sure what pool of money he is managing. In contrast, the amount of money the fund manager of an investment company has to manage is fixed at the outset, when the company raises its capital and lists onto the stock market. One advantage of this is that the fund manager can plan ahead without having to be concerned with who is buying or selling shares in the investment company he is managing: in other words, the fund manager has a fixed amount of capital to invest.

Strong Regulatory Protection

An investment company offers the investor strong regulatory protection. As they are companies, they are governed by the requirements of the relevant Companies Act of the country in which they are incorporated. This means annual and interim reports to shareholders, explicit duties for the board of directors responsible for the investment company and an annual audit. The assets of an investment company normally are held separately through a recognised global custodian, which ensures security of the company's assets, so that even if the fund manager goes bankrupt, the company's assets remain secure. Thus, there is no counterparty risk with investment companies as the company owns the assets outright.

Share Price Can Deviate From the Fund Value (or Net Asset Value)

The investment company's share price only indirectly reflects the underlying value of its portfolio of investments. Unlike ETFs and non-listed funds, investment companies are closed-end funds. Consequently, demand and supply between investors in the market place is the main determinant of the share price of an investment company.

In the short-term, there can be imbalances between demand and supply, leading to a share price that is either above or below the value of the company's underlying portfolio of assets (referred to as the Net Asset Value – or NAV).

An investment company whose share price is below its net asset value is said to be trading at a discount. Similarly, an investment company whose share price is above the underlying net asset value is said to be trading at a premium.

Chart 18.2 provides a real-life example. RIT Capital Partners plc is an actively managed mixed asset (or balanced) fund which has been listed on the London Stock Exchange since 1981. The chart highlights the progress of both the fund's share price and its underlying net asset value from 1995 to early 2012. The net asset value of the fund reflects the market worth of its portfolio of investments. However, when you go to buy shares in an investment company like RIT, the fund manager does not create new shares for you, as happens when you invest in a mutual fund, a unit trust or a unit-linked fund. Instead, you must buy shares from another investor in the market place. This interaction between buyers and sellers creates a price for the fund's shares, and this price may or may not equal the fund's underlying value. When there are more buyers of RIT's shares than sellers, the share price can trade above the underlying fund's net asset value (or at a premium). The corollary is also the case – an excess of sellers of RIT's shares over buyers will see its shares trade at a price below the fund's underlying net asset value (at a discount).

Chart 18.2: RIT Capital Partners plc: Share Price and Net Asset Value

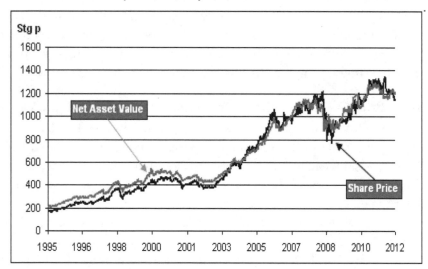

Source: RIT Capital Partners Annual and Interim Reports, Yahoo! Finance and GillenMarkets.

It is clear from **Chart 18.2** that RIT Capital Partners's share price has regularly deviated below, and sometimes above, the fund's net asset value over the 1995 to 2012 period for which I have drawn the chart. However, it is important to realise that the share price will follow the net asset value in the medium- to long-term.

A Discount is not Necessarily a Positive

A substantial discount to the underlying NAV can be a significant positive for the patient (medium-term) investor, as it offers the potential for additional returns over time. But an investor needs to investigate why a particular investment company is trading at that discount and satisfy himself regarding the risks. Often, a discount exists simply because the net asset value is lagging behind the decline in the share price. For example, early on in the property downturn of 2007-2009, many property investment companies traded at substantial discounts to their respective net asset values. This occurred because investors recognised that asset values would subsequently fall. Investors were correct, and in that case the discounts did not actually represent extra value.

No Distribution Costs

As an investment company raises the bulk of its monies at the outset, and simultaneously lists on to a recognised stock exchange, the costs associated with establishing an investment company are incurred upfront. However, as all other subsequent dealings in the shares of the investment company occur between investors in the secondary market, there are no further marketing and distribution costs incurred. This contrasts particularly with open-ended non-listed funds, which are always trying to take in new investors and have a sales force to do just that – which, of course, is an overhead base that the fund has to pay for.

The Capacity to Borrow can Boost Returns

With a fixed amount of capital, it is easier for the fund manager of an investment company to borrow from a bank in an effort to leverage the returns for investors. As long as markets move upwards over time, investors can get more bang for their buck, as the investment company can enhance the returns to shareholders through the use of borrowings. Like houses, borrowing to enhance returns works to the benefit of investors if the market rises over time. That said, the level of borrowings within most investment companies is fairly modest, often ranging between 10% and 30% of the assets in the company. In addition, not all investment companies borrow.

Geographic, Sector and Asset Choice

With nearly 350 investment companies listed on the London Stock Exchange, investors have a wide choice. Within equities, there are investment companies that specialise in the varied geographical regions of the world, like Europe, the US, Asia, China, and more general investment companies that provide exposure to the global stock markets. There are investment companies that specialise in generating an income by focusing on investing in a portfolio of high dividend-yielding shares. Other investment companies focus on investing in growth stocks, while yet others focus on specific sectors like the financial, healthcare or technology sectors.

Outside of equities, there are investment companies providing exposure to other asset classes, including government and corporate bonds, property, mining companies and commodities, private equity and hedge and absolute strategies in many regions of the world. In addition, there are investment companies providing mixed asset exposure – often referred to as balanced funds. Lastly, there are investment companies called 'Fund of Funds' that invest in a wide spread of other funds. They can provide exposure to a range of different fund managers with different investment strategies.

Key Advantages

The key advantages of investment companies include:

♦ They are vehicles through which investors can pool their resources, thus lowering the overall costs;

♦ They provide a spread of risk through diversification;

♦ They provide access to a wide range of asset classes;

♦ They provide access to professional fund managers;

♦ There is less administration and better visibility on pricing through constant pricing of the fund's shares through the trading day;

♦ There are no entry or exit costs or early redemption penalties, which are a feature of some unlisted funds.

♦ There is no minimum holding period.

OTHER CONSIDERATIONS

Other considerations for potential investors in investment companies include:

♦ Past performance not always being useful for predicting the future, and;

♦ The need for information sources.

Past Performance is Not Always Useful

Past performance may indicate the success or otherwise of a particular investment company, but, in isolation, does not necessarily give any guidance about future performance. Other factors to consider are the investment company's operating costs, the level of borrowing within the company, the sector or region that the company specialises in, the size of the investment company and the discount or premium to net asset value that the shares are trading at. Of more importance is the investment strategy that the fund manager is following.

Information Sources

Many UK fund management organisations (both large and small), operate investment companies. *The Financial Times* provides a list of investment companies each day. The website, **www.trustnet.com**, categorises investment companies and provides details of prices and track records, etc.

Once you identify an investment company, you can look it up on the Internet and should easily find an interim and annual report. Indeed, the fund management house that manages a particular investment company normally provides a monthly fact sheet for existing and potential investors to read. These fact sheets keep investors up-to-date with the progress of the company, its portfolio of shares and the performance of markets that the company is investing in.

The GillenMarkets website provides analysis and commentary largely on investment companies listed on the London Stock Exchange (LSE) for subscribers to the website.

CHAPTER 19
AN INVESTMENT PLAN: GETTING STARTED

To invest successfully, investors need a sound framework for making decisions and an ability to keep your emotions from corroding that framework.
Warren Buffett[20]

Warren Buffett did not say a 'great' framework: he said a 'sound' framework. With a bit of planning, everyone has the ability to adopt a sound approach to stock market investing.

GETTING STARTED

There are many ways to win a football match and many ways to succeed in business. Similarly, there are many ways to invest. Having an approach that you understand and that makes good investment sense, and then consistently applying that approach, is the most likely route to success in investing.

There is no silver bullet for investment success and you can treat anyone who suggests otherwise with a healthy degree of scepticism. To achieve the average returns that the markets offer is easier than you may think; to achieve above-average returns is far more difficult than many appreciate.

An investment approach that is likely to stand the test of time – which means surviving bear markets – should be capable of controlling risk and delivering the returns on offer in markets, at least. **Chapters 20** to **22** outline four separate approaches that an investor might consider when

---

[20] Buffett, W. (1973). 'Preface' in Graham, B., *The Intelligent Investor*, 4th edition, New York: Harper & Row.

investing in markets. These approaches, which are not mutually exclusive, include:

◆ Diversifying across the various asset classes (**Chapter 20**);

◆ Income investing in funds (**Chapter 20**);

◆ Value investing in the FTSE 100 Index (**Chapter 21**);

◆ Timing the markets (**Chapter 22**).

OPENING A STOCKBROKING ACCOUNT – SAVINGS AND PENSION MONIES

You will need to open a stockbroking account if you don't already have one. Your main choice is between a traditional broker and an online broker. A traditional broker provides a fuller service and mainly takes orders by phone, and provides execution-only and advisory accounts, and in some cases discretionary fund management services. The cost of transacting through traditional stockbrokers for private investors is higher than through online brokers.

The Internet, of course, has spawned an industry of online stockbroking services, which provide execution-only services with minimal ancillary services. The major advantage of dealing with an online broker is that dealing costs are substantially less than with traditional brokers. For example, if you buy Stg£1,000 worth of Tesco shares through a traditional stockbroker, the charge is likely to be *circa* 1% or a minimum of Stg£40; the same transaction through a UK online stockbroker would cost you Stg£15 or less. If you bought Stg£10,000 worth of Tesco shares though a traditional broker, the deal would likely cost you Stg£100; the same deal through an online broker would cost you circa Stg£25 and often much less.

SECURITY OF CLIENT ASSETS

The same regulations apply to all stockbrokers in regard to the security of client assets. For that reason, your assets are as secure with online brokers as they are with traditional brokers. Local directories or the Internet should provide you with a listing of traditional stockbrokers in your own locality. Traditional full service stockbrokers can buy or sell a share on your behalf on practically any market in the world. Few online stockbrokers have the same level of market coverage, although most of them can take phone orders for non-routine transactions. Hence, if you are intent on dealing in several markets, you may need to open a number of online accounts in separate geographic regions, or find an online broker that allows you to deal in several markets through the one account with them.

MANAGING YOUR OWN PENSION

Many countries, including the US and UK and, more recently, Ireland, have provided the regulatory backdrop for qualifying individuals to manage their own pension assets. Individuals with this flexibility have the option to invest their pension assets *via* the stock markets, and can choose to open either a traditional or online stockbroking account on behalf of their pension fund.

Now with the nuts and bolts of stockbroking accounts out of the way, let us examine how we might select our investments in practice.

CHAPTER 20
INVESTING ACROSS THE ASSET CLASSES

Is it possible, with a busy lifestyle, that an individual can control his/her own investments in a couple of hours a year, while at the same time gaining better control over the investment process, maintaining diversified exposure to a variety of asset classes and minimising the cost of investing? With either exchange-traded funds (ETFs) or investment companies or a combination of both, the answer is an unequivocal "Yes"!

It may be hard to believe but six investment decisions made at the outset probably will see you through a lifetime of successful investing, whether it is with your personal savings or pension monies. If it is your intention to diversify across the asset classes, then the six decisions might include investing in:

♦ A global equity ETF or investment company;

♦ A global property ETF or investment company;

♦ A global government bond ETF or investment company;

♦ A global hedge fund ETF or investment company;

♦ A selection of ETFs or investment companies offering exposure to the alternative assets, which includes private equity, timberland assets, precious metals among others; and, finally

♦ A global mixed asset ETF or investment company.

A simple strategy of adding to those positions over time would be an effective way to manage your pension monies or ordinary savings. Specific asset classes can be excluded or adjustments to the exposure to any particular asset class can be made if they become either obviously overvalued or seriously undervalued.

BUILD YOUR OWN FUND OF FUNDS …
AT MINIMAL COST

The world of ETFs keeps expanding. In the early 1990s, the first batch of ETFs introduced was equity ETFs. However, the range of assets covered has grown and today ETFs cover most of the major asset classes. **Table 20.1** highlights a sample of ETFs that provides exposure to several asset classes. There are many other ETFs that could be included in this table. However, those outlined will do the job required. Each individual ETF is well diversified in its own right. In addition, the portfolio of ETFs provides currency and geographic diversification. To assemble this portfolio through a low-cost online broker might cost you in the order of €250 or Stg£200 in fees. If you invested, say, Stg£50,000 into the portfolio outlined in **Table 20.1**, the costs would represent circa 0.4% of the monies invested. That is highly competitive compared to the entry costs to non-listed funds, which probably range from 2% to 5% of the funds committed depending on several other factors.

Once you are invested, you can simply add to selected ETFs over time depending on where you see value and other issues you may wish to consider. It might be worth glancing back over the Summary Conclusions outlined at the end of **Chapter 9**, as this will put into perspective which of the asset classes below you might exclude. In addition, through the GillenMarkets weekly investment bulletin, I provide a regular update on my views regarding the value or otherwise in the various asset classes, and in global markets.

Investment companies (trusts or closed-end funds) offer the same flexibility to build your own fund of funds through a stockbroking account. Like ETFs, several investment companies can be held simultaneously in one stockbroking account. This improves an investor's ability to achieve diversification, not only by region and asset class, but also by fund manager, while also reducing the administration involved. Because such products are already listed on a stock exchange, there is no further form filling required irrespective of whether you buy one or 10 funds. In contrast, the administration surrounding non-listed funds is onerous, in my view.

Table 20.1: A Fund of Funds Using ETFs

Exchange Traded Fund	Ticker	Asset Class	Region	Exchange	Currency
PowerShares FTSE RAFI AllWorld 3000 Equity ETF	PSRW	Equities	Global	London	Stg£
iShares FTSE EPRA/NAREIT Developed Markets Property ETF	IWDP	Property	Developed Markets	London	Stg£
iShares FTSE EPRA/NAREIT Asia Property Yield ETF	IASP	Property	Asia	London	Stg£
iShares JPMorgan $ Emerging Markets Bond ETF	SEMB	Govt. Bonds	Emerging Markets	London	Stg£
iShares Markit iBoxx Euro High Yield Corporate Bond ETF	IHYG	Corporate Bonds	Europe	London	€
SPDR Gold Shares ETC	GLD	Gold	n/a	US	$
Market Vectors RVE Hard Assets Producers ETF	HAP	Mining	Global	US	$
db Hedge Fund Index ETF	XHFD	Hedge Funds	Global	London	$

Table 20.2: A Fund of Funds Using Investment Companies (Trusts)

Investment Company (Trust)	Ticker	Asset Class	Region	Exchange	Currency
RIT Capital Partners	RCP	Mixed Asset	Global	London	Stg£
Berkshire Hathaway	BRK'B	Equities	US	US	$
Fidelity European Values	FEV	Equities	Eurozone	London	Stg£
Templeton Emerging Markets	TEM	Equities	Emerging Markets	London	Stg£
HG Capital Trust	HGT	Private Equity	UK/Europe	London	Stg£
Hansteen Holdings	HSTN	Property	Europe	London	Stg£
Ruffer Investment Company	RICA	Absolute Return	Global	London	Stg£
Blackrock World Mining Trust	BRWM	Commodities / Mining	Global	London	Stg£

Table 20.2 represents a list of investment companies (trusts or closed-end funds) covering several different asset classes. Again, the list is by no means an exhaustive list, and there are many other investment companies quoted on the London Stock Exchange and US stock exchanges that could have been included. Nonetheless, the funds included should do the job required.

Berkshire Hathaway is not strictly an investment company – it's more like an industrial holding group. Nonetheless, Berkshire has a diversified portfolio of world-beating companies, and I'd be happy to include it in any such portfolio.

Investing in stock market-listed funds does not preclude you from investing directly in shares – each to their own. Your principle aim is to buy into asset classes that are priced to deliver decent inflation-adjusted returns on a five- to 10-year view. Avoiding exposure to overvalued asset classes will ensure that you can optimise your returns from risk assets over the life of your investment programme.

INVESTING FOR INCOME ACROSS THE ASSET CLASSES

Many investors need to earn an immediate income from their investments. If that is your aim, then **Table 20.3** provides a list of high-yielding exchange-traded funds and investment companies. Clearly, an investor can buy individual companies offering above average dividend yields. However, I exclude individual companies or shares from **Table 20.3** on the basis that funds provide better diversification, which helps control risk. The list of funds includes global, UK, Eurozone and emerging market equities, private equity and a Eurozone non-investment grade corporate bond fund. At the time of writing, this list of funds offered an average income of just over 5% and compared well to bank deposit interest rates of below 1% and long-dated bond yields of below 2% in the developed markets. **Table 20.3** is a list of risk asset funds but the yield on offer suggests to me that the value and income lies in risk assets at this point in time. Clearly, events in the Eurozone and in the developed economies generally have been unsettling investors.

Table 20.3: An Income Focused Portfolio of Funds

ETF / Investment Company	Ticker	Exchange	Asset Class	Dividend Yield
WisdomTree International Dividend (ex-financials) ETF	DOO	US	Equities	4.7%
Edinburgh Investment Trust	EDIN-L	London	Equities	4.4%
iShares Euro Stoxx Select Dividend 30 ETF	IDVY-L	London	Equities	5.6%
WisdomTree European Small-cap Dividend ETF	DFE	US	Equities	4.1%
iShares Asia/Pacific Select Dividend 30 ETF	IAPD-L	London	Equities	4.6%
Princess Private Equity	PEY-L	London	Private Equity	7.7%
F&C Private Equity Trust	FPEO-L	London	Private Equity	5.5%
WisdomTree Emerging Markets Equity Income ETF	DEM	US	Equities	3.8%
State Street S&P Emerging Markets Dividend ETF	EDIV	US	Equities	4.6%
Merchants Trust	MRCH-L	London	Equities	6.5%
iShares Euro High Yield Corporate Bond ETF	IHYG-L	London	Corp Bonds	6.0%
Average Yield				**5.2%**

Note: Dividend yields were based on historic dividends and prices at 1 June 2012. ETF dividends were the average dividends paid out over the previous three years.

The lack of any yield from government bonds in the developed economies is the reason why none are included in **Table 20.3**. Spanish and Italian medium-dated government bonds are yielding *circa* 6% (again at the time of writing) and they could be included so long as an investor treats them as risk assets.

CHAPTER 21
ENHANCING RETURNS: VALUE INVESTING IN THE FTSE 100 INDEX

This chapter outlines a rules-based approach to selecting a portfolio of stocks from the UK FTSE 100 Index. The approach overcomes many of the difficulties private investors face when trying to assess whether to buy a new share or to hold or even sell an existing share. Some readers may wish to refer to the case study on terminology in **Appendix I** before reading on.

In **Chapter 8, The Difficulties of Stock Picking,** we examined some of the potential hurdles private investors encounter when trying to select individual shares. The principle problem is the difficulty in assessing the three major risks: business risk, financial risk and valuation risk. Before jumping straight into the specific approach to selecting FTSE 100 companies, I will examine these problems in more detail, and provide an explanation as to why selecting stocks in a non-subjective manner has significant advantages over trying to select them subjectively.

Figure 21.1 highlights the immense challenge that most private investors face in assessing the merits or otherwise of individual companies. It highlights some subjective or qualitative factors (left-hand side), as well as several numerical or quantitative factors (right-hand side) that make up the investment decision-making process.

It is much the same process as you might go through if you are in business for yourself and trying to decide on an expansion plan or an acquisition. In the stock market, where we are dealing with quoted companies, an investor might use this decision tree to help him decide on the quality of a particular company and the value on offer.

Figure 21.1: Investment Decision-making

It makes intuitive sense to try to assess a company's management, product positioning, ability to control its own prices, the threat from new entrants, etc. However, the difficulty with the subjective or qualitative factors is that they are hard to assess, even for more experienced analysts. Also, even if you do make a decent assessment of a particular company, there is no guarantee that your assessment is any better than all the other views that are already in the marketplace about a particular company. In short, the likelihood of a private investor assessing a company any better than has already been done by the many analysts and fund managers operating in the market is remote. On top of that, even if you achieve this, you still must ensure that you do not overpay.

I believe that it is commonsense for the vast majority of private investors simply to acknowledge that it is impractical for them to carry out the level of research required to be subjective about which shares should be part of their stock market portfolio. If you agree with me on this, and still want to build your own portfolio of shares, then you must find another way of selecting shares.

An alternative way to select a portfolio of stocks is to eliminate the subjective factors on the left-hand side, as **Figure 21.2** demonstrates. After all, if you cannot assess these qualitative factors, why bother even trying? It is not that they are irrelevant – rather, most investors cannot use them to make an informed investment decision. Instead, you are better off concentrating on what you *can* do.

Figure 21.2: Non-subjective Investment Decision-making

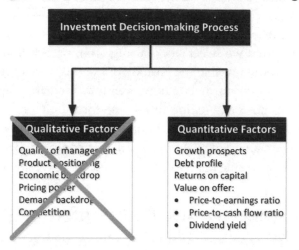

The quantitative, or numerical, factors on the right-hand side of **Figure 21.2** are easier to use in assessing the merits of one company *versus* another. By using numerical factors, we can measure the relative value on offer. And by concentrating on the numerical factors alone, it is possible for any investor to adopt an approach that:

♦ Obtains better value, at the time of purchase, than is on offer in the market generally;

♦ Removes subjectivity and emotion from the decision-making process;

♦ Has worked well in the past, in other words is 'time tested';

♦ Provides diversification, which is essential to controlling risk;

♦ Is easy to follow and implement; and

♦ Makes the 'what to buy' and 'when to sell' decisions obvious.

MAKE THE STOCKS IDENTIFY THEMSELVES

Any approach to stock selection that satisfies the above criteria removes much of the decision-making (and agonising) from the stock selection process. What is truly different with this way of assembling a portfolio of stocks is that the stocks that need to be included in your portfolio identify themselves.

If the buy and sell decisions are obvious, then the investor has limited input into what stocks are selected and when they are sold. This might offend your intellect, but we are after results and not an ego boost. We need to ensure that we select stocks using an approach that has proven itself to have worked well in the past. By doing this, we are removing the opinions of others – no matter how well-informed they appear to be. Equity analysts in stock broking firms who form opinions on stocks are intelligent, hard-working people, with good intuition and well-informed views. However, an opinion about a particular company from an analyst is not remotely the same thing as a tried and tested investment approach.

WE ARE NOT GOOD AT FORECASTING

An opinion from an equity analyst is an interpretation, a forecast; and human beings are not built for forecasting. That does not stop us trying, but neither does it make us any better at it just because we keep trying! A subjective view, no matter how well researched and written, is just that: a view. The mistake that many private investors make is to treat views from stockbroking analysts as 'gospel' simply because the analyst has more facts to hand and possibly has access to management. Many studies have shown that research from stockbroking companies provides no edge in the stock selection game.

BETTER TO JUST SELECT STOCKS BY VALUE

An approach to selecting stocks that simply measures values as they exist at the time has as good a chance of delivering the returns as trying to forecast which are the likely winners. In addition, as the approach is based on numbers, it can be tested back in time to see how effective it has been at producing returns, and how those returns compare to the returns generated by the market itself. For example, if you were to use the price-to-earnings ratio as the measure of value to select stocks from the FTSE 100 Index (as we will soon do), then surely it would be important to know whether this approach to stock selection has led to success in the past. The longer back in time we can evaluate the success, or otherwise, of this low price-to-earnings approach, the better. If you are to buy stocks in the UK market on the basis of a low price-to-earnings ratio, surely you would want to know whether this method of selecting stocks has delivered the market returns, higher than market returns or lower than market returns in the past?

Remember that if you wish to invest in the UK stock market, you always have the choice of buying an exchange-traded fund that will passively replicate the FTSE 100 Index for you, or to buy into an investment company actively managed by a fund manager, instead of buying individual companies' shares.

If we know the criterion for selecting stocks – in this case, the price-to-earnings ratio on FTSE 100 stocks – and can measure how effective it has been in the past, then we are heading towards finding a tried and tested approach to stock selection. If the approach is also easy to follow, it substantially increases the odds of you being able to use it. The approach should also ensure good diversification – somewhere between 10 and 15 stocks is sufficient.

If the measure of value we are using to select the stocks is clear and unambiguous, then a stock either matches the criterion or it does not. If not, then the stock is sold. Therein lie the 'what to buy' and 'when to sell' decisions. Subjectivity and opinion are removed; instead, we rely on facts. This also should help us to stay unemotional in volatile market conditions.

All stocks decline when markets decline and many stocks decline substantially in bear markets. A portfolio of stocks selected using some measure of value, like the price-to-earnings ratio, will decline also – sometimes less than the market and sometimes more than the market. However, that is not important, since such declines most likely represent temporary losses, not permanent ones. A well-constructed, well-diversified portfolio of stocks, selected using a measure of value that has been proven to work over time, will recover with the market, and often more than the market.

STOCK PICKING IN THE FTSE 100 INDEX

In the complex and often intimidating world of stock market investing, the idea that an approach so simple could result in superior returns intrigued me.
Michael O'Higgins[21]

Skewing your portfolio towards stocks that offer better value, while still ensuring good diversification, increases your chances of beating the market returns.

Knowing how an approach has worked previously, and over many stock market cycles, is essential to helping you to stay the course through both good and difficult times – and there will be difficult times.

In his excellent book on value investing published in 1998, US fund manager David Dreman[22] outlined a long-term study on value-based approaches to selecting a diversified portfolio of large-sized companies (by market capitalisation) in the US stock market. At the time, the approaches appeared to me to be within the grasp of every investor and also likely to be highly suited to the UK market. Dreman's study showed the results of selecting stocks in the US stock market using a couple of value metrics over a 27-year period, from 1970 to 1996 inclusive. He demonstrated that, over this period, a portfolio of large companies chosen on the basis of the dividend yield, the price-to-earnings ratio or the price-to-cash flow ratio delivered annual returns in excess of the market returns from 1970 to 1996 inclusive. **Chart 21.1** replicates a chart from Dreman's book *Contrarian Investment Strategies: The Next Generation.*[23]

---

[21] O'Higgins, M. (1991). *Beating the Dow,* New York: HarperCollins, Introduction, page xii.

[22] Dreman, D. (1998). *Contrarian Investment Strategies: The Next Generation,* New York: Simon & Schuster.

[23] Compiled using data from tables in Dreman, D. (1998). *Contrarian Investment Strategies: The Next Generation,* New York: Simon & Schuster, pages 161, 164 & 168. Permission kindly granted by Dreman Value Management.

**Chart 21.1: US Market: Top 300 Stocks (Top Quintile):
Annual Returns (1970-1996)**

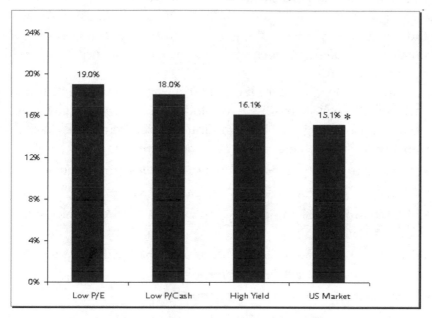

* Represents the market return and is the average annual return of the 1,500
stocks for each separate study.

In the Dreman study, the US Compustat database was sorted using the
following measures of value:

♦ The highest dividend yields;

♦ The lowest price-to-earnings ratios; and

♦ The lowest price-to-cash flow ratios.

For each separate study – the high yield, low price-to-earnings and low
price-to-cash flow – the top 1,500 stocks were selected. The performance
of the top 300 stocks chosen by the relevant measure of value (the stocks
with the lowest price-to-earnings ratio or price-to-cash flow ratio or the
highest dividend yield) was monitored for each value study. The top 300
stocks is referred to as the top quintile or top fifth (a fifth representing
300 out of 1,500 stocks).

The returns outlined in **Chart 21.1** are the annualised returns of these
top 300 stocks in each portfolio (rather than compound *per annum*
returns). In each case, the 300 stocks selected were held for one year, after
which the stocks that were no longer in the top 300 as defined by the

value metric were sold, and the new stocks that were now in the top 300 were added to the portfolio. Hence, the investor always held 300 US large capitalisation value stocks in his portfolio for the 27 years of the study, and simply altered the portfolio once a year to ensure it still contained the 300 stocks offering the best value, as defined by the value metric in question.

It struck me forcibly at the time that this was an approach that should work equally well in the FTSE 100 Index, or, indeed, in any market where there is a large pool of significantly-sized companies to choose from. In other words, here was an approach to investing:

♦ Where the 'what to buy' and 'when to sell' rules were obvious;

♦ That made business sense, as it was based on values;

♦ That controlled risk through its emphasis on large companies and diversification;

♦ That was easy to follow in practice and that had worked well in the past, in the US market at least; and

♦ That needed no forecasts of any nature.

Dreman's approach had a lot of appeal, and, in 1999, using the Company REFS[24] database in the UK, I tested the approach on the UK market back to 1995 and have kept the records for each year since then.

In practice, I selected the top 75 stocks in the UK market by market capitalisation, and selected the top 15 stocks (top quintile or top fifth) using the dividend yield, price-to-earnings ratio and price-to-cash flow ratio – three portfolios in all. I recorded the total returns for each year for each separate approach, and this has provided me with 17 years of credible data (1995 to 2011 inclusive) on how effective or otherwise the approaches have been in the UK stock market. **Chart 21.2** records the summary compound *per annum* returns of all three approaches for this 17-year period and compares them to the FTSE 100 Index: both the traditional market capitalisation-weighted FTSE 100 index and an equal-weighted FTSE 100 index.

Over the 17-year period from 1995 to 2011, the traditional FTSE 100 market capitalisation-weighted index delivered a compound *per annum* return of 7.4%. This return includes dividend income and excludes transaction costs. An equal-weighted FTSE 100 Index generated a 9.4%

---

[24]   www.companyrefs.com – devised by Jim Slater, 1994.

compound *per annum* return, suggesting that an equal-weighted ETF on the FTSE 100 Index would improve returns for investors. I'm surprised one has not yet been introduced by one of the major ETF providers.

Chart 21.2: FTSE 100 Index: Top 15 Stocks (Top Quintile) Returns *per annum* compound (1995-2011)

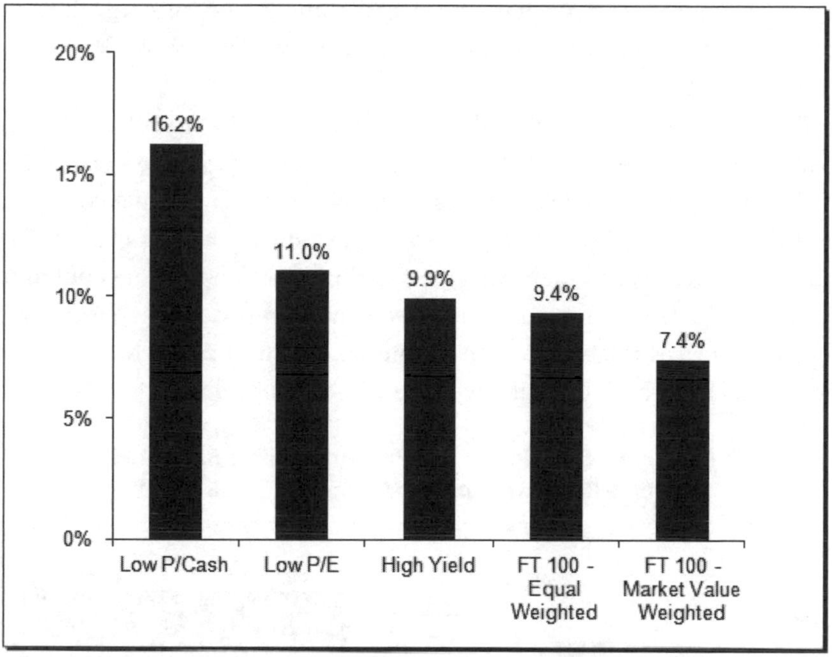

Source: Company REFS and GillenMarkets (annual dividend yield added to index price data to give an estimate of total returns annually).

Chart 21.2 provides us with proof-of-concept of value-based approaches to investing in the UK FTSE 100 over an extended period of time. For the remainder of this chapter, and for the sake of keeping things simple, I will now outline how to implement just one of these value-based approaches – the low price-to-earnings approach – and try and deal with some of the questions that readers naturally will have on it.

THE FTSE 100 LOW PRICE-TO-EARNINGS APPROACHES

Our universe of stocks is the top 75 stocks by market capitalisation in the UK stock market. They are all members of the FTSE 100 Index. I restrict the universe of stocks to 75, even though there are 100 companies in the FTSE 100 Index, as I wish to base my statistics on a stable body of companies and avoid the 'noise' potentially created by stocks that are constantly entering and leaving the index.

Before I outline the exact rules for selecting stocks from the FTSE 100 Index, I will rank the 75 stocks by the price-to-earnings ratio and split the list into groups of 15 stocks, or quintiles, with the top quintile containing the 15 stocks on the lowest price-to-earnings ratios (those stocks with low share prices relative to their earnings) and the bottom quintile containing the 15 stocks on the highest price-to-earnings ratios (those stocks with high share prices relative to their earnings). In **Chart 21.3**, I then examine the returns from each quintile over the 17-year period.

**Chart 21.3: FTSE 100 Index: Low Price-to-earnings Ratio Study –
Quintile Returns *per annum* Compound (1995-2011)**

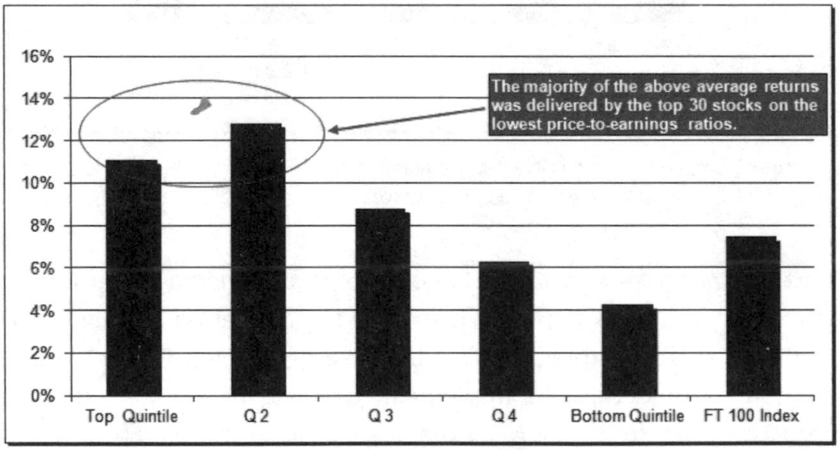

Source: Company REFS and GillenMarkets.

Chart 21.3 provides further proof-of-concept that the more value there is in your portfolio (assuming it is well diversified among larger stocks), the higher the subsequent returns. It can be no coincidence that the bottom 15 stocks (or bottom quintile), which represent the 15 stocks from the basket of 75 that were trading on the highest price-to-earnings ratios at the time of purchase, delivered the poorest returns over the 17-year period. Indeed, the fourth quintile, containing the 15 stocks that were trading on the next highest price-to-earnings ratios (at the time of selection) delivered returns somewhat better than the bottom quintile but lower than the remaining quintiles, which all contained stocks that were trading on a lower price-to-earnings ratio at the time of purchase. It is clear from **Chart 21.3** that the more value that exists in your portfolio (provided it is diversified among large companies), the higher the subsequent returns.

The only anomaly in **Chart 21.3** is that the top quintile, which represents the 15 stocks on the lowest price-to-earnings ratios, delivered lower returns than the second quintile over the 17-year period: I put that down to the banking crisis of 2008. Banks went bust in 2008 and they were mostly represented in the top quintile at the time. Nonetheless, it is clear from **Chart 21.3** that it is the top two quintiles, or the top 30 stocks on the lowest price-to-earnings ratios (from the basket of 75 FTSE 100 companies chosen by market capitalisation) that deliver most of the excess returns compared to the FTSE 100 Index. That being the case, we can move on and show how to select a portfolio of 15 stocks from this pool of 30 stocks. After all, if this pool of stocks has delivered better than average returns in the past, then surely it makes sense to fish in this pool when selecting a portfolio of stocks from the FTSE 100 Index in the future.

What to Buy

- ◆ List the top 75 stocks by market capitalisation (size) in the UK market (using some database like Company REFS);
- ◆ Rank this list by the lowest price-to-earnings ratio – the company with the lowest price-to-earnings ratio will be at the top of the list and so on down (Company REFS uses a forecast P/E ratio);
- ◆ Select the top 30 stocks trading on the lowest price-to-earnings ratios.
- ◆ You then have two choices:
  - ◊ Buy the top 15 stocks on the list – the 15 stocks on the lowest price-to-earnings ratios – referred to as the 'Top 15' low price-to-earnings approach;

◊   Alternatively, select one stock from each sector from the top 30
    stocks until a portfolio of 15 stocks has been assembled – referred
    to as the 'Sector 15' low price-to-earnings ratio approach;

♦   Within reason, invest the same amount of capital in each stock each
    year.

When to Sell

♦   Hold the portfolio of 15 stocks for one year and then re-do the
    exercise, selling any stocks that are not in the current 15 and buying
    the new stocks that are now included.

Table 21.1: FTSE 100 Index: Low Price-to-earnings Approaches:
Annual Returns (1995-2011)

Year	FTSE 100	Top 15 Portfolio	Out-/Under-performance	Sector 15 Portfolio	Out-/Under-performance
1995	20.3%	34.3%	14.0%	26.1%	5.8%
1996	19.3%	11.2%	-8.1%	10.0%	-9.3%
1997	24.4%	37.9%	13.5%	32.6%	8.2%
1998	15.6%	11.4%	-4.2%	2.0%	-13.6%
1999	16.4%	11.1%	-5.3%	10.3%	-6.1%
2000	4.6%	6.5%	1.9%	10.0%	5.4%
2001	-16.5%	12.8%	29.3%	5.6%	22.1%
2002	-17.0%	-3.0%	14.0%	-7.5%	9.5%
2003	8.3%	8.7%	0.4%	11.1%	2.8%
2004	12.4%	19.2%	6.8%	18.8%	6.4%
2005	15.8%	16.0%	0.2%	22.1%	6.3%
2006	22.0%	39.9%	17.9%	44.1%	22.1%
2007	12.7%	20.3%	7.6%	18.9%	6.2%
2008	-31.3%	-49.2%	-17.9%	-38.7%	-7.4%
2009	30.7%	64.0%	33.3%	58.6%	27.9%
2010	13.0%	12.5%	-0.5%	17.5%	4.5%
2011	-1.5%	-15.7%	-14.2%	0.7%	2.2%
1995-2011 (c.p.a. %)	7.4%	11.0%	3.6%	12.2%	4.8%

Source: Company REFS and GillenMarkets (annual dividend yield added to index and
share price data to give an estimate of total returns annually).

Note: Years 1995 to 2008 refer to the 12-month period from 1 November to 31
October; 2009 refers to a 14-month period from 1 November 2008 to 31 December
2009; 2010 and 2011 are calendar years.

Table 21.1 highlights the annual returns of both the 'Top 15' and 'Sector 15' approaches and their annual outperformance and underperformance compared to the FTSE 100 Index. **Charts 21.4** and **21.5** display the annual outperformance and underperformance in graphic format, which may be easier to follow.

Chart 21.4: FTSE 100 Index: Low Price-to-earnings 'Top 15' Approach: Annual out/underperformance (1995-2011)

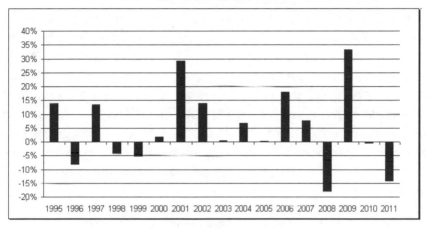

Source: GillenMarkets.

Chart 21.5: FTSE 100 Index: Low Price-to-earnings 'Sector 15' Approach: Annual out/underperformance (1995-2011)

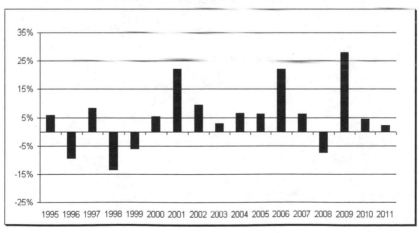

Source: GillenMarkets.

The consistency of the performance of the 'Top 15' low price-to-earnings approach has been good, with the portfolio outperforming the index in 11 out of the 17 years. The period of most significant underperformance was in 2008 during the banking crisis, when the portfolio declined in value by 49.2% compared to a decline of 31.3% in the FTSE 100 Index, an underperformance of 17.9% in that year. However, in 2009, the year of greatest outperformance, the portfolio delivered a return of 64%, some 33.3% in excess of the UK market return in that year.

For the 'Sector 15' low price-to-earnings approach, the consistency of the performance also has been good, with the portfolio outperforming the index in 13 out of the 17 years. Unlike the 'Top 15' stock portfolio, the period of most significant underperformance for the 'Sector 15' approach was in 1998 when the portfolio advanced in value by only 2.0%, compared to a gain of 15.6% in the FTSE 100 Index, an underperformance of 13.6% in that year. In 2009, the year of greatest out-performance, the portfolio delivered a return of 58.6% compared to a rise of 30.7% in the FTSE 100 in that same year, for an out-performance of 27.9%.

Chart 21.6: FTSE 100 Index: Low Price-to-earnings Approaches: Value of £10,000 invested on 1 November 1994

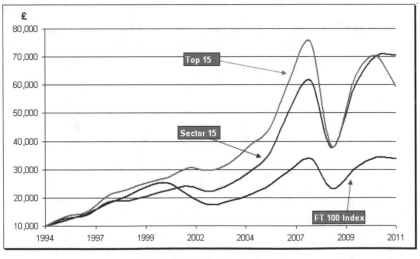

Source: GillenMarkets.

Chart 21.6 highlights that a £10,000 investment in November 1994 in the low price-to-earnings approach grew to £59,292 for the 'Top 15' approach and £70,559 for the 'Sector 15' approach by December 2011. The same £10,000 invested in a FTSE 100 ETF grew to £33,732. All figures are for illustrative purposes as I have ignored costs and taxes for the sake of simplicity.

The Approaches also Protect Against an Overvalued Market

As **Table 21.1** highlighted, both low price-to-earnings approaches delivered *per annum* compound returns of between 11% to 12% over the past 17 years. Indeed, if we start in 2000 (November 1999), the 'Sector 15 approach delivered *per annum* compound returns of 10.8% compared to 2.9% for the FTSE 100 Index. The UK equity market peaked in late 1999 at overvalued levels and has struggled to generate the long-term average returns since then. Yet, the value focused low price-to-earnings ratio 'Sector 15' approach continued to deliver double-digit returns. Its concentration on obtaining better value compared to what was on offer in the index is the most likely reason why it delivered better returns in the subsequent 12 years from 2000 to 2011 inclusive.

COMPOUNDING IN THE FTSE 100 INDEX

As we saw in **Chapter 4, The Power of Compounding,** the impact of greater returns kicks in most strongly after several years. **Table 21.2** now compares the contrasting scenarios for a pension fund investor of obtaining a 4% *per annum* compound return from cash deposits and a 10% *per annum* compound return using the low price-to-earnings 'Sector 15' approach to investing in the UK FTSE 100 Index. A 10% return is used compared to the slightly higher returns actually achieved by the UK low price-to-earnings approach over the past 17 years to account for the impact of the annual trading costs. As it is a pension investor, there are no tax implications. I assume the investor adds a more realistic €15,000 each year to his pension account, or €300,000 in total, and that he starts later in life, at age 45, than prudent retirement planning would probably advise.

**Table 21.2: Pension Fund Investing in Cash Deposits and the UK FTSE 100
Low Price-to-earnings (Sector 15) Approach**

End of Year	Investor A: 4% Return	Investor B: 10% Return
1	15,600	16,500
2	31,824	34,650
3	48,697	54,615
4	66,245	76,577
5	84,495	100,734
6	103,474	127,308
7	123,213	156,538
8	143,742	188,692
9	165,092	224,061
10	187,295	262,968
11	210,387	305,764
12	234,403	352,841
13	259,379	404,625
14	285,354	461,587
15	312,368	524,246
16	340,463	593,171
17	369,681	668,988
18	400,068	752,386
19	431,671	844,125
20	€464,538	€945,037
Starting at Age 35	€649,676	€1,622,726
Starting at Age 30	€874,925	€2,714,151

After a 20-year period, the investor who contributes €15,000 annually into his pension from age 45 and saves through cash deposits earning 4% *per annum* has a lump-sum of €464,538 at retirement. By investing in the UK low price-to-earnings 'Sector 15' approach, the same investor would have generated a lump-sum at retirement of €945,037, over double the returns generated from cash deposits.

Of course, these days, an investor can't get 4% from cash deposits but the 10% annual return is most likely still going to be available from the low price-to-earnings (Sector 15) approach (not straight line, of course). Indeed, the earlier the investor starts, the starker the contrast.

If he starts 15 years earlier, at a still realistic age of 30, then the lump-sum generated from a 10% *per annum* return over a 35-year year timeline to retirement at 65 is €2.7 million – and all from contributing €15,000 annually to the programme, or €525,000 in aggregate.

POINTS TO CONSIDER

There is nothing magical about the one-year holding rule. In the UK, most companies report to shareholders twice a year and this gives them time to perform – or, indeed, recover.

Of course, you are in for the full year. In between, do not try to second-guess the approach. For example, do not introduce stop losses (setting a pre-determined price which, if hit, triggers an investor to sell automatically). An investor should either accept the approach for what it is, or not follow it at all. By undertaking an annual review, you get to spring-clean your portfolio once a year, which assists you to remain in the 15 stocks that offer the best value, as defined by the low price-to-earnings ratio.

If the prospect of your portfolio performing worse than the market in any particular year unnerves you, then do not attempt to adopt the approach. Satisfy yourself with the market returns and buy an index product like an ETF or an investment company that is actively managed by a fund manager.

Why Only 17 Years of Data?

The reason my studies started on 1 November 1994 (in effect, 1995) is that this was the date the Company REFS database was first published and it provided me with real-time valuation data on the FTSE 100 Index, which I considered to be extremely reliable. As a result of using only data known to have been in existence at the time, there was much less chance of hindsight bias in the analysis. One might argue that 17 years is not enough time to prove anything. In his book, David Dreman details 27 years of data backing up his approach. Combined with my own, you could argue that the two together amount to a full 44 years of data.

Why Have These Approaches Improved on the Market Returns?

The next question that naturally arises is: why have the approaches done better than the market in the past? David Dreman points out that "investors overreact to events in a predictable fashion: they consistently overvalue the prospects of the 'best' investments and undervalue those of the 'worst' investments".[25] A disciplined approach to catching out-of-favour companies, possibly undervalued by the market, delivers better returns than the market.

By no means could I say that the approaches work for each individual stock identified or selected. Quite the opposite, in fact! There will be many losers among the 15-stock portfolios. Hence, diversification is essential and a portfolio of 15 stocks will contain winners and losers. Overall, however, the 15-stock portfolios identify a sufficient number of undervalued stocks, relative to the market, to deliver better returns than the market over time. As companies swing back from undervaluation to overvaluation, they generate above average returns.

The FTSE 100 low price-to-earnings approaches outlined in this chapter recognise that it is the mood swings of investors that is of paramount importance; even more important, it seems, than the underlying earnings growth of the companies. We saw this same phenomenon in the Coca Cola case study earlier in **Chapter 8, The Difficulties of Stock Picking**. Thus, a disciplined approach to buying the cheapest companies on offer, without regard to the outlook, pushes us into potentially undervalued stocks. Yes, there will be genuine losers identified along the way, but the approaches identify sufficient numbers of genuinely undervalued companies to deliver above average-returns overall, over time. And the approaches achieve that without having to forecast anything. It is a common misconception among investors that you have to 'forecast' in order to buy the right stocks.

No Need to Understand Terminology

Another factor worth highlighting in the low price-to-earnings value-based approaches, and other value-based approaches, is that it is not necessary to be an expert in terminology to be a successful investor in the stock markets. In these UK value-based approaches I outline here, an investor does not need to determine what the right 'price-to-earnings ratio' is. He or she simply needs to ensure that they are in the cheapest 15 stocks as defined by the lowest price-to-earnings ratio. By adopting such an approach, investors are assuming the market will make progress in

---

[25] Dreman, D. (1998). *Contrarian Investment Strategies: The Next Generation*, New York: Simon & Schuster, p.246.

the medium-term and are content to be in the stocks that offer the best relative value at the time of purchase.

A relatively simple approach to stock market investing can give you an edge over time, because the Achilles-heel of the stock market is that it overreacts in the short-term to events unfolding: both in its treatment of individual companies, and of the market as a whole. In the medium- to long-term, the market and investors are logical and do reward the right companies; it is in the short-term that the market can be irrational. The investor who has a plan to take advantage of that and can keep his emotions under wraps has every chance of generating better returns. In that regard, both of these FTSE 100 low price-to-earnings ratio approaches offer time-tested solutions for investing in the UK stock market.

In the short-term, investors make emotional decisions: selling companies whose prospects are deemed to be poor (or, at least, deteriorating) and buying those companies whose prospects look better. In doing so, investors tend to overpay for the stocks that are in favour and to undervalue those stocks with less favourable prospects. If you are armed with a definite plan based on 'values', or even 'relative values', which determines what you buy and when you sell, you have an edge on the market. By limiting your purchases to stocks that offer better value, you are loading the odds in your favour.

Benjamin Graham, the famous US value investor (who taught Warren Buffett at Columbia University in the late 1940s) also said that you can invest in the stock markets "by way of prediction" or "by way of protection".[26]

There is great wisdom in Graham's words, which he wrote over 60 years ago; nothing has changed in the stock markets since. What Graham was saying is that you can choose a portfolio of stocks by trying to predict which companies are best positioned to prosper in the years ahead. However, Graham also understood that you can approach stock selection by 'way of protection': by this, he meant that there is no need to predict anything in the stock markets so long as you protect yourself by selecting stocks with a 'margin of safety'. In that regard, Graham also

---

[26] Graham, B. (1949). *The Intelligent Investor*, New York: Harper & Row (p.198, 1973 reprinted edition).

said that "…the function of the margin of safety is, in essence, that of rendering unnecessary an accurate estimate of the future".

In these two FTSE 100 low price-to-earnings ratio approaches (Top 15 and Sector 15), by insisting on buying the best value at the time of purchase, an investor has introduced a 'margin of safety'. Here, the investor pays more attention to the value he or she has bought, rather than trying to predict the companies likely to deliver the best earnings growth. Many of the stocks you will end up buying will appear to have poor or dull prospects: that is why you are getting them cheap. It is management's job to improve the business; if they *do* manage to turn the business around, you get a double benefit. Earnings recover more strongly than investors in general are anticipating, and investors are then prepared to pay more for those same earnings than they were before. On the other hand, if you pay a high price for the earnings of a company that is expected to grow fast, then failure by the company to deliver on those expectations will hit the investor twice: earnings will not have grown as fast as expected, and the price investors are prepared to pay for those same earnings declines.

Don't Deviate from Large Stocks with this Approach

Using a single value factor like the price-to-earnings ratio should be considered only with large companies like those in the FTSE 100 Index. Investors should not for a moment consider adopting this approach for the selection of smaller stocks. Big companies are different in many respects from smaller ones: large companies tend to survive troubled times; smaller companies do not have the same survivorship odds. It's a bit like comparing a large tanker and a small yacht out on the ocean: each is equal, so long as the weather is fine. But brew up a good storm with the accompanying waves and suddenly the odds of survival change – the large tanker can survive heavy waves pounding it all day long; the smaller yacht can probably survive the first tough wave, but a consistent battering may see it disappear altogether.

It is the same in the stock markets. Against consistently tough economic headwinds, some smaller companies just don't survive. So, in the case of smaller companies, a price-to-earnings ratio is not a reliable guide to value. For larger companies, it is a more reliable measure of value.

In addition, the value-based approaches outlined here insist on proper diversification across 15 stocks. This should ensure that your portfolio is spread across a number of different sectors, although it is fair to say that in the 'Top 15' approach, a concentration of sorts will be inevitable. Some stocks will disappoint, while others will fare well. It is the overall result which you are after, and you should not concern yourself with the performance of individual companies.

The approaches force you to rely on a framework for building and maintaining a portfolio of stocks. To understand how an approach has performed in the past is critical. It is far better to rely on a time-tested approach than on opinions gathered from the media, analysts or friends. Opinions are forecasts and as Dreman says, "people do not know their limitations when it comes to forecasting".[27]

Choose Your Own Stocks

Of course, you do not have to follow the approach in as robotic a manner as I have outlined. If you examine **Chart 21.3** again, it is clear that it is the top 30 stocks, sorted by value, out of the FTSE 100 Index that have delivered above average returns over time. So, if you are confident enough in your own ability to analyse the three principal risks (business, financial and valuation) when selecting stocks, and wish to add your own flavour to your portfolio, then you can pick 15 stocks from this basket of 30 based on your own subjective views.

SOME FREQUENT QUESTIONS

Inevitably, readers will have questions regarding the approach outlined here. The first thing I should say is that this approach is far from perfect. Indeed, there may be other value-based approaches more suited to the FTSE 100. Nonetheless, the approach I have outlined here is easy to follow and I have now built up 17 years of data that provides proof that it has come through several difficult market conditions.

The following is a short, but certainly not exhaustive, list of questions on the approach that I have dealt with at the one-day stock market training seminars which I have delivered since 2005.

---

[27] Dreman, D. (1998). *Contrarian Investment Strategies: The Next Generation*, New York: Simon & Schuster.

What about profit warnings and dividend cuts that might come after an investor has bought particular shares outlined by the approach – do these not undermine the value that appeared to be there? What should an investor do when faced with these events during the year?

The short answer is that dividend cuts and profit warnings were a constant feature among the stocks selected in the portfolios over the 17 years from 1995 to 2011. You might be very tempted to sell on such news, but, then, how can you, a private investor, know what is priced in when you go to sell? A profit warning may already be priced in. Indeed, that may be the reason why the stock was available at what appeared to be a low valuation – because the market expected bad news. The bad news arrives and you sell, expecting the shares to fall further in price, but then you are mystified to see the shares rise just after you have sold. The point is that you do not know what the market has already discounted.

What about high debt levels and other indicators of financial risk in companies one is buying?

Undoubtedly, some of the companies you will be buying will have inappropriately high levels of debt, and, in recessionary environments, some of these companies will get into financial difficulties. However, as a private investor most likely not familiar with balance sheets and cash flow statements, how are you to assess such issues? Of course, if you are an experienced investor, then you have the choice of selecting your own 10 to 15 stocks from the top 30 value stocks, as outlined previously. You can use your own judgement to avoid those companies in the top 30 that you feel carry an above average level of financial risk. But, for all other investors, the diversification offered by spreading your monies across 15 stocks provides adequate protection. It certainly did over the 17 years that I have the data for, which included two recessionary periods in the early and late 2000s.

What about the fact that most of the companies selected are not growth companies?

One of the Holy Grails of investing is identifying companies that can grow their earnings year-in, year-out, irrespective of the ups and downs in the economic cycle, and that are available at cheap prices. If you could assemble a list of stocks with these characteristics, you could probably put your feet up once you had bought them, and just watch them grow!

However, they are rare, and it is even rarer to find them at good value. The fact is, there are just not that many companies that can grow in a consistent and reliable manner. In the late 1990s, investors mistook technology companies for growth companies and grossly overvalued them, and we know where that ended. The predictability attached to earnings of technology stocks is way below average, making them especially difficult to value. Hence, an approach to selecting a diversified portfolio of stocks that does not focus on growth is at no immediate disadvantage, in my view.

Stock market returns are generated from dividends received and capital gains, and if the capital gains delivered from value-focused portfolios largely come from a recovery in valuations, as opposed to growth in underlying earnings and cash flows, then so be it.

But if it is all so easy, why aren't the professional fund managers following these approaches?

Some fund managers do adhere to value-based approaches, but they appear to be in a minority. The pressure to deliver returns close to the market returns is an industry hazard, and any fund manager who lags behind the market return for an extended period is taking what they describe as a 'career risk' (he or she risks being sacked).

Take the example of the fund manager who is managing a pension fund on behalf of a large international company. The fund manager decides to adopt the 'Sector 15 Low Price-to-earnings Approach'. If you examine **Table 21.1**, you will notice that this approach lagged behind the FTSE 100 returns by a cumulative 21% over a four-year period, between 1996 and 1999 inclusive. Now, picture the fund manager sitting down at an annual review meeting with the trustees of the pension fund, who collectively probably know very little about investing, and discussing the underperformance. Clearly, the fund manager believes his approach is good and is sure the underperformance is temporary and likely to be corrected when those insanely-valued technology stocks implode. However, it is not himself that he has to convince but his clients, who have been reading all about the success of technology stocks in the marketplace. These 'knowledgeable' trustees are more likely to tell the fund manager why he should be in technology stocks after they have sacked him.

In response to such a career-threatening risk, the fund manager rightly concludes that he would be better off shadowing the index. It's okay to be adrift of the index return by a small margin – that can easily be explained by a few good one-liners full of industry bluff; but to lag the index consistently and by a wide margin over a few years is to risk losing not only the investment mandate but also your job.

Why don't we employ stop-losses?

I have often been asked in my one-day seminars whether one should use stop-losses with the approaches. A stop-loss is where an investor puts in a predetermined price that he is willing to sell at. It can be done automatically in the US markets but not in the Irish or UK markets.

My answer has always been that stop-losses are not an investor's tool – they are a trader's tool, and trading markets is an entirely different discipline. If one were to put a stop-loss in and it was hit, and you were sold out of those particular shares, how do you know the shares would not then start reversing their decline and fully recover, and possibly more? In a general market decline, perhaps all your shares hit their predetermined stop-loss limits, only for the market to regain its poise and in a few months all your stocks are higher in price than when you sold them.

Since 1995, the UK market has edged upwards on average, admittedly interrupted by two severe bear markets. Employing stop-losses is to introduce a timing mechanism into your investment strategy. If you are to consider doing that, then you had better know whether it leads to superior results or to unnecessary costs and reduced returns. These UK FTSE 100 low-price-to-earnings approaches I have put forward here are time-tested. If you wish to introduce further rules such as stop-losses, then you had better do some homework first!

These questions and answers above are just a sample of the many I have been asked over the years. No matter which way you cut it, the value-based approaches I have outlined are not the Holy Grail of investing but they do offer investors an easy-to-follow plan that can achieve market returns – and often above-average returns – with minimum effort, whilst controlling risk. The price for superior performance is that investors have to put up with periods of underperformance.

As is often said, investing may be simple in theory but, in practice, it is far from easy. It is one thing to own a portfolio of stocks in a downmarket, but to be underperforming in a downmarket is emotionally difficult. At these times, everyone else – media articles, friends and other fund managers – will be telling you why your approach no longer works and the pressure to abandon it can become overwhelming. This is why it is important to know the facts about how the approach has performed in the past.

Getting Through the Global Credit Crisis

Tables **21.3** and **21.4** highlight the pressure an investor was under in real-time. **Table 21.3** is the performance of the 2008 low price-to-earnings portfolio (Sector 15) in the huge down year of 2008. The year covered was 1 November 2007 to 31 October 2008.

Table 21.3: FTSE 100 Index: Low Price-to-earnings 'Sector 15' Portfolio: Performance (1 November 2007 to 31 October 2008)

Company	Industry	Return
Royal Bank of Scotland	Banking	-83.0%
British Airways	Airlines	-67.9%
Aviva	Assurance	-47.2%
Kazakhmys	Mining	-80.3%
Wolseley	Building Materials	-57.1%
Legal & General	Insurance	-45.5%
Royal Dutch Shell	Oil / Gas	-17.8%
AstraZeneca	Pharmaceutical	16.7%
Next	General Retail	-48.3%
Centrica	Utility	-13.2%
British Energy	Nuclear	43.3%
WPP Group	Advertising	-41.0%
BT Group	Fixed Telecom	-61.4%
Average Returns (inc. Dividends)		**-38.7%**
FTSE 100 Index Return		**-31.3%**

Note: There were only 13 separate industries represented in the top 30 low price-to-earnings ratio stocks on 1 November 2007.

Source: Company REFS and GillenMarkets (annual dividend yield added to index and share price data to give an estimate of the total returns).

The portfolio underperformed the FTSE 100 Index in that dreadful year by 7.4%, and, but for British Energy and AstraZeneca, the performance would have been a good deal worse. You would have been wondering what kind of an approach you had adopted, with two stocks down 80%, a further two down 60% and your portfolio down almost 40% overall.

It was what you did next that determined whether you recovered substantially or not. On 1 November 2008, many of the stocks in **Table 21.3** were no longer selected by the approach, and it was difficult indeed to sell them out; none of us likes taking losses – especially when the losses are so great. Surely the stocks that had been battered the most would recover strongest? But that is not the approach. On 1 November 2008, your job was to get back into the 15 stocks that offered the best value at that time as defined by the approach. You must not forget that, while you may be selling stocks with good recovery potential, you are also buying stocks with possibly even greater recovery potential. We must be unemotional about the selections and remind ourselves that the overall portfolio losses are not permanent.

Table 21.4: FTSE 100 Index: Low Price-to-earnings 'Sector 15' Portfolio: Performance (1 November 2008 to 31 December 2009)

Company	Industry	Return
Eurasian Natural Resources	Mining	205.9%
Old Mutual	Other Financial	127.9%
HBOS	Banking	-29.4%
Prudential	Assurance	113.6%
BT Group	Fixed Telecom	25.1%
Royal Dutch Shell	Oil / Energy	18.3%
International Power	Utility	46.4%
Next	General Retail	108.1%
WPP Group	Advertising	68.0%
TUI Travel	Travel & Leisure	41.0%
Royal Sun Alliance	Insurance	-6.8%
Vodafone	Mobile Telecom	31.5%
AstraZeneca	Pharmaceutical	16.5%
Rolls-Royce	Engineering	54.1%
Average Returns (inc. Dividends)		**58.6%**
FTSE 100 Index Return		**30.7%**

Note: There were only 14 separate industries represented in the top 30 low price-to-earnings ratio stocks on 1 November 2008.

Source: Company REFS and GillenMarkets (annual dividend yield added to index and share price data to give an estimate of the total returns).

Of course, you also caught lots of big recoveries, including the mining stock Eurasian, Old Mutual, Prudential and Next in 2009. **Table 21.4** covers a 14-month period from 1 November 2008 to 31 December 2009 and shows an overall portfolio return of nearly 60%.

IMPLEMENTING THE APPROACHES IN PRACTICE

If you are just getting started and can save only, say, €250 a month at the outset, then clearly you cannot buy the 15 stocks. In this instance, you have two choices. The first is to buy any one of the 15 stocks in the current list each time you have saved enough money and, eventually, you will end up with a portfolio of 15 stocks. Alternatively, you can start investing in a FTSE 100 index product (such as an ETF) at the outset, which will give you instant diversification. Then, when you have a sizable enough portfolio where the costs of dealing are efficient, you can switch into one of the FTSE 100 value approaches by buying a 15-stock portfolio in one go.

All the information required to follow the FTSE 100 value approaches is available to subscribers at **www.gillenmarkets.com**. Essentially, the work is done for you and all you have to decide is which, if any, of the approaches is best suited to your temperament.

A Note for the Investment Professional

The Sharpe ratio, which is a measure of the risk taken (based on volatility, which academia labels as risk) *versus* the return provided, was higher by a significant margin for both of the FTSE 100 value approaches outlined in this chapter. In other words, the returns of these two value-based approaches were not just higher than the FTSE 100 Index, but they were higher while taking less risk. The efficient market hypothesis has argued in the past that this is not possible but, as highlighted in many books on value investing, the efficient market hypothesis is full of holes.

CHAPTER 22
TIMING THE MARKETS

*There are two possible ways to take advantage of the recurring wide
fluctuations in stock prices, by way of timing or by way of pricing.*
Benjamin Graham[28]

Graham's above quote ranks as one of the very best I have had the
pleasure to read on investing. **Chapter 21, Enhancing Returns: Value
Investing in the FTSE 100 Index** highlighted an approach to investing in
equities that generates above average returns over time by selecting
portfolios of stocks containing better value than is available in the market
as a whole. Through Graham's eyes, these approaches take advantage of
the recurring wide fluctuations in stock (or asset) prices 'by way of
pricing'. But there is another way to take advantage of the recurring
wide fluctuations in stock prices: 'by way of timing', or timing the
markets.

Timing the markets can form an investment strategy in its own right –
if you choose, you can use the indicators outlined in this chapter to guide
you as to when it is safe to enter the markets and when it is timely to exit.
Technical indicators do not form a central part of my own approach to
investing, but I do like to use them to better understand the likely near-
term direction of markets. For others, and that could be you, technical
indicators could dictate how you invest. Each to their own!

TIMING THE MARKETS

Technical analysis is the study of the price action in markets in an effort
to determine the likely trend ahead. Occasionally, if correctly interpreted,
the markets reveal where they are next most likely to go, but, as I have

---

[28]   Graham, B. (1973). *The Intelligent Investor*, 4th edition, New York: Harper &
Row, page 95.

said several times – and don't mind repeating – there is no silver bullet in investing, and approaches to market timing do not offer up the Holy Grail of investing. Both technical analysis and fundamental values have advantages and disadvantages when used to time the markets and neither can be mastered without understanding, homework and discipline.

Technical Analysis – The Study of Price Action

Technical analysis is used to decipher the likely short-, medium- and long-term market direction.

However, as this book is about investment and not speculation, I will be elaborating on technical price signals that provide clues regarding the direction of markets solely on a medium- to long-term basis. I will not be discussing or examining technical signals used to try and determine short-term market movements, as they are of use only to the speculator. Here, we are interested in catching the big moves – the switch from primary bull to primary bear markets – and not the secondary or daily movements in between.

The idea that you can read the market signals – to sell out before downturns and re-enter before upturns – is seductive. God knows, if you listen to the propaganda from spread-betting companies, you would be convinced that it is easy to make money in markets that way; nothing could be further from the truth.

Like fundamental analysis, technical analysis demands study, patience and respect. However, if you take the time to understand the language of the market, you will free yourself from having to react to every move the market makes, or from being dependent on outside commentators' interpretations of what is going on.

What few understand is that it is not opinions in printed form that matter – the market is the opinion-former. Think about it for a moment: the market itself is made up of professional fund managers, professional traders, private investors, private speculators, market makers, stockbrokers, analysts and many other participants. Anyone who has a view expresses it in the market by either buying or selling – their actions (or lack of action) give voice to their views.

When buying outweighs selling, the market moves up, and when selling outweighs buying, the market moves down. All the buyers are buying for reasons they feel are correct, based on information they have received or analysed. Similarly, sellers are selling for reasons they also believe to be correct. The point is that all the information that is out there is being interpreted by a myriad of different parties, and then expressed in the market. They are not expressing their opinions with words but with positive action. So we can justifiably conclude that everyone's view is already – and always – in the market. That does not mean that the majority is always right, but it is the best guide we have about market direction.

Looked at from this stance, if there is bad news on the economy heading our way, the majority view will sense that and express it in the market by increased selling. Likewise, when the economy is improving or has stopped deteriorating, then the majority will sense it and buying will outweigh selling. Only the price action can tell when buying outweighs selling or when selling outweighs buying. This may sound like commonsense but, to see the market action in this way, one must be dispassionate, remove one's own view and analyse the movements of the market in a cold, analytical way.

As everyone's view is in the market – and often these views are expressing things that are not yet obvious in the real economy – the market can be seen as a forward-looking indicator, pointing the way to improving or deteriorating economic and business conditions. For that reason, the stock market can be seen as a leading indicator of the likely business conditions ahead. For example: after the terrifying decline from 2007 to early 2009, there was a recovery in the global stock markets that got underway in mid-March 2009. As I recall, many commentators denounced the recovery as nothing more than a 'dead-cat bounce' – but the market recovery continued. Enough investors formed the view that the efforts of the central banks and governments would be sufficient to turn economies around. When the majority positive view outnumbered the detractors, the market had to rise. In that case, investors got it right as the economy indeed did start a recovery soon after, and the recovery justified their buying ahead of time. Hence, the market foresaw the economic recovery that followed the global credit crisis.

Many investors, particularly private investors, are bewildered when the market rises in the face of bad news in the media. Their mistake is that they do not understand that the bad news may have been priced in already. If it is priced in and the news is even incrementally better, then that is reason enough for the market to rise.

Lower Lows and Lower Highs Define a Bear Market

In technical price action terms, and in its very simplest form, the hallmark of a bear market is lower lows, and when a reaction against the prevailing trend sets in (a rally in a declining market), the market makes a lower high than previously. **Chart 22.1** highlights this, during the bear market that started in early 2000 and ended in late 2002.

Chart 22.1: S&P 500 Index: 2000-2003 Bear Market

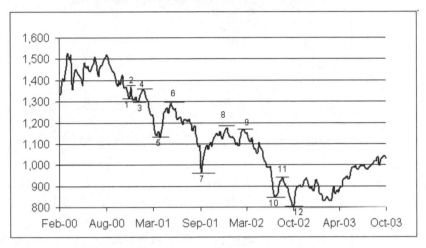

Source: GillenMarkets (chart based on weekly closing prices).

In late 2000, the S&P 500 Index made a lower low, just above 1,300 (1 on Chart 22.1) and a further low just below 1,300 (3 on the chart). It rallied in this region twice in quick succession, but during both rallies, the highs were lower than previously and so it made two lower highs (2 and 4 on the chart). From there, another steep decline set in, and the market made a new lower low at around 1,140 around April 2001 (5 on the chart). Again, the market tried to rally, but the high peaked at just below 1,300 (6 on the chart) and was lower than the previous rally high. Thus, we had another lower high and so on.

Higher Highs and Higher Lows Define a Bull Market

Similarly, the hallmark of a bull market is higher highs, and, when a reaction (or sell-off) sets in, the market makes a higher low than previously. **Chart 22.2** highlights this, during the bull market that started in early 2003 and ended in mid-2007.

Chart 22.2: S&P 500 Index: 2003-2007 Bull Market

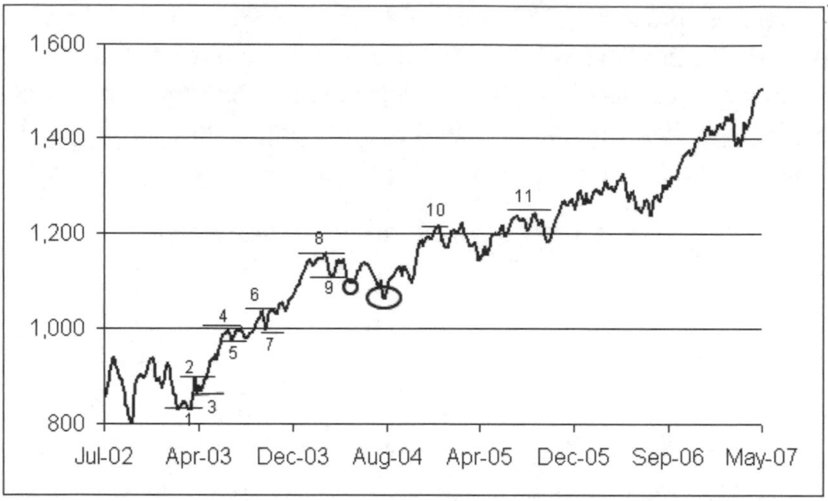

Source: GillenMarkets (chart based on weekly closing prices).

The bottom of the 2000-2002 bear market occurred in August 2002 but the recovery only really started in March 2003. On **Chart 22.2**, 1 marks the initial higher low at *circa* 828 on the S&P 500 Index – the lows in early 2003 were higher than the August 2002 low. From there, the index made a recovery high to 895 in late March 2003 (2 on the chart). A small reaction set in, but the low (3 on the chart), at around 868 in mid-April 2003 on the index was above the low of late March 2003. Next, the market pushed ahead again and made a series of new highs until it stabilised for a few weeks just over the 1,000 mark (at 4 on the chart), before pushing higher once again. By early 2004, the market had pushed significantly higher, before a series of reactions set in once again, which, at the time, resulted in two lower lows (the black circles on the chart) and signalling a possible turn in the market. However, just to prove that no indicator is infallible, the market turned upwards once again in August 2004 and made more new highs (10 and 11 on the chart) and so on.

History rhymes in the market. As **Chart 22.3** highlights, the recovery from the global credit crisis started in March 2009, and the familiar sequence of higher highs and higher lows is obvious once again – although not without some inconsistencies.

Chart 22.3: S&P 500 Index: Recovery from the Global Credit Crisis (2009-2011)

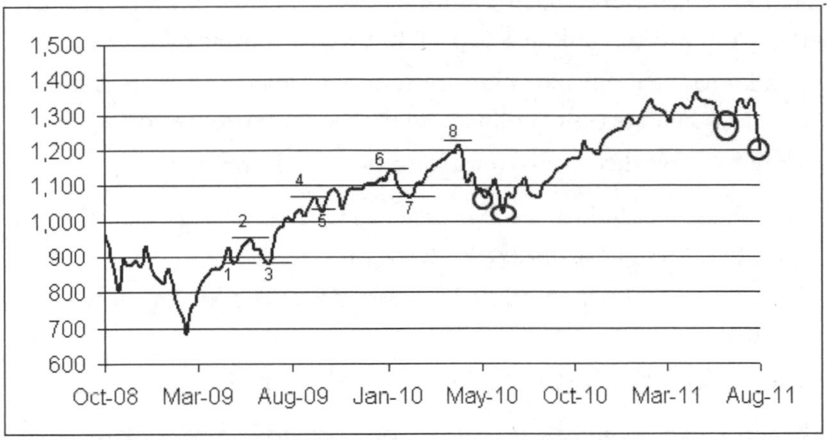

Source: GillenMarkets (chart based on weekly closing prices).

Using higher highs and higher lows as our guide, the first real sign that the S&P 500 Index had turned up (on this measure) was in May 2009, when a reaction against the rise from March 2009 ended with a possible higher low (1 on **Chart 22.3**) – the low having occurred in early March 2009 (a daily chart would have shown a series of higher highs and higher lows earlier in the recovery). In June 2009, the market made a higher high (2 on the chart) and the subsequent reaction against the now rising trend ended with a very slightly higher low (3 on the chart) before powering ahead to a new higher high (4 on the chart) and so on.

The recovery that started in mid-March 2009 had two inconsistencies. In July 2010, the market made a lower low (the first two black circles on **Chart 22.3**), which opened up the possibility that the market had turned down. But it resumed its uptrend soon after, no doubt fooling many who were of a bearish disposition and calling for the market to go even lower. Following that lower low signal, the probability that the market had turned down had risen strongly – but the signal proved to be a false one, in that instance.

TECHNICAL INDICATORS

There are a plethora of technical indicators that one can put forward on markets, but those I outline below all have two common factors:

♦ Similar to the FTSE 100 value approach outlined in the previous chapter, their success or otherwise can be measured; and

♦ They have worked well over a long period of time.

The two technical indicators that provide both 'buy' and 'sell' signals on markets that I will now discuss in detail are:

♦ Dow Theory, and the updated version, Dow Theory for the 21st Century;

♦ The 30- & 50-Week Moving Average Indicator;

and then some technical indicators that provide 'buy' signals only on markets:

♦ The Coppock Indicator;

♦ Capitulation Indicators: The 30-Week Moving Average Capitulation Indicator and the Schannep Capitulation Indicator.

DOW THEORY

Dow Theory, which is a technical indicator for the US markets only, was first outlined in a series of articles by Charles Dow, the first editor of *The Wall Street Journal*, over 100 years ago. The theory was refined by a number of Dow Theorists thereafter, such as William Hamilton and Robert Rhea. Dow Theory is based on the higher highs, higher lows principle (for bull markets) and the lower lows, lower highs principle (for bear markets). In addition, Charles Dow used two indices, the Dow Jones Industrial Average Index (DJIA) and the Dow Jones Transports Index (DJTI), insisting that a new high or new low in one index had to be confirmed by a similar movement in the other index before a signal that the market had turned was valid.

More recent research by Jack Schannep, author of *Dow Theory for the 21st Century*,[29] highlights that a signal from two out of three of the major US indices (DJIA, DJTI and S&P 500) also works. Dow Theory for the 21st

---

[29]   Schannep, J. (2008). *Dow Theory for the 21st Century: Technical Indicators for Improving Your Investment Results*, New York: Wiley.

Century issued a 'buy' signal on the US stock markets on 23 March 2009 when the Dow was 7,776 and the S&P 500 Index was 769, just over two weeks after the actual bottom on 9 March 2009 following the global credit crisis.

Dow Theory for the 21st Century gave that 'buy' signal on 23 March 2009 using the following signals:

♦ All three indices (DJIA, DJTI and S&P 500) had rallied from the 9 March 2009 lows;

♦ On 20 March, two out of the three indices had a reaction against the prevailing trend and declined by a required 3% (both the S&P and DJTI declined by more than 3%);

♦ From these reaction lows, which were higher than the lows made on 9 March 2009 (a higher low), both the S&P 500 and DJTI indices advanced to new highs on 23 March 2009, thus making higher highs. The turn in the market thus had been called.

Charts 22.4 and **22.5** highlight how and when Dow Theory for the 21st Century called the turn in the US markets in March 2009. The US markets have a significant influence on global markets, at least over the short-term, so what happens on them is worth keeping a close eye on.

Chart 22.4: DJ Transportation Index (Jan-Mar 2009)

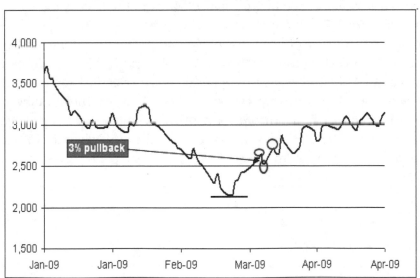

Source: GillenMarkets.

Chart 22.5: S&P 500 Index (Jan-Mar 2009)

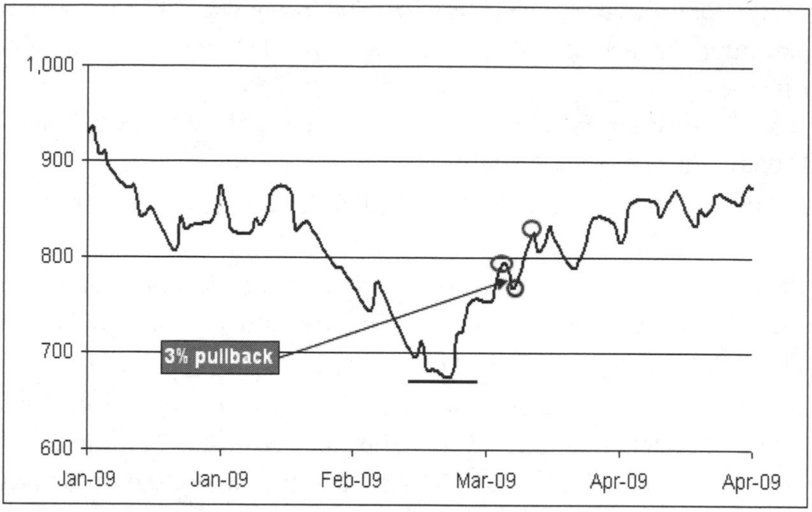

3% pullback

Jan-09 Jan-09 Feb-09 Mar-09 Apr-09 Apr-09

Source: GillenMarkets.

The Track Record of Dow Theory and Dow Theory for the 21st Century

In his book *Dow Theory for the 21st Century*, Jack Schannep updated the original Dow Theory. In **Chart 22.6**, I outline the long-term gains for an investor in the S&P 500 Index. From 1954 to 2011 inclusive, the returns from the S&P 500 Index to a 'Buy & Hold' investor were 10.4% *per annum* compound inclusive of dividends reinvested. Using the traditional Dow Theory technical indicator added 1.4% *per annum* to these returns to deliver an 11.8% *per annum* compound return over this same 57-year period. Using Jack Schannep's improved Dow Theory technical indicator (which he labels Dow Theory for the 21st Century) added 3.7% *per annum* to the S&P 500 Index 'Buy & Hold' return to deliver a 14.1% *per annum* compound return over this same 57-year period from 1954 to 2011.

Chart 22.6: S&P 500, Dow Theory and Dow Theory for the 21st Century: Track Records (1954 to 2011)[30]

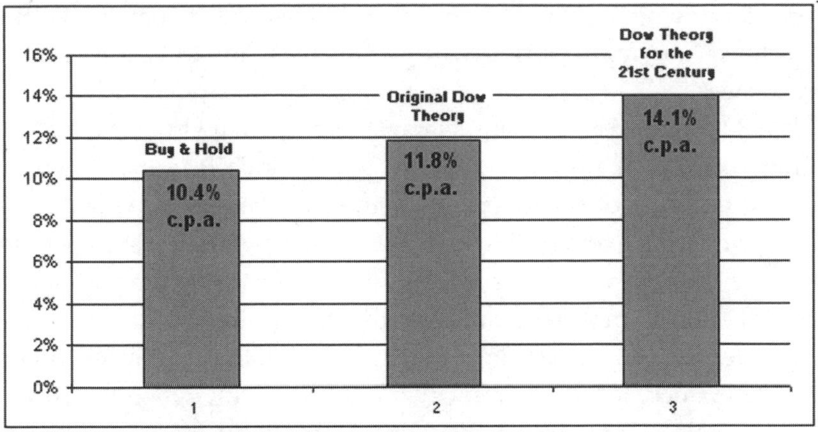

Source: www.thedowtheory.com.

Dow Theory for the 21st Century also generates a 'Buy' signal when the US stock market 'capitulates'. Schannep found that following a selling frenzy (or capitulation) the US stock market always went on to trigger a Dow Theory 'Buy' signal. For that reason, his upgraded version of Dow Theory recommends that investors buy an initial position on the 'Capitulation' signal and ahead of the actual Dow Theory 'Buy' signal. Schannep has his own proprietary indicator – known as the Schannep Capitulation Indicator (developed in the 1960s) that tells him when the US stock market has 'capitulated'. I outline this indicator in more detail later in the chapter.

THE 30- & 50-WEEK MOVING AVERAGE INDICATORS

Next, we examine the combined 30- & 50-Week Moving Average Indicator as a market 'buy' and 'sell' signal. I describe this technical indicator as one that is slower to react to turns in markets but useful in highlighting trending markets – markets that are in either a defined uptrend or defined downtrend. This particular technical indicator was

---

[30] Returns are compound *per annum* from 31 December 1953 to 31 December 2011 and include dividends reinvested.

discussed at length in Mark Shipman's book *Big Money, Little Effort*.[31] Similar to the other technical indicators outlined in this chapter, the 30- & 50-Week Moving Average Indicator is mechanical in nature, with no subjectivity or input required by the user (apart from using a spreadsheet).

The 30- & 50-week moving averages are calculated by obtaining the average price of the market over the last 30 and 50 weeks. There is a practical example of how to perform the calculations in **Appendix III**. Like any moving average, the 30- & 50-week moving averages help iron out the short-term volatility apparent in the underlying market, and can assist investors to more easily identify the underlying trend.

The defining characteristic of this indicator is that a 'buy' signal on a market (or stock, fund or currency) is generated only when the 30-week moving average line crosses upwards through the 50-week moving average line. Similarly, a 'sell' signal is given only when the 30-week moving average line crosses below the 50-week moving average line. It is a slower-moving indicator than the Dow Theory for the 21st Century indicator but it can be used on any market. Although the main benefit of the indicator, in my view, is that it can keep an investor out of deep bear markets, it gives fewer signals and thus tends to get an investor out of the market later into a downturn and back into the market later in a recovery.

If you examine **Chart 22.7**, a 'sell' signal was given in January 2008 when the 30-week moving average declined down through the 50-week moving average at that time. As both the 30- and 50-week moving averages were declining, the probability that the market was in a defined downtrend had risen significantly. This 'sell' signal in January 2008 kept investors out of the worst bear market since 1937. A Dow Theory 'sell' signal was given earlier in November 2007. In September 2009, a 'buy' signal was given when the 30-week moving average rose upwards through the 50-week moving average. By then, both the 30- and 50-week moving averages were rising. With both averages rising, the probability that the market was in a defined uptrend had risen significantly.

---

[31] Shipman, M. (2008). *Big Money, Little Effort: Practical and Effective Strategies for Stock Market Investment*, London: Kogan Page.

Chart 22.7: S&P 500 Index: 30- & 50-Week Moving Averages (2005-2012)

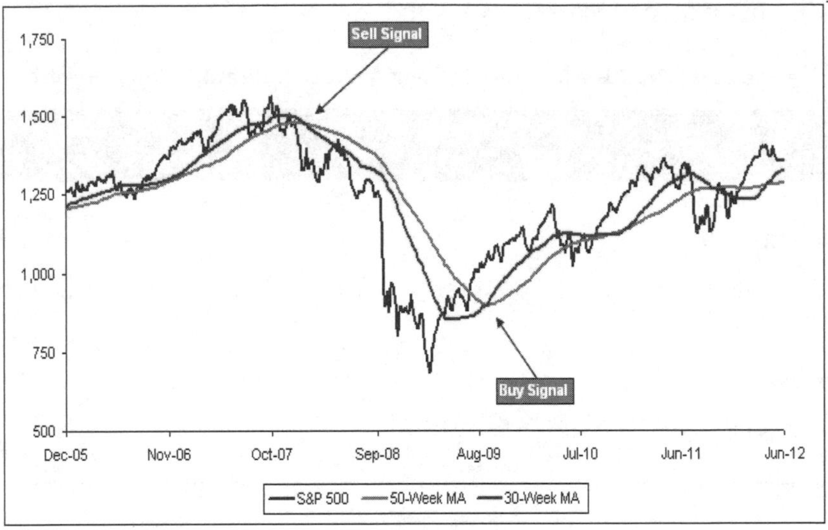

Source: GillenMarkets.

The markets turned in March 2009, but the turn was so sharp that the slower 30- & 50-week moving averages didn't give a 'buy' signal until early September 2009, when the S&P 500 Index had risen to 1,043 – or some 56% from the low on the weekly charts. A false signal was given in November 2010, but it reversed itself within a few weeks with no major damage done. Overall, the 30- & 50-Week Moving Average Indicator has been quite effective on the US market from 2002 to 2011.

Like any other technical indicator, of more importance is whether it has a good long-term track record of calling market turns and delivering returns to the investor who follows it in a disciplined way. My research confirms that the 30- & 50-Week Moving Average Indicator has worked in approximately two out of every three occasions. That said, I would still advise any investor to study the track record of the 30- & 50-Week Moving Average Indicator in the particular market you might be looking at, as the indicator has a varying track record in different markets. In particular, one must recognise that this indicator has limited value in ranging markets (markets that are trading sideways with no defined uptrend or downtrend). Like the Dow Theory for the 21st Century Indicator, the proof of the pudding is in the eating. **Table 22.1** provides a summary of the track record of the 30- & 50-Week Moving Average Indicator on several markets over varying timelines.

Table 22.1: The 30- & 50-Week Moving Average Indicators: Track Record

Market	US	UK	Eurozone	Ireland	Japan	China	India	Brazil
Starting Date	1950	1969	1971	1972	1959	1992	1987	1995
No. of wrong calls	7	6	8	7	10	9	3	4
No. of right calls	15	9	11	12	13	4	7	6
Success Rate	68%	60%	58%	63%	57%	31%	70%	60%
Worst Loss	-8%	-12%	-27%	-20%	-26%	-30%	-29%	-39%
Best Gain	179%	174%	143%	144%	219%	182%	110%	128%
Worst Cumulative Loss	-8%	-12%	-37%	-29%	-28%	-50%	-40%	-39%

Source: GillenMarkets.

Note: The signals recorded are from the starting dates noted in the table and up to mid-2011. A cumulative loss represents the loss made on successive wrong signals.

With the exception of China, where my index data only goes back to 1992, the success rate of this indicator varies from 57% in Japan to 70% in India. Of course, if your goal is to limit the downside risk in markets, then the indicator scores well. With the exception of China, the worst single and cumulative loss was -40% in India, while the best single gain was 219% in Japan. Hence, it seems the indicator controls the downside risk reasonably well. Clearly, however, the indicator has not worked on the Chinese stock market, which has been a restricted and largely government-manipulated market. That is probably changing, though. Nonetheless, if you are going to rely on this indicator, it is as well to do your homework. If you don't know how the indicator has worked in a particular market in the past, then how can you have confidence in it for the future?

Next up is a discussion and analysis of two technical indicators that provide 'buy' signals only:

♦ The Coppock Indicator; and

♦ Capitulation Indicators (the 30-Week Moving Average Capitulation Indicator and the Schannep Capitulation Indicator).

THE COPPOCK INDICATOR

The Coppock Indicator was devised by Edwin Coppock (of the US), who was asked by the church, for whom he was an advisor, to identify a good time to buy into the markets for long-term investing. He countered by asking the church how long it took, on average, for people to get over a bereavement. The church felt it took on average 11 to 14 months. Coppock knew that the impact of bear markets on an investor was psychologically similar to bereavement. So, if it took 11 to 14 months on average to recover from bereavement, Coppock figured that he should not expect recovery in markets after a recession-led decline until the same time had passed.

He set about developing a technical indicator to help him better gauge when markets had turned. The Coppock Indicator, as it is now known, represents the sum of a 14-month rate of change and an 11-month rate of change, with the combined rate of change then averaged out over a 10-month period with a higher weight attached to the most recent month and progressively less weight to the other nine months. It sounds complex but it is very simple to measure using a spreadsheet, and I have provided a practical example of how to set up such a spreadsheet in **Appendix IV**.

The Coppock Indicator gives 'buy' signals but it is not designed to give 'sell' signals. Nonetheless, as a 'buy' indicator, it has an excellent long-term track record. Significantly, the Coppock Indicator gave 'buy' signals on global stock markets in late February, March, April and May 2009 (some markets registered a Coppock 'Buy' signal before others). A 'buy' signal is given when the indicator drops below zero and then turns upwards from a negative position.

The Coppock Indicator is a monthly indicator. As **Chart 22.8** shows, the last buy signal on the S&P 500 Index was given at the end of May 2009. The indicator must now drop below zero and record an increase from a negative position (it must record a less negative reading) before any further 'buy' signal is generated.

However, like many technical indicators, the Coppock Indicator does not work all the time. But, as **Table 22.2** highlights, it has worked exceptionally well on the key US S&P 500 Index over many years.

Chart 22.8: S&P 500 Index: Coppock Indicator (1971-2011)

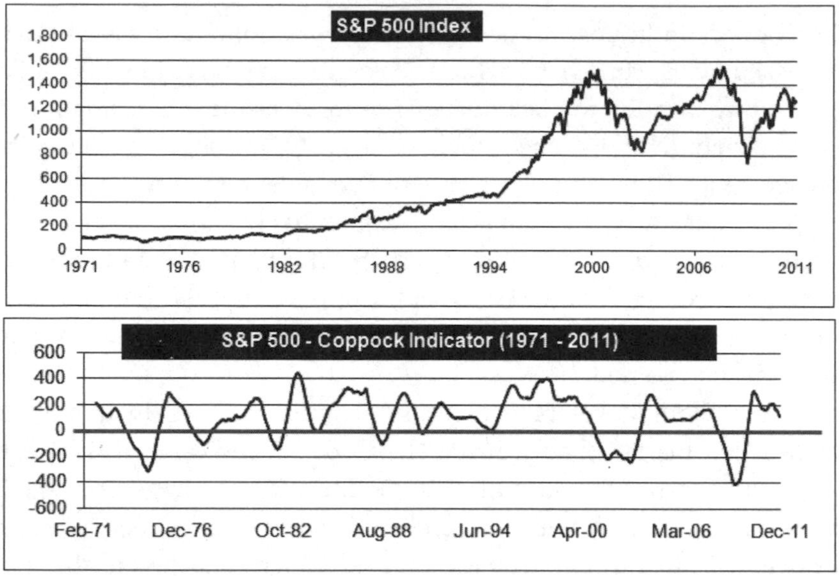

Source: GillenMarkets.

Table 22.2 provides an analysis of the returns on the S&P 500 Index one, three and five years after a Coppock 'buy' signal was given. Since 1970, there have been only 11 Coppock 'buy' signals given. In 10 out of those 11 occasions, the returns from the market were positive one year later, and often substantially so. After a three- and five-year period, returns were always positive, with the average return after three years clocking in at 42%, and 88% after five years. By any measure, these are exceptional batting averages. The returns following the Coppock 'buy' signal in December 2001 were negative one year later, and below average on a three-year and five-year view. Perhaps that can be explained by the fact that the S&P 500 Index still was substantially overvalued following the peaking of the US equity bull market in early 2000. Despite the sell-off in the US equity market following the terrorist attacks in September 2001 and the subsequent rebound in late 2001 that led to the Coppock 'Buy' signal on 31 December 2001, the US equity market was not cheap enough to support a real recovery in prices.

Table 22.2: The Coppock Indicator: Track Record of 'Buy' Signals on the S&P 500 Index since 1970

Signal Date	S&P 500 Level	Subsequent Returns		
		1 Year	3 Years	5 Years
31 Jan 1970	78	29.6%	15.6%	47.9%
30 Apr 1978	98	4.1%	35.9%	66.0%
31 Aug 1982	118	38.9%	59.5%	173.5%
31 Dec 1985	167	26.3%	47.1%	111.3%
30 Sep 1988	271	29.3%	43.4%	70.0%
28 Feb 1991	370	11.3%	25.4%	73.9%
31 Jan 1995	470	35.7%	112.9%	199.6%
31 Dec 2001	1,148	-23.4%	4.7%	23.5%
30 Nov 2002	935	14.5%	33.7%	58.5%
30 Apr 2003	916	22.0%	43.1%	51.3%
31 May 2009	919	18.5%	42.5%	
Average returns		**18.8%**	**42.2%**	**87.6%**

Source: GillenMarkets.

Returns are price returns only (dividend income not included).

The advantage of using technical indicators like Dow Theory for the 21st Century, the Coppock Indicator and the 30- & 50-Week Moving Average Indicator is that you are not influenced by market sentiment, which is always bullish near market tops and bearish near market bottoms. Technical indicators cut through the talk and let you see clearly what investors are actually doing – not merely what they are saying or what the media is reporting.

CAPITULATION INDICATORS: BUYING PANIC ALSO PAYS HIGH RETURNS

Markets may not panic often, but they do panic. When the economic or business news flow is unambiguous and sufficiently bad, investors can panic and markets can enter a tailspin as selling overwhelms buying. This phase in markets is referred to as 'capitulation'. History teaches us that panicked markets that capitulate often represent the bottom of bear markets or close to it, and can signal an ideal time to buy into markets.

The two market panic or capitulation indicators we will now examine are:

♦ The 30-Week Moving Average Capitulation Indicator; and
♦ The Schannep Capitulation Indicator.

The 30-Week Moving Average Capitulation Indicator

We saw in **Chart 22.7** that a moving average, like the 30- or 50-week moving average line, provides a smoothed picture of the underlying market trend. At times, the market moves ahead, sometimes far ahead, of the underlying trend. At other times, the market moves below, often far below, the underlying trend.

It is well-known that bull markets end in a whimper, often marked by range trading. But it is also well-known that many bear market bottoms are made when investors throw in the towel and sell irrespective of underlying values. Such occasions are referred to as 'capitulation'.

I measure this phenomenon in markets by calculating the percentage a particular market has declined relative to its 30-week moving average. This provides me with a picture of the speed of decline. **Chart 22.9** highlights that, since 1970, a decline of 20% or more relative to its 30-week moving average (on the European equity markets) represented an extreme market decline, as it has occurred only nine times over that time frame.

Table 22.3 highlights the returns to an investor who bought when the European equity markets declined by 20% or more relative to the 30-week moving average over the next year, three years and five years.

The returns are impressive for both the short- and medium-term investor. Over this 40-year period, following a 20% decline against the 30-week moving average, which has occurred on only nine occasions, the European equity markets have delivered, on average, a 17% return the following year, 21% over the subsequent three years and 53% over the subsequent five years.

Chart 22.9: European Equity Index (excluding the UK Market): Deviation from 30-Week Moving Average

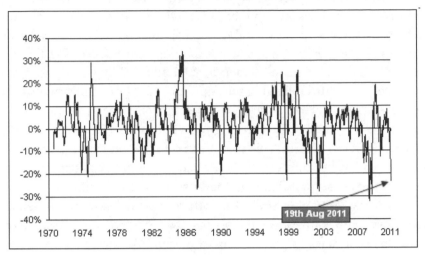

Source: Compilation of indices.

Note: End of week prices used.

Table 22.3: 30-Week Moving Average: Track Record of Capitulation 'Buy' Signals on European Markets since 1970

	Subsequent Returns		
Signal Date	1 Year	3 Years	5 Years
16 Sep 1974	29.0%	48.9%	118.5%
6 Nov 1987	22.7%	29.1%	43.3%
28 Sep 1990	18.9%	49.3%	67.8%
2 Oct 1998	46.3%	32.5%	1.1%
14 Sep 2001	-18.1%	-11.1%	23.3%
19 Jul 2002	-8.8%	21.6%	64.9%
10 Oct 2008	19.4%	-6.3%	
16 Jan 2009	28.9%	6.5%	
19 Aug 2011			
Average returns	17.3%	21.3%	53.2%

Source: GillenMarkets.

Note: Where the European equity markets capitulated by 20% relative to the 30-week moving average, I took the first week that they did so and ignored the subsequent weeks even if they too remained 20% below the 30-week moving average. Returns are price returns only (dividend income is not included).

The five-year return following capitulation in October 1998 was just 1.1%, but, as we now recognise, the developed equity markets were at their most overvalued levels in the late 1990s, so that we might conclude that an investor who buys following capitulation when markets are substantially overvalued is still at risk of poor returns. Likewise, the one-year returns following capitulation in 2001 and 2002 were negative and the three-year return following the September 2001 capitulation also was negative, most probably due to the fact that European stock markets were still overvalued relative to long-term norms at these times.

The corollary, of course, is that returns following capitulation when fundamental values are better than average should result in out-sized returns. The latest capitulation in the Eurozone equity markets occurred on 19 August 2011, after several months of bad news on the sovereign debt crisis, and gathering evidence of the potential for a double-dip recession, sent markets globally into a tailspin. As the Eurozone equity markets were trading on single digit price-to-earnings ratios and offering dividend yields of 4.5% to 5%, I argued at the time on my own website that the Eurozone markets were cheap compared to historical norms, and that following capitulation the medium-term (3 to 5 year) gains were most likely to be well above average. We shall see!

The Schannep Capitulation Indicator

In *Dow Theory for the 21ˢᵗ Century*, author Jack Schannep outlines a Capitulation Indicator, which he developed back in the 1960s and which is ideal for timing your entry into the US equity market near the bottom of bear markets. Mr. Schannep recommends using this indicator to initiate entry into the US equity market ahead of any signal given by the Dow Theory for the 21ˢᵗ Century.

The Schannep Capitulation Indicator works in a similar, but slightly more complicated, way to the Coppock Indicator and I quote directly from *Dow Theory for the 21ˢᵗ Century*:[32]

> *Schannep uses a short-term oscillator to measure the percent of divergence between the three major stock market indices (Dow Jones Industrial Average, S&P 500 and the New York Stock Exchange Composite) and their 10-week, time-weighted moving*

---

[32]   Most of us are unlikely to be able to replicate this indicator in real time, but it is monitored for you by Jack Schannep and his team at **www.thedowtheory.com**.

averages. Market bottoms are identified when the divergence between the three major stock market indices is 10% below their respective 10-week, exponentially time-weighted moving averages, and has only been signalled 11 times in the last 50 years. The date used is the first day the level was attained. This Indicator has identified 10 of the last 14 bear market bottoms, including the last seven market bottoms on a real time basis! It had no signal at four other bottoms – some bear markets end with a whimper – and has never generated a false or extraneous signal.

Although the signals that this capitulation indicator has provided are available for review going back to 1953, **Table 22.4** highlights only the signals given on the S&P 500 Index since 1970. This is done so that I can provide a useful comparison with the 30-Week Moving Average Capitulation Indicator highlighted in **Chart 22.9** and **Table 22.3**.

Table 22.4: The Schannep Capitulation Indicator: Track Record of Capitulation 'Buy' Signals on S&P 500 Index since 1970

Signal Date	S&P 500 Level	Subsequent Returns		
		1 Year	3 Years	5 Years
25 May 1970	70	41.6%	53.7%	28.9%
23 Aug 1974	72	17.8%	36.4%	51.8%
30 Sep 1974	64	32.0%	51.9%	72.0%
19 Oct 1987	225	23.1%	38.9%	84.4%
3 Dec 1987	225	20.7%	43.9%	90.09%
23 Aug 1990	307	28.4%	48.3%	81.4%
31 Aug 1998	957	37.9%	18.4%	5.3%
20 Sep 2001	985	-14.1%	14.0%	34.6%
19 Jul 2002	848	17.2%	45.0%	83.2%
9 Oct 2002	777	33.7%	54.0%	101.5%
7 Oct 2008	996	6.2%	16.0%	
11 Dec 2008	852	26.7%	47.0%	
23 Feb 2009	743	47.3%	77.4%	
08 Aug 2011	1,119			
Average returns		**24.5%**	**41.9%**	**63.4%**

Source: www.thedowtheory.com. Returns are price returns only (dividend income is not included).

Table 22.4 highlights that the one-, three- and five-year returns following a signal from the Schannep Capitulation Indicator are even more impressive than those highlighted by the 30-Week Moving Average Capitulation Indicator, although the indicators are used on different markets so that it is not quite comparing apples with apples. After only one year, the average return has been 24.5%. After three years, the average return has been 41.9% and 63.4% after five years.

The one-year return following the capitulation signal on 20 September 2001 was the only loss recorded using this indicator since 1970. As was highlighted earlier in this chapter (and in detail in **Chapter 12, Equities (Shares)**), the US equity market was substantially overvalued in the early 2000s and a 'buy' signal from even such a reliable indicator as the Schannep Capitulation Indicator must be less reliable against a backdrop where fundamental value is so poor.

I think it is fair to conclude that we are spoilt for choice when it comes to 'buy' signals near bear-market bottoms. Not all bear markets end in 'capitulation' but, of the two capitulation indicators, the Schannep Capitulation Indicator has a superior track record to the 30-Week Moving Average Capitulation Indicator I have traditionally followed. The Coppock Indicator, on the other hand, is somewhat slower at identifying the turns in markets, and its subsequent one-year average returns have not been as strong as those for the Schannep Capitulation Indicator. However, as the Coppock Indicator identifies all the market turns, the subsequent five-year average returns have been stronger than either of the capitulation indicators.

Summary

In summary, Schannep's Dow Theory for the 21st Century, the 30- & 50-Week Moving Average Indicator, the Coppock Indicator and the capitulation indicators (both the 30-Week Moving Average and Schannep Capitulation Indicators) are proven tools for timing markets. Like any timing indicator, however, none are infallible and they do not work all the time. In the ranging market conditions of the past two years, few technical indicators have worked effectively and even Dow Theory for the 21st Century has given a number of false signals. That said, this serves to further highlight that no approach works all the time. Readers with a particular interest in Dow Theory for the 21st Century and Schannep's Capitulation Indicator can buy the book where a lot more detail is available. In addition, Jack Schannep has his own subscription website (**www.thedowtheory.com**) where he monitors these indicators.

As I mentioned at the start of the chapter, using medium-term timing indicators is a valid investment strategy in its own right. My own view is that, if they are used while also keeping an eye on the value on offer in the market relative to long-term norms, they can make for an excellent risk-controlled approach to entering markets, or deploying additional capital into markets.

CHAPTER 23
THE FINANCIAL SERVICES INDUSTRY

Since qualifying as a Chartered Accountant in 1985, I have served my time, not as a practising accountant, but in the financial services industry. Although I would probably struggle to put a decent set of accounts together, I remain proud of the qualification and it equipped me well for work in an alternative industry. After all, accounting is the language of the financial and investment markets. While I can say confidently that the local accountant who avoids selling investment products serves his client in an uncompromising way, experience tells me that I cannot say the same about the financial services industry.

In the area of professional services, the local accountant charges for his time. This ensures that the accountant is on the same side of the table as the client. Likewise, so does the tax advisor, solicitor, doctor and dentist. However, in many countries, this is not so in financial services!

THE INVESTMENT ADVISOR AND THE CLIENT ARE ON OPPOSITE SIDES

As things currently stand, the financial services industry in many regions places the client and the financial advisor on opposite sides of the table, each with conflicting objectives. The client, quite rightly, wants to know the full range of choices on offer to him, and that the best value for money will be obtained. The majority of financial advisors, on the other hand, are incentivised to sell a product rather than to provide genuine independent financial advice. In many cases, the term Independent Financial Advisor (IFA) is a misnomer. Instead of there being a network of independent financial advisors working towards the best interests of the clients, mostly there is a network of product sellers. Of course, I must not tar everyone with the same brush, and I acknowledge that there are a minority of financial and investment advisors who operate on a fee basis.

FUND MANAGERS ARE NOT THE PROBLEM

This is not to say that there are not good fund managers and good investment products. There are. But the customer rarely gets to deal with the fund manager. The customer deals with an intermediary, who should provide him with the facts about different fund managers and different products. But since intermediaries are paid by product providers (banks, insurance companies, fund management companies, among others) with a vested interest in selling products, the customer has little chance of a fair service. The simple facts are that costs are unreasonably and unnecessarily high, and the full product range is rarely put on display.

Investing directly in shares carries the lowest cost and, consequently, can be expected to deliver the optimum returns although, as we have seen, the risks of error are higher. As ETFs have no entry costs, minimal annual management fees and no exit fees, they allow the investor to compound at a better rate. Investment companies (investment trusts or closed-end funds) are managed actively by fund managers, and annual management fees therefore are higher. However, as they are also stock market-listed products, they, too, have minimal entry costs and no exit fees, and the concept of early redemption fees does not exist. For this reason, returns to investors over a 10- and 20-year view are higher for stock market-listed funds than for non-listed funds, which trail, hampered by heavy distribution and marketing costs.

Why is it, then, that non-listed funds make up the vast bulk of client savings and pension portfolios in many economies, when cheaper and, in many cases, superior investment products are available? The reason is that those cheaper, superior investment products offer no commissions to financial advisors. Is this really independent advice ...?

THE SYSTEM NEEDS TO CHANGE

There is a general move away from commission-based investment product selling and I strongly support that move. However, such moves are in their early stages and until commissions are banned outright, it is my view that the client always will come second. A *Retail Distribution Review Consultation Paper*[33] issued by the Financial Services Authority in the UK in June 2009 proposed a ban from the end of 2012 on product providers from offering commission to secure sales and, in turn, a ban on advisor firms from recommending products that automatically pay commission. The recommendations in that review, including alterations following industry discussion, currently are being implemented in the UK and are a step in the right direction. Similar moves in the Eurozone to end the conflict of interest between advisors and clients is long overdue. The industry is unlikely to inflict its own wounds, and the catalyst for change has to come from financial regulators.

THE STOCKBROKING COMMUNITY

In the past, Wall Street (stockbrokers) has thrived mainly on speculation, and stock-market speculators as a group were almost certain to lose money. Hence, it has been logically impossible for brokerage houses to operate on a thoroughly professional basis. To do that would have required them to direct their efforts to reducing rather than increasing their business.
Benjamin Graham[34]

I worked in stockbroking companies for many years and, indeed, helped to found one in 1999. In my experience, Graham's comment way back in 1949 is as valid today as it was then. It is practically impossible for the stockbroker to be on the same side of the table as the client. Of course, I am referring to the private client side of brokerage firms, and not the institutional side, and there is a significant difference.

The institutional side of a brokerage firm can be classed as the professional side, as here a broker is dealing with a fund manager in pension funds, insurance companies and other investment outfits. Fund managers are professionals: they know their own business and form their own views, and, in the main, use the brokerage houses as a way to outsource research. They pay for that service with commissions on trades subsequently executed through a particular stockbroking company.

---

[33] www.fsa.gov.uk/pages/Library/Policy/CP/2009/09_18.shtml.
[34] Graham, B. (1949). *The Intelligent Investor*, New York: HarperCollins Publishers (p.49, 2005 reprinted edition).

The stockbroking companies have to vie for business with up-to-date information and good analysis. It is a competitive marketplace like many other industries, with those who provide the best service gaining additional business. Here, the stockbroker – be that the institutional equity salesman or the equity analyst – knows that he is dealing with a professional on the other side of the table. It is a case of 'buyer beware', as the analyst and brokerage firm can offer only their best opinion.

The confusion starts when the brokerage house then tries to offer the same service to its private client customer base. As Graham's quote demonstrates, many clients of brokerage firms want to speculate, and they get exactly what they ask for – opinions, views and up-to-date information. Overall, however, speculating leads to losses, just like gambling at the bookies. That said, if clients want to speculate, then the brokerage firm is perfectly entitled to serve that need.

The difficulty arises when dealing with customers who want investment advice and not a service geared towards speculation. Private investors don't necessarily understand the difference between investment and speculation, and certainly the ambitious private client dealer has no incentive to clarify the issue. The fact remains that brokerage firms thrive on increasing levels of turnover, so that proper investment advice, which, on occasion, may be to do nothing, is incompatible with the brokerage firm's goals. This most likely explains the significant level of dissatisfaction expressed by many clients regarding the service of traditional stockbroking companies.

Much of the research output from stockbroking companies is not, in my view, suitable for a private client audience. That research is produced for professional investors who both pay for it and know how to interpret it. Before the advent of the Internet, it was nearly impossible for private clients to get access to reports written by equity analysts. However, the Internet made the distribution of professional research notes to a wider audience almost inevitable.

The Internet has facilitated the introduction of low-cost online dealing (where no advice is provided). It also has facilitated the provision of low-cost independent investment advice online. However, investment advice delivered online really only works for those who have already attained a reasonable understanding of investment matters.

CHAPTER 24
3 STEPS TO INVESTMENT SUCCESS

PUTTING IT ALL TOGETHER

In the **Introduction**, I suggested that there were only three steps required to make a success out of investing.

1. The Power of Compounding

An appreciation of the powers of compounding is an easy first step. As we saw in **Chapter 4, The Power of Compounding**, there are a couple of key elements to compounding, including the amount you commit to an investment plan, the rate of return you compound at and the length of time you continue with it. Time is a vital part of obtaining the benefits of compounding. Indeed, you have to put in at least six to seven years before compounding starts to impact. But when it does kick in, it works phenomenally well.

2. A Defined Investment Approach

Having a defined investment approach is the second step. There are many options open to you, including:

♦ Trading markets;

♦ Investing across the various asset classes;

♦ Investing for income in funds;

♦ Investing in individual stocks; and

♦ Timing the markets.

Trading or speculating in markets is widespread. However, it is much more difficult than most private investors appreciate to trade markets successfully. As I highlighted in **Chapter 2, Common Investing Errors**, asset values rise over time and speculating or trading for short-term gains does not give you the time to benefit from this. What is rarely understood, or explained, by those who promote market trading is that the risks are substantially higher than they are with investing. In addition, you are up against professional traders in banks, fund management companies and hedge funds. As in most areas of life, the professionals tend to win – especially in trading markets where they can control risk better. That said, if trading markets appeals to you, then you should learn an approach that provides you with an edge, and I recommend you start by reading *Way of the Turtle* by Curtis Faith and *Reminiscences of a Stock Operator* by Edwin Lefevre (see **Appendix V, Recommended Reading**).

A straightforward defined investment approach is to spread your investments across a selection of asset classes. This can lower risk through diversification, but it is also important to invest in the asset classes that offer value or at least to avoid those asset classes that are dangerously overvalued relative to history.

There is a truth in investing and it is that the more value you buy the better will be your returns. With bank deposits, this is easy to determine – higher interest rates provide better returns. Government bonds should be seen in the same light; higher bond yields provide a better income. Today, after a 30-year rise in bond prices in the developed world, bond yields in the US, UK and Germany are below 2% (at the time of writing). It seems plain commonsense that there is little value and no income to be had from long-dated government bonds in the developed markets. A reasonable, but by no means exclusive, guide to value in property is the rental yield, and the earnings and dividend yield in stock markets. For example, the Eurozone equity markets are offering a starting dividend yield of close to 5% as I write. Despite the current heightened risks in the Eurozone, that simple yield is still far more attractive than bank deposits and long-dated government bonds. As we saw in **Chapter 12, Equities (Shares)**, while the US equity market remains somewhat overvalued relative to long-term norms based on the price-to-10-year average earnings ratio, the Eurozone, Japanese and Emerging markets all score well using the same measure of value.

There are question marks hanging over hedge and absolute return strategies and funds that employ them and returns vary by fund. If you do invest in this asset class, then at the very least spread your exposure over several hedge or absolute return funds. Commodities and precious metals generate no income. While their returns have kept up with inflation over the long-term, they have been lower than those generated by property and the stock markets. In addition, their returns have been highly concentrated and erratic. Hence, it is not obvious that you need separate exposure to these asset classes outside the indirect exposure provided through equities.

Chapter 18, Ways of Gaining Exposure to the Markets highlights the various fund options open to you. It is relatively easy and cost-efficient to build your own fund of funds using exchange-traded funds and investment companies listed on stock markets. While this simple approach qualifies as a defined investment approach, you need to ensure that you are either obtaining value or at least avoiding clearly overvalued asset classes.

As outlined in **Chapter 20, Investing Across the Asset Classes**, a focus on income investing in funds also is a solid, conservative approach to risk assets, and suitable for investors who need to generate an immediate income from their assets. A high yield is normally an indication of value so that a focus on income funds achieves both diversification and a value bias.

Chapter 8, The Pitfalls in Direct Stock Picking highlighted the often underappreciated difficulties private investors face when trying to select individual shares. Few private investors can assess the three critical risks in companies: business, financial and valuation risk. Any one of these risks can lead to a permanent loss of value in a particular share. The global credit crisis ruthlessly uncovered these risks, and investors that were over concentrated in companies with too much leverage suffered permanent losses.

However, **Chapter 21, Enhancing Returns: Value Investing in the FTSE 100 Index** provided a solution to this problem and outlined a defined investment approach for those who prefer to invest directly in companies listed on markets. The approaches outlined in **Chapter 21** ensure diversification and a focus on value in large capitalisation companies in the UK market. The returns from these approaches were higher by 4% to 5% *per annum* than the returns from the FTSE 100 Index over the full 17-year period from 1995 to 2011.

Investing in growth companies is also a legitimate approach to selecting stocks. However, it is not the focus of this book. In any event, the returns generated by the value-focused approaches that I have outlined in **Chapter 21** prove that it is not necessary to find growth companies in order to generate satisfactory returns.

Chapter 22, Timing the Markets examined a number of defined approaches to medium-term market timing. These approaches give you the option of timing your entry into and exit from markets. That said, as is surely obvious by now, no one approach works all the time.

3. Controlling the Volatility

The third, and final, step to investment success is to ensure that volatility in markets does not upset your long-term investment plans. **Chapter 6, Understanding Stock Market Volatility** provided both an understanding of why the markets tend to be so volatile, and an appreciation that volatility is not the same thing as risk.

There is a major difference between temporary declines in prices and the risk of a permanent loss. Diversification, through funds or otherwise, an avoidance of leverage and a focus on value should allow you to ride out bear markets (down markets) and ensure that you recover with the markets, and hopefully more.

ONLINE DEALING AND INDEPENDENT ADVICE

The advent of online dealing has substantially lowered the cost of investing in markets. The Internet has also made it easier to access independent investment advice. If you wish to be a DIY investor, to reduce your reliance on product sellers, then the tools are now readily available to you. As I said in the **Introduction,** anyone can be a DIY investor – from parents with the children's allowance to individuals with the flexibility to manage their own pension to anyone else who is in a position to save some of their monthly income. My wish is that you now feel empowered to take control of your own financial and investment future.

CHAPTER 25
GILLENMARKETS

GillenMarkets is a website dedicated to 'Uncovering Value for Investors' across the various asset classes including equities, property, bonds, commodities and a range of alternative assets. Subscribers to the website can access:

♦ A weekly investment bulletin with analysis of events in global markets;

♦ Research notes on recommended stocks and funds;

♦ A section offering advice on asset allocation along with lists of stocks and funds suitable for each asset class;

♦ Tables highlighting funds offering above average income;

♦ Tables outlining the stocks that match the UK value-based FTSE 100 approaches referred to in **Chapter 21**;

♦ A facility to monitor the performance of your own stocks and funds on the website;

♦ Access to the market timing indicators referred to in **Chapter 22**; and

♦ An e-Learning centre.

If you are based in Ireland, we run one-day investment training seminars, which are open to members and non-members alike, at various intervals during the year.

Email: info@gillenmarkets.com.

Web: **www.gillenmarkets.com.**

SECTION IV
A SHORT STORY

Of the many important investment messages in this book, I thought it would be useful to highlight in a short story the major risk of speculating rather than investing. In planning the book, I commissioned the short story *A Villa in the Sun* from Virginia Gilbert, an experienced writer and director. I found it a gripping tale and I hope you enjoy it as much as I did.

ABOUT VIRGINIA GILBERT

Virginia is a BAFTA-nominated, award-winning writer and director. She writes and directs for film, radio and television. Her screenwriting work has been placed on the BritList and she was named as a 'Star of Tomorrow' by Screen International. She also writes short fiction, and has been published internationally. Her short stories have been shortlisted for the RTÉ Francis MacManus Award and BBC Radio 4 broadcast a season of her work. Her debut collection of short fiction was shortlisted for the Scott Prize 2011. She is currently finishing her debut feature film as writer-director, *A Long Way from Home*, based on her original short story of the same title, starring Oscar-winner Brenda Fricker, James Fox and Natalie Dormer. The film is scheduled for release in 2013.

CHAPTER 26
A VILLA IN THE SUN

David Davis had always felt that his name suited him. The solidity of the repetition, the strength of it – people remembered his name, the roundedness, the two large capital 'D' initials. Whether he'd grown to suit his name or whether it was the other way around, mattered little. What mattered was that it worked. He loved his name, loved saying it into the phone by way of greeting. There was only one person he didn't do that with: Mark. When Mark rang, David never wanted to dally.

"So? What's the story?"

"Pretty good, David, pretty good."

David felt the familiar heat spreading through him, the little quiver of excitement that set the hairs on the back of his neck on end.

"Yeah?", he replied, as casually as possible. "Go on."

He could hear Shona calling for him from upstairs and quickly went to his study door to shut her out. Let Maria deal with whatever it was that was bothering the silly mare now.

"You're online?", Mark asked.

"'Course."

"Take a look at *The Irish Times*."

David obeyed, frowning slightly as he scanned the headlines. "Job cuts at Pfizer … Teachers strike imminent …"

"Further down." David could hear the suppressed mirth in Mark's tone. "D'you see it yet?"

And there it was. Small, three-quarters of the way down the page, but unmistakable nevertheless.

"Wow."

"Yep! Thought you'd be pleased."

David clicked on the link, scanning the story. "'Google announced late last night that its operating system, Android, has overtaken the iOS platform. Originally envisaged for only three devices, within the space of two years, Android sits on over 100 smartphones, with numbers set to rise.' Shit. Thought I saw some activity going on this morning."

"Activity?", Mark allowed himself a short, sharp laugh. "I'd say so. You're up 6%."

David clenched his free fist high above his head in triumph, though he regretted the gesture slightly, for at that very moment the door to his study banged open.

"David, I've been calling you for hours! Didn't you hear me? We have to go!"

Shona stood, angry, in the doorway.

"Just give me a second ..."

"You want me to call back?" David could hear the edge to Mark's tone.

"No! No ... hang on ... Shona," he appealed, putting the phone to his chest, "just give me one minute. There's something I've got to move on fast."

"There's always something! You're supposed to come to the store with me – we've got so much to do before they come!"

"It's only Frank and Moira, for God's sake! And we've still got two days! What the hell do we need to prepare, anyway?"

Shona visibly bristled, and David knew he'd said the wrong thing. For though it was true that it was merely his brother and sister-in-law coming out, yet again, for a holiday – a brother and sister-in-law who were impressed with the most minor of things – that wouldn't wash with Shona. She needed an audience, however humble, and the engine of her days was geared towards presenting herself and her life to whomever it was that was coming to view it. Thus endless preparations, doings and re-doings of arrangements, of stuff, to show them off to their best advantage, was the price David had to pay for a moment's peace.

"Okay. I'm right with you," he told her, smiling as winningly as he could, aware that every second's delay could be costing him. "Let me finish off and I'm all yours."

Pouting, but placated, Shona left the room.

"All right?", Mark queried.

David sat back down at his desk, switching screens on his laptop impatiently. "So ... what's the next move?"

✑ ✑

The day was turning into a real scorcher and David was grateful for the cool of his study. When they'd originally bought the villa, the room had been used as a children's playroom by the previous occupants: gaudily decorated, the walls bashed and bruised. But David had been able to see beyond the damage to recognise it as a room of quality, affording him a lovely view out over their entrance drive, and, because there was only one set of windows, coolness and shadows when the shutters were closed.

He could hear Shona giving orders to Maria and the two handymen she'd seconded from next door. She'd insisted on getting some wicker chairs for the terrace – chairs she claimed she'd had her eye on for some time – and chairs that David, for his part, could see little merit in, for they were highly uncomfortable and terribly overpriced. The ones they had were perfectly serviceable, and barely a year old. Nevertheless, the acquisition of the new furniture had made her happy, boosting her mood and getting her excited about the arrival of her in-laws. David had paid just enough attention in the boutique store to make Shona think he gave a hoot, and had been able, on the quiet, to place a couple more calls to Mark.

"You're sure?", Mark always felt the need to offer a tiny warning before David did the inevitable.

"Yes."

David felt that surge of confidence that always preceded the taking of a major position in stocks. Years back, when David had been doing well with his business and was starting to have a bit of spare cash to play with, he'd enlisted the services of an investment advisor, Andrew. 'The little grey man' was what David had called him – spouting facts and figures like a trumped-up accountant. His advice had always been of the cautious variety.

"Don't go putting everything on a 'Big One', David," he'd drone, "you need to spread the risk across a wide variety of investments; you need to diversify. A global equity fund would be just the thing, or a mixed asset fund, if you want a little bit more excitement."

And David had listened and had obeyed, not knowing any better, until he realised that Andrew was nothing but a wimp. No one got anywhere in this life without taking the odd risk or two, and sure as hell, no one had ever gotten rich playing it safe. Andrew certainly hadn't made him rich – at least, not rich enough. Fifteen years he'd done what he was told, cautiously investing in his mixed asset fund and what sort of a return had he seen? A measly 6% *per annum* on a modest investment! Sure, it was a little better than if he'd shoved his money in a bank, but it wasn't nearly enough. Not when he'd overhear other businessmen, in the clubs or at the charity dinners he and Shona attended with regularity, talking about their brokers and their deals and their payoffs. Other people's money seemed to grow a great deal faster than David's.

And it was then that David had met Mark.

Business had been fantastic at the time, and David, flush with the success of Ireland's building boom, was riding high. At the golf club's annual Christmas party, Mark had sidled up to David, as casual as could be. David Davis. Now there was a name Mark knew. What a shame David hadn't heard of Mark, because Mark had a feeling they could do great things together.

And Mark had been right.

"David, I'll be straight with you – a man like you, a man of the world, a man of business – you know the way things work. You want to play it safe? That's fine – that's absolutely fine. You'll get yourself a nice house, couple of cars, maybe even a little holiday place in France somewhere – the Dordogne, maybe, not the Cote d'Azur, but still, nice enough. You'll do all right, 'course you will. But – and this is a big 'but' David – you could do so much better. So much better. You just need the right advice, that's all. Someone who gets what you're about, someone who knows just when and how to take the right risks that get you the rewards. No mucking about, no funny business. But I'll tell you what – you don't up your game a bit, you'll fall behind. And I've a feeling that's not in your nature. After all, would I be right in thinking that a recent valuation of your company put it at close to one million? Not bad, David – not bad at all. You didn't get to where you are without some calculated risk, right?"

David knew he was being flattered, knew enough to spot a come-on when he saw one, but there was something about Mark Slater that appealed to him. Something canny and to-the-point. Smart. And though David did not consider himself reckless, and knew better than to blindly follow his gut instinct about someone, he also knew that carrying on with Andrew was a dead-end. Besides, Greenbaker stockbrokers had a client list he could not argue with. Everyone else David knew was with them, and he was in the big league now. Why the hell shouldn't he?

He'd kept things slow and small, more to test Mark's mettle than anything else. Mark hadn't let him down.

"Big positions with some debt on top – leverage. CFD accounts – Contract-for-difference – is what I'm looking at, David. They're absolutely the best way to take quick advantage of changes in the market."

Whether it was sheer bloody luck or whether Mark was as sharp and on the ball as he seemed David didn't know initially, but the first few trades that he authorised were resounding successes. What's more, Mark hadn't hidden anything – he'd explained his rationale and process to David step-by-step, had involved him in the minutiae of things, as a proper confidante. The more David understood, the more he realised he had stepped into the world he had truly been born for. Mark had his finger on the pulse of the market, and David sensed that, with enough experience, he could, too.

Of course, David knew better than to consider Mark a friend. Mark and his firm got their commission every time David made a trade, regardless of whether or not he gained or lost. Jesus, David had paid his firm 35 grand in the past six months alone! And David couldn't deny that he'd had his share of bad luck. Mark hadn't always got it right and unexpected things happened sometimes. But – and it was a big but – Mark had always rallied round and worked extra hard after things hadn't gone their way. David couldn't fault him on that. No, if it were just the commission Mark was after, he wouldn't go that extra mile when things weren't great, wouldn't put himself out the way he did. So, okay, maybe Mark wasn't a friend, in the strictest sense of the term, but he sure as hell was an ally. After all, they'd been in business together a while now and David spent more time talking to him than anyone else in his life. More often than not, Mark knew what he was thinking before David did himself. Especially in the last 18 months or so, after the sale of David's business. He'd made a cool €2.5 million on it, quite a bit more than he'd expected given the state of the economy at the time. Mark had sent him an enormous hamper to congratulate him, and had taken him out for a celebratory dinner.

"Well done, David. Freedom at last!"

"Yeah. Yeah, I suppose."

"So what are you planning to do? You'll have a hell of a lot of time on your hands."

David had shrugged, and Mark had paused, looking at him, tilting his head to one side, as if in response to a tricky question. In a softer tone, more measured, Mark had said, "There's something up, isn't there? You're worried".

David had started. He hadn't realised he'd given himself away so easily.

"I know you, that's all," Mark told him. "I know when there's something on your mind. Talk to me, David. Tell me what I can do."

So David had. And Mark's response was more than he could have hoped for – far, far more than the sort of support he'd have got from a friend.

"We'll double your money, David. Six months, tops. And then you'll really be laughing. Look, no one wants to face an uncertain future – no one. You're quite right to be concerned. You've done extremely well for yourself, but you're a family man – wife, kids. Responsibilities. Let's be honest, a million quid doesn't go that far these days. No point having slaved your guts out all these years only to end up counting the pennies in what should be the time of your life. We've worked together, what, two years now? I'd say it's gone pretty well, wouldn't you?"

"It's gone great, Mark. Just great."

"So don't fret. You've done all the hard work, David. Now you get to reap the rewards. We'll get you sorted."

David had drunk to that. And now, the moment had come.

"I'm going to say it one more time, David, because you know I have to. You've been doing brilliantly recently. Vodafone, Nokia – that deal with Microsoft. You played a blinder there. You could hold on, you know, with Google. Things might even rise a little more ..."

"No ... you know the way it works. Now's the moment."

There was a short pause on the end of the line, and David could almost feel the frisson of Mark's excitement, so palpable was it. But Mark would not give in to it, not quite yet.

"I just need to remind you, David ... you stand to gain a good deal, but there's always the chance ..."

"Come on, Mark ... let's get on with it."

So David sold his Google shares for a 6% gain – well, 5% after costs. But as he had used the borrowing facility available on the CFD account, his gain came to 8%! In one trade! He had been right. He had been absolutely right to trust in Mark. To trust in himself. Just one or two more breaks like this one and he'd be set for good.

"You opened the champagne yet?" David could hear the laughter in Mark's tone.

"Not yet. I want to know what's next."

"Of course you do. Well, …"

Word on the street – or at least, in the rarefied corridors of Greenbaker stockbrokers – was that Ennobank, the massive Dutch institution, was rumoured to be acquiring Spencers, the ailing British bank. Were the rumour to become fact, Spencers' share price would be set on fire and things were already moving.

"We're likely to hear something definite tomorrow – Wednesday at the latest. But I wouldn't wait if I were you, David. We're not the only ones who've heard about this, so if you want to get a good deal, I'd move fast."

"And just out of interest, where did you hear about this?"

"Just strong rumours, David, but suffice to say, the boys in our research department believe the rumours make complete sense. As you know, we specialise in covering the European banking sector, know management in all the banks, know what makes sense, who's doing what."

Hadn't Mark told him to stay out of bank stocks last year, and how right he had been, if this news was anything to go by. David felt the sudden surge of energy that let him know he was getting in the zone: that place in which the magic happened, in which everything came together – his head, his heart, his gut. Each nerve, each sense was alert and alive. The wood of his desk almost throbbed under his hand, he was aware of every muscle in his body, taut and strained, as if in anticipation of the starter's whistle. David's mind raced. Mark wasn't a bullshitter. Okay, once or twice he'd let him down, got things wrong, but those had been small bits and pieces, nothing serious. Mark had never been wild or reckless. There was no reason to think he would be now, not when he knew David had so much at stake, now that he'd sold the business. No, they were in this together. All the way.

"Yes." The adrenalin surged through David. That one little word lit up his mind in a brief explosion of excitement.

"Yes?"

"Yes."

"Good. I don't want to sound dramatic David, but this may very well be the best decision of your life. Right … let's get on with it …like I say, things are already moving."

They went back and forth for 10 intense minutes and it was done. A million of David's capital plus the same amount in borrowings from the CFD facility. A €2 million commitment in total to Spencers Bank, in anticipation of imminent good news, which, as Mark put it, was "the banking sector deal that was waiting to happen".

Shona mistook her husband's energy that afternoon for passion, and indeed, it was passion, of sorts. But when he left her, tousled and exhausted, he made his way downstairs and spent the hours through until dinner scanning the net, checking the markets, refreshing his news browser constantly, his energy increasing. It had been a revelation to David, the ease with which he could make money, now that he had time on his hands to take it really seriously. Though perhaps it shouldn't have surprised him, for he knew he'd always had a natural ability for it. It made him regret the years he'd spent with dreary, boring Andrew, squirreling his money away without really thinking about it. If only he'd known then what he knew now, he could have really been a player.

Still, no point dwelling on the past. The fact was, David Davis had done very well for himself – and was about to do even better. It amused him to hear the way in which old friends and acquaintances talked of his success: wry, half-sarcastic, half-disappointed. He'd exceeded all expectations, had achieved beyond anything he'd ever imagined, had outstripped his contemporaries in becoming the man he was today: David Davis, capital Ds, self-made success, founder and seller of his own building firm. Wealthy. On his way to retiring early at barely 50, and now, reinventing himself as a financial whizzkid. The pleasure of playing the markets outstripped any professional triumphs he had ever experienced – even the success of his business, the buying out of a couple of smaller firms – everything. The thrill of it was second to none. He was now a professional investor, thinking big, acting big. What he was doing now seemed to David to be the crystallisation of everything he'd always loved about doing business, everything he'd always loved about himself and his temperament: harnessing his skill, accessing the best information, assessing risks, keeping his eye on the ball at all times, moving fast, listening to his gut when he was uncertain, learning to say no when he really wasn't feeling something: it was pure, unadulterated pleasure. He'd never felt so fit and strong, mentally and physically, in his entire life. It was as if he'd finally found his true vocation.

Shona insisted they dine on the terrace, and, at close of business, with a reassuring e-mail from Mark that all they had to do now was wait, David allowed himself a brief half-hour of pleasant and relaxed contemplation, made all the sweeter by the fact that Shona received a phone-call from her best friend Ailish, and retreated inside to gossip and chat for an hour. The villa had been a bit of a stretch for him and, initially, he'd been uncertain. High off the back of selling the business, he'd wanted to keep his cash for the markets. But Shona had had her heart set on it – she'd talked of it for years, holidaying out in the Riviera, or Tuscany, in rented places – how she longed for a place of her own, in a good hot climate, with sun and sea and all the rest of it. Besides, they were the only couple they knew who didn't have a proper holiday home! It looked miserly, and David didn't want people to think he was becoming a Scrooge in his old age, did he?

And then she'd found the place online, and they'd visited and David had seen that his wife had fallen head-over-heels in love. Her enthusiasm had been infectious. After all, didn't David deserve it? Hadn't he only made a fortune, after working himself half to death all his life? Wasn't it about time he learned how to relax and enjoy himself a little? He could afford to – in fact, he couldn't afford not to! And yes, David had to agree he was very taken with the charming view and the spacious rooms and the close proximity to one of Europe's best golf courses (not that he'd had a chance to use it yet). So he'd borrowed the €1.1 million needed and bought the place. Now, if things continued going as well as they had been, he'd be paying off his mortgage overnight. Of course he would. Mark wouldn't fail him. He wouldn't fail himself.

God.

Between the million in cash and same again of CFD borrowings, he was in for a cool two million. Two million euros, all riding on the possible announcement of the acquisition of one bank by another.

God.

Have I pushed this one too far?

He had been using gains to pay off some of the mortgage on the villa which was now down to €1 million. Then there were the cars, the yacht, the renovations on the house back home. All the extras – golf clubs, gyms, spas, housekeeping, college for Grainne, subsistence for Rory – the list was never ending. He did a quick calculation – €2 million on the bank deal left €0.5 million in cash and the mortgage was €1 million. Of course, he wasn't earning any longer but he planned to fix that in a few months.

No.

He wasn't going to think this way. This was just a natural reflex, that was all. Perfectly normal to have a moment of doubt after taking on such a big position in the market. Sure, hadn't he felt this way before, when stakes were high and he'd had to make decisions? Of course he had. It was natural. It would pass. It always did. No pain, no gain. He'd take this little, momentary pain for the massive gains to come.

Dabbing the sweat from his brow with his napkin, David rose from the table and strolled down onto the lawn. The Mediterranean grass felt different from the grass back home: dryer, more springy, more buoyant, somehow. He kicked off his sandals and let the rough blades scrape across the soles of his feet, distracting his thoughts, calming him. Beyond the garden and the pool, the sea glimmered azure blue in the sunset. The summer was truly upon them. Which meant that poor Frank would be lobster-red by the end of his first day.

Frank Davis. Now there was a name most people didn't remember. David smiled to himself. He and his brother could not have been more different – physically as well as everything else. David, for example, tanned a deep, copper brown, used, as he now was, to the Spanish heat. Frank, however, only had to look at the sun to burn and blister, and no matter how long he spent desperately trying to even himself out, rid himself of the blotches and patches of red and white, he'd invariably end up going back home looking like a sore and defeated jigsaw puzzle.

Defeated – yes, that was the word for him. Life had not been kind to Frank – well, not as kind as it had been to David. But then, David didn't credit life with having much of a hand in things. Nor did he credit God, or Buddha or any other force that might or might not be out there. No – he had no truck with fate or chance or luck. You made your own – all of it – and anything else was a big fat lie. Thus David had made himself into the envied and admired man he knew he'd always meant to be, whilst Frank, earnest, diligent Frank, had slogged away at life, his minimal returns equal to the minimal effort he put in. And now, with both of them in their early 50s, both in the prime of life, it seemed to David that justice had prevailed: the law of nature, of man, not of God: the law of getting what you deserved, getting out what you put in.

David had long since given up urging his younger brother to do more, be more, take more risks. It wasn't in Frank's nature. To say that David despised him for it would be too strong, but there had been between them for many years a wall of coolness. This was less to do with something said or done, than it was with David's implacable frustration with Frank's lack of ambition. Of courage. His refusal to lift his head above the parapet and take action. Frank's mild resistance to any schemes or offers David pushed his way, any urgings or suggestions intended only for his own benefit, had enraged him. He saw his younger brother's refusal as pathetic parochialism, took his unwillingness to make something better of himself as a harsh reflection on his stock – on him, David – and it had gnawed at him. For David felt that behind it all was a pettiness in Frank – a sour grapes aspect to his resistance. Frank liked to joke that "the rising tide lifts all boats", especially when David had just been successful with a trade, as if all David's work, all his skill, was nothing more than just getting lucky. It was sad, really, that Frank should be so transparent.

Nevertheless, though the brothers might have let things lapse, left to their own devices, the wives had made an effort, phoning for birthdays, sending Christmas cards and presents for the kids. Moira, Frank's wife, was a good sort, and she made things a little easier between the brothers, with her simple cheerfulness and uncomplicated admiration of the wealth and luxury that was beyond her. There was no side to her – no envy, or malice that David could detect – and though a bit of envy might have pleased him, it was really to her credit, for it must have irked her over the years, the decades, the way in which one brother soared ahead whilst the other, her own husband, kicked his heels in the dirt. But she never complained – at least, not in David's hearing. She appreciated. She was a good audience. It was really thanks to her that David had taken to inviting them out to summer in Spain since they'd got the villa. Besides, they were all getting older now. No point in squabbling. They were what they were, that was certain. Nothing would change that now.

Shona came back out, clutching her wine, flushed from the excitement of the conversation, and the drink that had accompanied it. She called to him from the terrace:

"You'll never believe it, but Miles Ronan has only gone and left his wife!"

David indulged her for a good 15 minutes, enjoying once more the anticipation of his next imminent triumph, before going back inside to his study.

෬ ෮

It was a magnanimous gesture, going to fetch Frank and Moira personally from the airport. David could have sent a car, of course, or ordered them a taxi, but ever since the first summer, when they'd been robbed by an unscrupulous driver who'd taken them all round the houses, racking up the bill to nearly €100, David had thought it best to take charge. He'd almost fought with Frank over that – how could he have been so stupid? He knew the villa was a mere half-hour from the airport, David had told him! So why had he allowed the taxi driver to …? Well, never mind. Frank had borne his loss well, uncomplaining, laughing off his idiocy, shrugging at the jibes and barbs. But still. Ever since, David had taken it upon himself to fetch them, not least because it afforded him the opportunity to take the car out for a proper spin.

He was edgy. There had been no news on the Spencers' front and David felt the urge to pace, to move, but he remained glued to his computer and his phone. Mark had called him first thing, and though his words had been light enough – "nothing yet, hang on" – there had been a slight hint of concern to his tone: tiny, but enough for David to pick up on.

"David! Two minutes!" Shona banged on his study door as she passed, gathering her things for the drive. His phone beeped through a message – it was Rory, their eldest.

"Moored in Saint Tropez. Can you give me Pierre's number for the restaurant? Having to really work hard to impress young Kirsty. Might need a little bit extra for this one."

David smiled, shaking his head. Rory was a chancer, all right – took after his old man. He'd had a gap year before university, but had insisted on a second one after graduating, swearing that he'd knuckle down once he'd got the travel bug out of his system. David couldn't see it happening for a while yet, but then, what was the harm? Let the boy enjoy himself – God knows he'd worked hard enough to give his kids the best. What point denying them? Besides, of the two of them, Rory was the only one who seemed to appreciate his Dad's generosity.

Grainne had decamped to London to live in a grotty bedsit and study fashion, grimly taking handouts on the side, but with an expression that made David feel that she was doing him a favour, not the other way around. Still, he mustn't complain. At least she was settled, finally – or seemed to be. He'd not yet had the dreaded phone call informing him yet again that she'd made the wrong choice and needed to switch degrees.

"David!" The door opened abruptly. Shona, groomed and glossy, ready to present herself to their guests, stood impatiently, dangling the car keys at him.

"Let's go!"

"Give me one second …"

Quickly, he replied to his son. He'd have Mark organise a wire transfer to him. As he was about to hit 'send', the telephone rang, and David pressed the wrong button, deleting his message. Cursing himself for his clumsiness, he saw that it was Mark himself, as if aware his services were about to be needed.

"Perfect timing! Was just about to call you. I need you to get some money to Rory."

Shona rolled her eyes and tapped her foot. David turned away from her.

"Mark?"

"David. Listen to me. We need to talk."

David frowned. Mark's tone, usually so friendly and upbeat, as if he'd just scored a winning goal, was flat.

"David, I'm going to say this one more time – we're leaving! Now!" Shona had come close to him and he could smell her strong perfume.

"Wait, Shona. Mark … I'm on my way out the door …"

"This can't wait, David."

David hesitated. He felt a tight little ball form in the pit of his stomach, recognising the sign. Fear. He was anticipating fear. And for the life of him, he couldn't fathom why.

"David!"

Shona looked at him, and her expression changed.

"What now?"

"Hang on, Shona. Mark, give me one second."

She'd be in a foul temper for the rest of the day, that much was certain. Shona loathed doing menial tasks on her own, and going to the airport to collect her brother and sister-in-law was right up there on the list. But it couldn't be helped. Once he'd heard the front door slam and the engine start, David went into the living room, pouring himself a tiny little finger of whiskey to calm the nerves that had sprung so unwarrantedly.

"So?", he said to Mark, as casually as he could. "What's cooking?"

৽ ঞ

Frank and Moira were happy to be alone for an hour or two. The flight had been a little stressful, what with the horribly early start and the rude flight attendant who had refused to seat them together: "You're supposed to select your seats in advance, sir – that's the point." After that, a car journey in heat and traffic with Shona, who, for whatever reason, was in a snappy mood. All in all, they were glad of a moment or two's peace and quiet – a moment to remind themselves that they were actually on holiday.

"I wonder why David didn't come?" Neither had had the opportunity to discuss things yet.

"Could be anything. Work, perhaps."

"I think he and Shona've been fighting." Moira lay back on the bed, legs and arms outstretched, luxuriating in the size of it.

"Maybe. Though she said it was work, didn't she?"

"Yes, but you know what she can be like."

Frank began unpacking as Moira lay there, eyes half-closed, face half-lit by the sunlight streaming through the window.

"I'm sleepy!"

"I'm not surprised. It's been a long day already."

"And it's not even noon!"

She rolled over so that her head was closer to him by the wardrobe, her feet hanging off the other end. "I'm getting hungry."

"We're having lunch here, I think. That's what she said."

"Good. I don't want to go out. It's a bit rude though, don't you think? To not even say hello?"

"He's busy, Moira – that's all it is. After all, he does live here half the year – he's not on holiday. He's got work to take care of."

Frank's tone was a little sharper than he'd intended and he saw the fleeting look of hurt pass across his wife's face. He sat down on the bed, one of her dresses in his hands, and leaned down to kiss her.

"Sorry," he told her.

"Shona's mood's infected you."

"It hasn't. I won't let it. Promise. Let's just settle in and relax."

It was a loyal, sacrificial gesture on the part of his wife, Frank knew, to traipse out to David's villa again for another holiday. Moira longed to travel – longed to make better use of their annual trips and see new places – but the pull of fraternal reconciliation had taken priority and Frank loved her for it. She had been the one to push him to accept David's invitation. She had always been the one to keep their relationship alive. For Moira, an only child who had lost her parents young, family – siblings – were sacred. Nothing and no one should get in the way – not even a deep desire to see the world, to spend their hard-earned money on something far more enjoyable and rewarding. That belief in the bonds of family was what had made her an exceptional mother herself. And an exceptional wife. Not to mention a kind and tactful sister-in-law, for God knew neither Shona nor David were easy. And after more than 30 years, Frank was more grateful to Moira than ever.

He had never pretended that his relationship with David was good. It never had been, even when they were kids. Frank didn't quite know how it had happened that they should be so close in years, yet so far apart in temperament and psyche. There had been something implacable about David from the start – something restless and unappeasable. There was no line David wouldn't cross, it had seemed, and, looking back, Frank realised that it had only been when David had achieved authority of his own – when he set up his business and had people working for him – did he finally knock a little of the edge off himself and become slightly less volatile. No doubt his colleagues and business partners had borne the brunt, but Frank wouldn't know about that. When it came to their professional lives, neither brother had been entirely honest with the other.

"Perhaps I should just nip downstairs and see if everything's all right?"

Moira was getting restive. She hated tension, especially when it was not of her own making.

"I'd leave them for a little while. We'll go down in a bit. Relax – go on, lie down again. I'm nearly finished here."

Frank hung his summer suit up carefully. He'd been caught out the first year at the villa – they both had – by David and Shona's insistence that they eat out at expensive restaurants. Frank had had nothing suitable to wear with him, having to borrow something from David. Moira too, had brought an evening dress along – nothing too fancy, but enough so that she wouldn't stand out in public for being underdressed. Unfortunately for Moira that first trip, there had been no time to rush out and get something suitable, and of course, none of Shona's clothes would fit her. Shona stuck religiously to an exercise and beauty programme that kept her skinny as a rake. Moira, though by no means hefty, had allowed time to take its toll on her body and was a good few sizes larger.

"We could all look like that if we had nothing better to do than run around a park", she'd sniffed at Frank, humiliated by the experience. "But some of us have jobs, you know."

It was one of the only times he'd heard her complain about her in-laws, or even make the vaguest of references to the discrepancies in their lives, and he'd comforted her willingly. A lesser woman might have taken it worse than Moira – might really have made an issue of how successful David was in comparison to Frank – but Moira never did. Perhaps because she knew that success was relative, and that all the wealth in the world couldn't buy what she and Frank had together.

Although, if Moira wanted to, she could buy herself a new evening dress. Ten, if she really wanted. It was a source of great personal pride to Frank that he had always managed to provide for his family, for his wife and kids: that no matter what the circumstances or vicissitudes of life and work and the economy, he'd always put food on the table and a roof over their heads. They'd not gone without and though, granted, they may not have had much to flash about, they'd done well, kept things going, been able to hold their heads up and be counted. They both had comfortable pensions, Moira's from the school and his from the library, but better than that, they'd both been of the same mind when it came to savings and security. Both were frugal by nature, both were happy to put off the gratification of now for the happiness of later, and both had determined, early on, to save little and often for their twilight years. Years that were fast approaching. Sometimes it seemed remarkable to Frank that they were in their 50s. He didn't feel it when he woke, didn't really see it when he looked in the mirror or at his wife. It didn't feel real, somehow – he felt no different now than he had done 30 years ago – if anything, he felt more himself than ever. Yet here he was, decades of work behind him and only a decade or so ahead, fit and healthy and blessed with a happy marriage, loving, independent kids, and with a nice little nest egg to finally reward him.

He hadn't yet let on to Moira just how well they were doing – not that he was hiding it, only that he'd wanted to tell her the good news in a nice setting – walking along the beach, perhaps, before dinner. Their pensions aside, which would have seen them both through the years ahead, they also had the security of their house, the mortgage fully paid off as of a year ago. But aside from that – the house and the pensions – their little nest egg was building up very nicely indeed. Far more nicely than Frank had ever dreamed of. It had been the one good bit of advice his older brother had ever given, and perhaps the only bit of advice Frank had ever taken from him. David, who had been flying high with his company, taking advantage of the sudden demand for building work that European money had brought the country, had taken Frank out for a birthday lunch, more than two decades ago now. Though David had spent most of the meal boasting, a little nugget of valuable information had slipped out.

"I've got myself a financial advisor."

"What – an accountant?"

David had laughed at that, Frank remembered, though there had been little laughter in his eyes.

"No, brother dearest, not just an accountant – a professional investment advisor. Andrew Roberts, that's his name. He's good, by all accounts – went to business school in London. He tells me where to put my money. I tell you what, Frankie-boy, that man's going to teach me how to make a fortune, and no mistake."

"I see. So how much of your fortune d'you pay him, then?"

David could tell Frank was out to irritate him. Jealous, of course.

"He gets a commission, fair and square, when he sells me an investment product. But that's not the point, Frank. This guy, Andrew, there's nothing he doesn't know about getting your money working for you. After all, money doesn't just make itself, you know. Global equity funds, European property portfolios, mixed asset funds – he knows his stuff."

"What – investments and things?"

"And things?!" David had mocked him, as if they had been ten again. "Something like that. I tell you what, Frank, there's no limit to the amount you can make if you're canny. If you've got a nose for it. And good advice. Though to be honest, I reckon I'll have picked up most of what this guy's got to offer in another little while and then I'll really be laughing."

It had all gone over Frank's head at the time – the nuts and bolts of it. Once David had got started, there was no shutting him up, and Frank knew his brother was out to intimidate him. He'd refused to be riled, however. Instead, he'd just nodded mildly, interjecting here and there with the odd "that's nice", or "sounds interesting", visibly infuriating David. But upon leaving the lunch and returning to his little desk behind the library counter, his mind kept going over some of what David had said. Frank knew nothing about savings and investments – only that both he and Moira diligently put aside a little bit in their special account each week for a rainy day, and that they both had pensions – but the notion that your money could work for you if you had the right advice: that alone amongst David's ramblings seemed to make sense. And so, after long discussion with Moira, they made an appointment to see an investment advisor themselves.

"We can't afford to lose money", Moira had blurted out anxiously at the start of the meeting. Frank had squeezed her hand, feeling, as if by osmosis, her acute embarrassment. Heartened by his support, and with a quick glance in his direction to confirm it, she'd carried on. "And we need to be clear on the costs – all the costs. We're not millionaires, you know, and we don't pretend to be."

"Don't worry, Mrs. Davis. Why don't I talk you through some of the possibilities on offer and the costs involved?"

And thus had begun Frank and Moira's education in the world of investment. As with the conversation with David, a great deal of the language and terms had passed Frank by, but their advisor was patient and apparently happy to explain things over and over. He was a nice boy, Ian, fresh out of college by the looks of things, and very determined to make them feel relaxed and comfortable. They had been lucky with him, no mistake.

"So let me get this straight … we invest regularly in this global equity fund and our investment is spread across a wide range of companies?"

"That's right, Mrs. Davis. The advantage of a fund like this is that it's diverse and well spread – has a holding in some 1,800 companies across the globe, many different economies and sectors: declines and losses on any one particular company will be more than balanced by the returns from another, if you see what I mean. The point is, the risk of a permanent loss is hugely mitigated. Sure, there'll be ups and downs, but each time the market declines, you're buying more with your monthly savings at lower prices."

"And what kind of returns are we looking at here? Is it that much better than just saving in a high-interest account?"

"Let me put it this way. A high-interest bank account might earn you … what? 3%? 3.5% *per annum* at the most? The stock markets have delivered a 9% annual return for the past 100 years, Mr. Davis – not each year, but over time. Your job – my job – is to see you get those returns if they are available. After costs, of course, that could be 8% *per annum* to you and Mrs. Davis – a return that would still see you double your money in nine years. The key here is that you're willing to invest regularly and over a long period of time. Time and regularity are the winning elements. Markets fluctuate – I can't pretend they don't. But overall, over time, returns increase – you'll be doing a heck of a lot better than having your money just sitting in a savings account. So if you can commit, if you can hang in there, even when things seem rough, you'll be looking at quite a lump sum. Because – and this is rather nice, actually – everything improves in the end. It might not be a law of nature, but it is a law of the markets. And that's really the only assumption you have to make – that the global economy, global businesses and the global markets will continue to make upward progress over the next 15 to 20 years, which is the time frame we're looking at here. That's what they've done over the past century. That's the trend. There are no watertight guarantees I can make you, but what I can tell you with certainty, is that time is the friend of the owner of assets. And, of course, you can also save in cash deposits – some risk assets alongside assets with no risk."

Ian hadn't pressed them for a quick decision, and indeed, it took them some time to make up their minds. After long discussion and endless goings over of the potential risks and rewards, Frank and Moira began to regularly invest a portion of their earnings in a simple global equity fund. After a while, they just stopped thinking about it, trusting to the mysterious laws of the market. And now they had been rewarded for it.

Unlike David's lavish ways – throwing great wads of cash at whatever happened to be hot and pulling out just as fast – Frank and Moira had been pleased to note that their regular instalments, though not making them millionaires overnight, were earning better for them than they had realised in the early years. And now, Frank had had a phone call two days before they'd left for Spain – just an update, nothing special. But Frank hadn't looked at a statement for a while and, when his advisor casually mentioned the size of the nest egg they were now sitting on, he'd been amazed.

"Are you sure? Are you sure that's what it is? You've not added on a zero, or anything?"

Ian had laughed. Of late, he had been more used to clients asking him the opposite, worried that a zero or two was missing. He was no longer as fresh-faced as he'd been when Frank and Moira had first met him, not by a long shot. But he was pleased for Frank Davis. Though certainly not among his most glittering, exciting clients, Davis was a workhorse: slow and steady, modest and reliable. Twenty years the man and his wife had been making monthly payments into their portfolio, and there was another 10 years of investing to come, before they retired. Never once had they asked to go for something more fashionable or trendy, gamble a little more, make some miracles happen. No, Frank and his wife had been content to know that they were earning just a little better than they would have with a bank. And so it was a pleasure to tell the man – twice, three times, so strong was his disbelief – that he now had an investment worth over €250,000. That amounted to an 8.5% compound *per annum* return on the monies invested. Deposit interest rates had averaged only 3% over the same period. Frank and Moira were sitting on nearly €300,000. Nice and handy for retirement. Might even get a little villa of their own in Spain one day for that.

"Moira, love – there's something I'd like to – "

"Lunch! Downstairs!"

Shona's voice was shrill and sharp. Moira sat up quickly.

"What, Frank? What is it?"

He kissed her warmly. "Nothing at all. Nothing that can't wait."

∽ ∾

He'd had bad times before. Plenty of them. And he'd got through all right. No sweat. He'd get through again. 'Course he would. That's what he was about. That was who he was. No gain without loss, sometimes. No rewards without a certain amount of punishment. That was life, right? That was the way things worked. You aim high, you have to take a beating sometimes. All that trouble in the late 1980s, when things were really tough. He'd got through that, hadn't he? The foolish gamble on the Bulgarian hotel investment – okay, that had stung, but it hadn't killed him. He'd cut his losses, cut back for a while, and had gotten lucky on the deal in Poland. But this time …

"You really are looking ever so well." Moira was smiling at him. Vaguely, David seemed to recall she'd already said that to him at least twice during the course of lunch. What was he supposed to say in return? I see you've piled on a few more pounds, Moira, love. Might want to re-think that hairdo.

"Thanks."

"We've both been looking forward to seeing you, haven't we, Frank?"

"Yes. Very much. Lovely of you to have us again."

God. God. Have to think. Have to keep my head straight. Have to breathe. Have to think.

Frank and Moira were struggling. Neither Shona nor David would look at them – had looked at them since they'd sat down to lunch. A fight, then – they must be fighting. Unless they'd done something …? Frank could see Moira worrying about it as she ate her tapas, trying to conceal her hunger. Shona hadn't eaten a thing, and David was morosely engaged in pushing his food around his plate.

"So, David. What's been happening?" Frank kept his tone light, hoping that the innocuous question might break the ice a little.

"What do you mean?", David jumped down his throat. Frank was thrown. Moira shot him a worried look.

"Nothing! Only I was just wondering how you are, that's all. Work and everything. The kids." He looked at Shona, appealing for help, but none was forthcoming.

"I got a nice text from Grainne the other day." Grainne loved her Aunt Moira, and kept in regular touch. "She seems to be doing well."

"She'd want to be!" David suddenly burst out. "With all the faffing about she's been doing these past few years. Costing me a fortune, that girl is."

It was then that Frank realised something serious had happened to his brother – something to do with money. He watched as his brother pushed back from the table, rattling the plates and dishes with the force of his movement.

"Excuse me", David muttered, leaving the room.

Shona rose to follow, but for once, Frank pulled fraternal rank. "I'd leave him for a moment, if I were you", he told her, kindly. "I'd let him be a little while."

ॐ ॐ

If they were talking about him in the dining room, David couldn't hear it. Shut away in his study, the BBC blared out the news.

"… well, Sarah, the long awaited announcement of the purchase of Spencers Bank by the Dutch Ennobank has turned into a nightmare announcement for Spencers' shareholders. It appears that Ennobank had been in secret negotiations to buy Spencers for weeks now, just as the rumours had hinted at, only for Ennobank to back out at the last minute, when its review of Spencers' loan portfolio uncovered a potential black hole, revealing losses of Stg2 billion. An announcement from the Bank of England is due within the next hour as to whether they're planning an investigation, but already, market confidence has plummeted with the unexpected news and expectations that Spencers will need to raise fresh capital. Spencers' shares are down 50% .."

50%! They'd been down 30% when Mark had called him with the initial breaking news. A further 20% drop in the space of a few hours. How much further could they decline? He was down €1,000,000 already. He couldn't see straight, the sweat was running down into his eyes.

"Mark …what the hell?!"

"Calm down, David …"

"Where the hell did this come from?! Your lads sniffed the acquisition alright, just like everyone else in the market it appears but what about the black hole! How could you guys hear rumours about the acquisition but not know about a giant bloody hole in its balance sheet?!"

"Believe me, David, I'm as shocked as you are – all of us are. This was kept so under wraps …"

"I don't give a toss about that now. Just tell me what I need to do! Jesus – it's like a bloody circus out there!"

On David's television screen, swarms of media crews and reporters, national and international, were assembled outside Spencers' headquarters.

"Listen … calm down, David. You need to keep a clear head."

"Just tell me! I'm down €1,000,000 already! I should just wait this one out, right? I mean, it'll all blow over, no? This kind of thing must happen all the time." David's free fist clenched tight, his nails digging hard into his palm. The back of his shirt was sticking to him.

"It's not quite as simple as that." Mark's tone was brisk, efficient. There was no hint of humour. "You need to add more money to cover your margin; either that or you have to get out now – sell."

"What? What the hell are you talking about? More money? I've already got a million of my cash in the position!" David longed to break something, longed to smash his fist deep and hard into something – anything – to get himself out of his head, to quench the panic he was feeling, if only for a moment.

"You know the deal, David. You're in for €1,000,000 of your own, and €1,000,000 of the borrowing facility from the CFD account."

"Yeah, but why the hell do I need to put more money in?!"

"I've told you before, David, CFD account borrowings isn't like taking a mortgage out – if prices start falling, you've got to top up the margin …"

"What? You've never told me this before! Mark!"

"I have, David. I explained it at the start." There was a coldness to Mark's voice now.

"No you bloody didn't …"

"Oh yes, David. I did."

And even as David was about to reply, vague memories of a conversation drifted back to him, hazy with time and distance. That lunch – that celebratory lunch when he'd sold the business. "Sure, the CFD account borrowing facility can have its downsides – there's definitely a bit of added risk there – but I really wouldn't worry about it too much. Unless things go really crazy – which they very rarely do – there's nothing to think about." Nothing to think about. Except his life.

"Right now, David, with the loss on this trade, you need to add €500,000 to the account or sell in the market now."

"But hang on – just hang on one minute! You're telling me I have to put more money in and we don't even know if we'll see anything back yet?!"

"Look …we don't know what's coming. The investigation could throw up positive surprises. You're right, this could all blow over."

"Don't give me any of that wishy-washy bullshit, Mark. We don't know what the hell's going to happen. What are the analysts saying? How bad might bad be at Spencers?"

There was a pause on the end of the line. David, who had been pacing furiously, stopped in his tracks. Though the television was still on, all he could hear was Mark's silence. Dry mouthed, David broke it.

"Tell me."

"If things don't go our way, David … The view from our research team is that Spencers might need to raise significant capital to plug the gap – the trouble is, who will give it to them? Worst case scenario is that we could be looking at a government bailout and a much larger loss to come for shareholders."

Which would eliminate most of the capital I earned on the sale of my business. David was surprised at how calmly the thought rang in his head, as though the news of his potential ruin was nothing more important than the announcement of a train delay or bad weather when a picnic had been planned.

"You're down 50% as it stands. And government intervention would lead to another big drop. But that's not a given – not yet. Don't let's get ahead of ourselves."

David didn't leave his study for the remainder of the day. He ignored the pleas and then the wails of his wife; refused to answer Frank's reasonable request that he come out and talk. The hours passed, each minute containing within it a portion of the value David had put on his life. At last he knew what the abyss looked like: a cool, shadowy room, far from home, with technology beeping out its messages of doom.

The shares never rallied and an announcement later in the day that the government had decided to intervene with a sizeable cash injection of Stg£3 billion left the shares down 75%. David could not stump up the extra margin to hold on for any recovery. He sold his shares for a loss of €1,500,000. Bad luck – that was what it was. A piece of monumental bad luck. It happened. Of course, it happened. He was good at this, David. No one could have seen this coming. No one. Even Mark agreed – in fact, after their heated conversation had cooled and a couple of hours had passed, he couldn't have been more apologetic. He was going to go all out for David now, together they were going to find a sure thing and would have him restored within the week. Of course they would.

Of course.

ॐ ॐ

"Well – you'll take him a slice of cake. And at least tell him I was asking after him."

"We will of course. Thanks, Maureen. You're very good."

Frank and Moira gathered up their things. Though both claimed they visited their elderly neighbour of 30 years to keep an eye on her, give her a bit of company, both knew that the reasons for their almost daily visits were the other way around. Maureen O'Shea was like family to them and Frank and Moira took great comfort from her presence.

"And you keep your strength up – both of you. These are difficult times, my dears – difficult times."

Armed with the cake, they went home. It no longer felt odd to Frank to be bringing back treats for his brother, no longer felt as strange as it once had that his brother was part of his domestic life for the first time in nearly 40 years. For the crisis that had engulfed David Davis had thrown him back on his roots, in a way none of them had ever imagined.

When the first big loss had come to light that fateful Wednesday afternoon in Spain, neither Frank nor Moira had had any idea just how bad things would get. David, wan and pale, had made an appearance in the early evening, as Frank and Moira sat on the terrace, convinced that something terrible was happening between himself and Shona, certain that they'd walked into a major marital crisis. For Shona also had spent the afternoon locked away upstairs, all pretence of normality and good hostessing forgotten. Moira had been on the verge of suggesting that she and Frank get on the next flight home, when David appeared to tell them of the real situation.

The way he spoke of it, they didn't realise that it was merely the tip of an iceberg. He'd told them that he'd taken a big hit on the markets – far bigger than he'd intended – but that he'd work it out in no time. The words sounded comforting enough, but something about the exhaustion in David's face, the eyes that stared unfocused into the distance for too long, the delayed responses to questions, as if he were very far away, told Frank that his brother was in uncharted territory. When the next morning, David did not appear for breakfast, and Shona came down red-eyed and make-up free – the first time they had ever seen her in so natural a state – both Frank and Moira knew that something unstoppable, uncontrollable was happening, A force beyond them – beyond any of them – had taken hold, and was catapulting their nearest and dearest towards disaster.

What neither of them understood at the time was that the force came not from outside, but from within. Only later – weeks later – did it become clear that David, trying to repair the damage inflicted by the Spencer bank position, had continued to trade but then wiped out the remaining monies he had made from the business it had taken him years to build up. He was now in debt with no income. It had never been obvious, before, the nature of the activities David was engaged with – what it had been that had kept him so busy and preoccupied, so energetic, since selling his business. It was the sort of thing you saw in films or on TV, or read about in newspapers. It had never remotely occurred to Frank or Moira that what David was doing each day was laying himself on the line, taking chances on the whims of the markets, trying to second-guess fate. Oh, he might have had the best advice in the world, but there were some things in life no amount of good advice could foresee.

After the Spencers Bank debacle, David had gamely tried to trade his way back up, but something in the air had changed. Either his luck had run out, or his desperation had taken over, for everything he touched turned to shit. Superstition became David's goddess: strange little rituals and obsessive behaviours took the place of robust self-confidence and certainty. Never had it been so starkly clear to Frank that his brother – his successful, entrepreneurial brother: rebellious, hater of authority, unappeasable, implacable – had become nothing more than a desperate gambler, no matter how he might try to dress it up.

It was amazing how quickly a life could fall apart. Decades of work meant little in the face of collapse. A few months, that was all it took. Done and dusted, just like that. First, the villa had to be sold, and the yacht. Then the Spanish cars. Two of the three Irish cars. Determined to keep their house, Shona and David sold as many of their personal items as held any worth, but the juggernaut of debt rolled ever onwards, impervious to their wishes. Of course, they wouldn't get a fraction of what they'd paid for the place, but there would be something, at least. Just a little something to tide them over, until … None of them knew what 'until' might mean. Shona couldn't handle it and had fled to London, to the solace of her daughter's little bedsit. Grainne, at least, was relatively robust. She had a part-time job, and her college had taken pity on her and helped her get a grant. Rory was a different matter. Appalled by the overnight disappearance of the family's wealth, he'd thrown himself on the mercy of his playboy friends, and was keeping going for the moment, though it couldn't last much longer.

And David? What of David Davis, man of friends and connections, man of business and stature? Subject of gossip merchants and hushed conversations in the clubs and bars he used to frequent. A warning figure, a symbol of doom, an unlucky talisman. Those he knew before feared to come near him, lest he somehow taint them with his misfortune. Even in the depths of his misery, he understood it. The lucky ones – for that was how he thought of the majority of his contemporaries now – needed to feel that their success, their luck, was down to something special within them: that it was something to do with who they were, some unique quality, some blessed quirk of temperament or personality that protected them from the harm that had befallen David. He understood it. For he himself had never believed in God or fate or destiny, had always felt man built his own luck, forged his life in his own image. So, to discover, 50 years or so in to his life on earth, that he was not as he had thought: that he was a man who had courted disaster, that he was someone damaged and dysfunctional and cursed … It was a shock far greater than the loss of his fortune.

Though he was unable to do so at the time, David would later thank his younger brother for the firm and swift action that he took. Frank, for his part, would be eternally grateful only for the restoration of David to his whole self. For David's decline, when it came, had been the most frightening experience of Frank's life. The inaccessibility of David's pain, and the inability of anyone around him to get within, to come close to reawakening him to what he had, not what he had lost, was terrifying. Though it seemed like a drastic step, Frank had moved David in with him and Moira, tending to him closely for the first while, like a child.

Frank had never before felt the pleasure of fraternal protection. For he did feel protective towards David, in spite of all the recklessness that had led him to this point. It had come instinctively, as soon as David had laid bare the squalor of his situation. The over-borrowing. The speculating. The buzz of the deal, the buzz of the unknown, the thrill of winning, the endless phonecalls, the hunt for the next big thing. The cavalier investments made on a nod and a wink with cronies on the golf course. The reckless spending. The unheeded warnings and advice. But above all else, the belief. The blind, insane belief that because things were going well, they always would. Because everyone else was mad, madness was normal. That because he'd had some luck – more good than bad – he was a lucky man. Invincible. Infallible. Subject to different laws than the ordinary person. Had David's situation not been so grave, Frank would have scorned him. Everything he'd suspected about his brother's true nature: his hatred of authority, his sense of superiority – everything he'd resented yet worked so hard not to resent – had been true. And yet ... he was his brother.

Back home, David was asleep upstairs. Ever since he'd come to them, he'd spent a good portion of each day asleep, as if only there, only with them, could he get some respite, some real rest. It was healing, Frank knew – healing, restorative slumber – that would arm him just a little from the buffetings of the world outside. It kept him from giving in to despair, and above all else, Frank needed to protect him from that.

Downstairs in the kitchen, Moira started the supper while Frank sat at the table, idly shuffling the newspaper.

"I know what you're going to say."

Frank looked up, startled. He'd not said a word, nor indicated that he was about to. Even so, a thought had begun to formulate in his mind.

"I don't think we should, Frank. I really don't."

"Moira ..."

She wasn't looking at him. When she next spoke, he caught glimpses of her reflected in the kitchen window, standing, as she was, by the sink, peeling vegetables. There was a steeliness in her voice, her stance, that Frank had never encountered from her before.

"You know I asked him, don't you? I asked him, Frank. 'Why? Why did you do it? Why did you risk everything, over and over?' Because that's what he did, Frank. Oh, it started small enough – a bit of spare cash here and there, throw it out there, see what happens. But he had too much time on his hands, and as he got more successful, as some of his wild gambles paid off, he risked more and more. Everything he owned.

He never imagined it could all go wrong. But one wrong move, one turn of the markets that he hadn't anticipated, one announcement that didn't get made ... So I asked him. 'Why?' I said to him, 'What was the reason for it? Hadn't you enough to be satisfied with? Didn't you have more than enough?' And do you know what he said, Frank? Do you know how he answered me?"

Frank shook his head, mute. Moira turned to him, her eyes bright, almost feverish, with anger or excitement, he couldn't tell.

"He told me, 'I had no reason except to go on and on. Doing it became its own reason. In the end, there was no point to it at all. It was pointless. Utterly pointless.'"

Frank gazed at her, uncertain. In a gentler tone, she continued:

"That's what's dangerous, Frank. Not David himself, not what he might yet do, but that need inside him. That's what we must beware of, that's what we mustn't indulge, however much we're tempted. We've spent our lives, Frank. Our lives. We will feed him and clothe him and love him and support him, but we will not trust him with our money."

She was right, of course. She, who had urged him all these years to keep things sweet with his brother, not to cut him off, not to rise to the petty taunts and upsets he created.

And so it was, that Frank and Moira helped David in every way they could as he looked for a job and sought to find a new home, but refused to let him know of their nest egg, quietly growing, taking the odd knock, but not letting them down. And some years later, when David was more or less back on his feet and in need of some respite, Moira and Frank would invite him out each summer, to vacation in their villa in the sun.

COMMENTS ON 'A VILLA IN THE SUN'

Virginia Gilbert has expertly captured the difference between investing and speculating and the emotional drive behind that search for quick profits. The stock markets are open all day, they are highly liquid, and give the impression that activity is good, or that without constant activity you cannot get the returns. Of course, nothing is further from reality. For many reasons, the markets fulfil the gambling instincts in human nature. David Davis fell right into the trap of thinking he could make money on hunches, a quiet word from a supposedly knowledgeable broker and speed. No doubt, many readers will recognise these traits – in others, if not in themselves.

David Davis had spent a lifetime building up his business but, for some reason, he thought he could take short cuts in the markets. If it was trading markets as opposed to investing that he was interested in, then he should have knuckled down to find out how to trade and control risk. Although this book is not about trading markets, what I do know is that trading is a damn sight more difficult than investing. Trading demands greater discipline, greater control over your emotions and the will to find and learn an approach to trading that can add value.

David, of course, got the buzz from trading and fooled himself for long enough that it was skill: that, in some way, he or Mark had an edge on the market. In reality, all David had achieved was to have taken more risk than the market. And like any area of life, excessive risk has a habit of flooring you just when you are at your most confident. David grew so confident that he put his entire assets into one deal. It may seem an extreme example but which reader will call it unrealistic, after the shocking events of 2008 when household banking names went bust?

Poor old Frank and Moira are labelled as the bores and I suppose that is the way investment is viewed. But their steady regular investment programme did the job it was supposed to do – and as it most likely always will. They did not try to overreach, and their more realistic expectations were achieved despite, as they said themselves, a few declines and bumps in the road along the way. When you buy a property, there is not much else to do but to wait for it to appreciate in time (assuming a fair price has been paid for it at the outset). So ask yourself why you should demand more activity when you invest through the stock markets?

APPENDIX 1
STOCK MARKET VALUATION TERMINOLOGY

In an interview for a job as an accountant, when asked what 2 plus 2 was, the first applicant answered "4", the second "22" and the third said "what number would you like it to be?" As the joke goes, the third applicant got the job. Accounting is not an exact science and interpretation of what is true and fair at times may need a subjective interpretation.

Thankfully, to benefit from the defined stock picking approach outlined in **Chapter 21, Enhancing Returns: Value Investing in the FTSE 100 Index** does not require you to be an expert in terminology. Becoming expert in understanding how to value a business is complex and best left to experts. But demystifying some key valuation terminology can help boost confidence and reduce the fear factor, which is my aim in this appendix.

DETERMINING VALUE

Price-to-earnings Ratio

When you buy a share in a business there are several ways of determining the value of what you are buying. You can compare the share price to the earnings, in which case you can express the value as the number of times you are paying for the earnings. This is referred to as the price-to-earnings ratio (or P/E ratio). A company with a market capitalisation (or market value) of €100 million and after-tax earnings of €10 million is said to be trading on a price-to-earnings ratio of 10 (100 / 10 = 10). Alternatively, you can express the earnings of the company relative to its market value as a yield. In this case, €10 million of earnings represents 10% of €100 million, so the earnings yield is 10% (10 / 100 expressed as a percentage).

Price-to-cash flow Ratio

Likewise, you can compare the price you are paying for a company to the annual cash flows it is generating. Continuing the example, assume the company earned €10 million but generated cash flows of €9 million. A company with a market value of €100 million and cash flows of €9 million is said to be trading on a price-to-cash flow ratio of 11.1 (100 / 9 = 11.1). Alternatively, you can express the cash flow that the company is generating relative to its market value as a yield. In this case, €9 million of cash flows represents 9% of €100 million, so the cash flow yield is 9% (9 / 100 expressed as a percentage).

Dividend Yield

Dividends are paid out of earnings and cash flows and are not the full value that resides within a company. Nonetheless, dividends are real (and sometimes more real than earnings) and also can be compared to the price you are paying for the business. In this case, assume the company pays out a dividend of €5 million from its earnings of €10 million. As the business is valued at €100 million, the dividend represents a 5% return on the €100 million valuation. In stock market terminology, the dividend yield is 5%.

Price per Share (the Share Price)

It is convention in the stock market to look at everything on a per share basis. In this example, the company's market value is €100 million. But, as it has 50 million shares in issue, each share is worth €2. Said another way, the price per share is €2.

Since convention talks about a 'price per share' (or share price), then to compare earnings, cash flows and dividends to the price you are paying, you must compute the earnings per share, cash flow per share and dividend per share.

With 50 million shares in issue, earnings of €10 million translate into earnings per share of 20c (€10 million / 50 million shares). Now the share price can be compared to the earnings per share (EPS) to give a price-to-earnings ratio of 10 (200c / 20c = 10) or an earnings yield of 10% (20 / 200*100 = 10%).

On the same basis, the dividend of €5 million works out as 10c a share, and when compared to the share price of 200c (or €2), the dividend yield is still 5%.

CASE STUDY: CRH PLC

CRH plc is a member of the FTSE 100 Index, and is separately quoted on the Irish Stock Exchange (ISEQ). The group also has ADR shares (American Depository Receipts) listed on the New York Stock Exchange.

Chart A.1 displays a chart for CRH plc, the Irish-based global building materials group (Cement Roadstone Holdings plc). On the right-hand scale is CRH's share price, or price per share, and on the left-hand scale is CRH's earnings per share (the lighter shaded bars) and cash flow per share (the darker bars). The chart shows this information for CRH from 1988 to 2010 inclusive, a 23-year period.

Chart A.1: CRH plc: Earnings, Cash flows and Price (1988-2010)

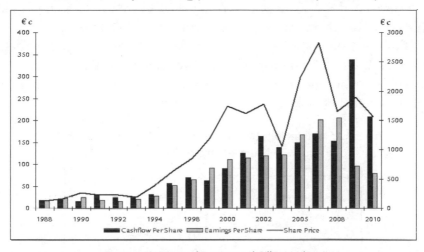

Source: CRH *Annual Reports* and GillenMarkets.

It is fairly obvious from the chart that CRH's earnings (EPS) have grown steadily over time and that CRH's cash flows have grown similarly.

It is worth remembering that earnings are an accounting concept, whereas cash is the fact. While growth in earnings highlights a company making good progress, it is important that those earnings are converted to cash, as it is cash that pays the bills, taxes and dividends. Earnings that are not eventually matched by cash flows are suspect earnings and perhaps not real. But determining this is complex, and not the subject of this book. The only point I make here is that, in CRH's case, it is obvious that reported earnings have been matched by cash flows, not in each year, but over time.

A publicly-quoted company like CRH usually pays a dividend to shareholders. These dividends are paid from earnings and cash flows. The remaining earnings and cash flows are retained in the business to fund growth, which should be reflected in a higher share price (capital gains) over time. Hence, the full value of the business is determined by the earnings and cash flows, and not simply from dividends.

The second important point to note from **Chart A.1** is that where earnings and cash flows go, the share price eventually follows. In CRH's case, its share price has moved up over time to reflect the growth in its earnings and cash flows. Of course, following the global credit crisis of 2007-2009, construction activity remains subdued in the major developed economies where CRH operates. This has impacted both its earnings and cash flows and the share price has followed them down. At times like this, a solid dividend yield can be a useful indicator of value.

Table A.1 outlines the valuation calculations using aggregate data, whereas **Table A.2** outlines the same valuation calculations on a per share basis, which is more normal practice. You will notice that the value calculations in both tables provide the same answers.

Table A.1: Terminology Case Study: CRH plc (31 December 2010): Using Aggregate Data

Share Price	1565c	
No. of shares in issue (m)	718	
Earnings (m)	€574	
Cash flows (m)	€1,501	
Dividends (m)	€449	
Valuation Metrics		
Market Capitalisation (m)	€11,236	(€15.65 * 718m)
Price-to-earnings Ratio	19.6	(11,236 / 574)
Earnings Yield	5.1%	(574 / 11,236*100)
Price-to-cash flow Ratio	7.5	(11,236 / 1,501)
Cash flow Yield	13.3%	(1,501 / 11,236*100)
Dividend Yield	4.0%	(449 / 11,236*100)

Note: (m) equals millions.

**Table A.2: Terminology Case Study: CRH plc (31 December 2010):
Using Per Share Data**

Share Price	1565c	
No. of shares in issue (m)	718	
Earnings (m)	€574	
Cash flows (m)	€1,501	
Dividends (m)	€449	
Per Share Values		
Earnings per share	80c	(574 / 718*100)
Cash flow per share	209c	(1,501 / 718*100)
Dividend per share	62.5c	(449 / 718*100)
Price per share	1565c	(€11,236m / 718)
Valuation Metrics		
Price-to-earnings Ratio	19.6	(1565 / 80)
Earnings Yield	5.1%	(80 / 1565*100)
Price-to-cash flow Ratio	7.5	(1565 / 209)
Cash flow Yield	13.3%	(209 / 1565*100)
Dividend Yield	4.0%	(62.5 / 1565*100)

Note: (m) equals millions.

Market Capitalisation or Market Value

The value of a company like CRH in the marketplace is the number of shares it has in issue, multiplied by its share price on any given day. At 31 December 2010, CRH's share price was 1565c (€15.65) and it had 718 million shares in issue at that time. If you could have bought all of its shares at that price, you would have paid €11,236 million (€11.2 billion). Hence, we can say that this was CRH's market capitalisation (or market value) at that time.

Price-to-earnings Ratio (P/E Ratio)

At any point in time along **Chart A.1**, an investor could ask what he had to pay for CRH's shares. At 31 December 2010, CRH reported earnings per share of 80c. Compared to CRH's then share price of 1565c, an investor was paying 19.6 times earnings (1565 / 80 = 19.6). In other words, the price-to-earnings ratio was 19.6.

Earnings Yield

Similarly, an investor could compare the earnings to the price – in other words, buying 80c of earnings for a 1565c outlay is equivalent to an earnings yield of 5.1% (80 / 1565 x 100).

Price-to-cash flow Ratio

CRH generated cash flows[35] of 209c per share from its operations in 2010. If you bought CRH shares at 31 December 2010, you were paying 7.5 times cash flows (1565 / 209 = 7.5) – the price-to-cash flow ratio.

Dividend Yield

In 2010, CRH paid a dividend of 62.5c per share out of its 80c of earnings or 209c of cash flows. If you had bought the shares for 1565c at the end of 2010, the shares were offering you a dividend yield of 4.0% (62.5 / 1565 x 100) at the time of purchase.

SUMMARY

Hence, when you buy a share, it is a relatively simple matter to compare the price you are paying to the company's earnings, cash flows or dividend per share. The company's *Annual Report* provides you with the historical earnings and dividend per share data. With the earnings per share, you have to adjust for profit or losses on non-recurring items. Thankfully, this figure is normally outlined somewhere in the Chairman's or Directors' report. The cash flow per share figure is harder to determine. Forecast data normally can be obtained from a full-service stockbroker if you are dealing with one (as opposed to an online stockbroker). I believe the above provides you with sufficient knowledge on terminology to remove the fear factor, and allow you to follow the investment approach for selecting stocks in the FTSE 100 Index outlined in **Chapter 21**.

The good news is that it is not necessary that you know the right price-to-earnings ratio to pay or dividend yield to receive for a given stock. As you will see in **Chapter 21,** it is much more straightforward than that.

---

[35] Defined as operational cash flows (including associated income) less interest and taxes and before capital expenditure, divided by the average number of shares in issue in the year.

APPENDIX 2
GUARANTEED STRUCTURED PRODUCTS

Guaranteed investment (or structured) products are not a separate asset class. But their popularity has increased substantially in the past few years (certainly in Ireland) in response to investors' increased awareness of the threat of capital destruction following the global credit crisis in 2008 and Eurozone sovereign debt crisis in 2011. For this reason, they are worth commenting on.

Guaranteed investment products offer the investor capital protection and the opportunity to benefit from a portion of the upside in risk assets. The capital guarantee can cover all of your investment or a percentage of it, normally ranging from 80% to 100%. The guarantee is for a set period, which results in most guaranteed investment products having a defined lifespan ranging from three to five years. They might seem like the ideal product choice for the conservative investor but, in my view, guaranteed structured products carry serious deficiencies and they are most certainly not the Holy Grail of investing.

After a painful decade for both equity and property investors in the 2000s, the idea that you can invest in a risk-asset fund with the prospect of much higher than cash deposit returns, and where the downside is limited via a guarantee, has significant attractions. For the investor, a guaranteed product appears to offer equity-like returns without the risk. But, in perhaps four out of five occasions, the upside is likely to prove illusory, because most of the time markets range with an upward bias, and the high costs within guaranteed products weigh too heavily on the normal returns available.

Without too much of a stretch, one can estimate the aggregate costs within a guaranteed product to be *circa* 2% to 3% *per annum*, to pay for the guarantee and product manufacturing and selling costs. My own estimates suggests that global stock markets are currently priced for annual returns of *circa* 6% to 8% over the next 10 years, and losing 2% to 3% annually to costs seriously handicaps the purchaser of these products. The conclusion that I have come to is that guaranteed investment products reward the seller, not the investor!

Instead of looking for a guarantee, investors might instead consider putting 50% of their intended investment into cash deposits earning interest, and the other 50% into a global equity exchange-traded fund. If the world stock markets decline by, say, 20% over the same four to five-year timeline as the alternative guaranteed product, the investor's equity investment will be down 20%. Overall however, the investor is down only 10% in capital terms, when you factor in that half the monies were in cash deposits. Indeed, the interest earned and dividends received possibly will eliminate the loss entirely over a four to five-year period. In addition, the investor will participate in 50% of any upside in equity markets, as well as still owning the investment at the end of the period. In other words, guaranteed investment products serve no useful purpose most of the time, other than to pander to investors' fears and reward the sellers of these products.

APPENDIX 3
CALCULATING THE 30- & 50-WEEK MOVING AVERAGES

FTSE ALLSHARE INDEX SPREADSHEET EXAMPLE

Date	FTSE ALL SHARE Price Index	30-Week Moving Average	50-Week Moving Average
29-Jan-10	2660		
05-Feb-10	2597		
12-Feb-10	2633		
19-Feb-10	2742		
26-Feb-10	2737		
05-Mar-10	2861		
12-Mar-10	2879		
19-Mar-10	2892		
26-Mar-10	2923		
02-Apr-10	2944		
09-Apr-10	2962		
16-Apr-10	2950		
23-Apr-10	2946		
30-Apr-10	2863		
07-May-10	2640		
14-May-10	2722		
21-May-10	2611		
28-May-10	2673		
04-Jun-10	2645		
11-Jun-10	2663		
18-Jun-10	2712		
25-Jun-10	2609		

Date	FTSE ALL SHARE Price Index	30-Week Moving Average	50-Week Moving Average
02-Jul-10	2505		
09-Jul-10	2653		
16-Jul-10	2665		
23-Jul-10	2744		
30-Jul-10	2715		
06-Aug-10	2754		
13-Aug-10	2717		
20-Aug-10	2681	2743.3	
27-Aug-10	2684	2744.1	
03-Sep-10	2800	2750.8	
10-Sep-10	2840	2757.7	
17-Sep-10	2845	2761.2	
25-Sep-10	2889	2766.2	
01-Oct-10	2890	2767.2	
08-Oct-10	2924	2768.7	
15-Oct-10	2948	2770.6	
22-Oct-10	2967	2772.0	
29-Oct-10	2936	2771.8	
05-Nov-10	3033	2774.1	
12-Nov-10	2990	2775.5	
19-Nov-10	2960	2775.9	
26-Nov-10	2931	2778.2	
03-Dec-10	2975	2789.4	
10-Dec-10	3012	2799.0	
17-Dec-10	3044	2813.5	
24-Dec-10	3108	2828.0	
31-Dec-10	3063	2841.9	
07-Jan-11	3104	2856.6	
14-Jan-11	3115	2870.0	2833.9
21-Jan-11	3061	2885.1	2843.2
28-Jan-11	3055	2903.4	2851.6
04-Feb-11	3110	2918.7	2859.0
11-Feb-11	3144	2934.6	2867.1
18-Feb-11	3154	2948.3	2873.0
25-Feb-11	3109	2961.4	2877.6

Average of the 30 weeks from 29 Jan 2010 to 20 Aug 2010

Average of the 50 weeks from 29 Jan 2010 to 14 Jan 2011

Date	FTSE ALL SHARE Price Index	30-Week Moving Average	50-Week Moving Average
04-Mar-11	3109	2973.3	2881.9
11-Mar-11	3026	2983.6	2884.0
18-Mar-11	2974	2993.3	2884.6
25-Mar-11	3066	3006.1	2886.7
01-Apr-11	3117	3016.6	2890.0
08-Apr-11	3138	3026.6	2893.9
15-Apr-11	3110	3035.4	2898.8
22-Apr-11	3122	3043.2	2908.4
29-Apr-11	3155	3052.0	2917.1
06-May-11	3110	3058.2	2927.1
13-May-11	3091	3063.0	2935.4
20-May-11	3100	3067.4	2944.5
27-May-11	3095	3072.7	2953.2

APPENDIX 4
CREATING YOUR OWN COPPOCK INDICATOR TEMPLATE

For the index of your choice, the following guidelines should allow you to create your own Coppock Indicator. The next page has the actual calculations for the FTSE AllShare Index leading up to the 'Buy' signal at the end of May 2009.

1. In Columns 1 & 2, note the end of month date and value for the previous 14 months.
2. In Column 3, note the index value for 14 months ago. In Column 4, express that difference as a percentage.
3. In Column 5, note the index value for 11 months ago. In Column 6, express that difference as a percentage.
4. In Column 7, add the 14- and 11-month percentage differences together.
5. In Column 8, multiply Column 7 by 10.
6. In Column 9, drop down a month and multiply Column 7 by 9.
7. In Column 10, drop down a month and multiply Column 7 by 8.
8. And so on – in each successive Column, drop down a month and multiply by one less until you come to Column 18.
9. In Column 18, sum Columns 8 to 17.
10. In Column 19, divide Column 18 by 10.
11. After point 10, you have a weighted average of the end of month data stretching back 24 months.
12. Only readings that have a value for each of the Columns 8 to 17 are included in the series.
13. Now plot the series on a chart (optional).
14. The indicator provides a buy signal when it dips below zero and then gives a less negative reading.

FTSE ALLSHARE COPPOCK SPREADSHEET EXAMPLE

1	2	3 14 mths	4 % change	5 11 mths	6 % change	7 Add 2 +4	8 Col 7 x 10	9 Col 7 (-1 mth) x 9	10 Col 7 (-2 mths) x 8	11 Col 7 (-3 mths) x 7	12 Col 7 (-4 mths) x 6	13 Col 7 (-5 mths) x 5	14 Col 7 (-6 mths) x 4	15 Col 7 (-7 mths) x 3	16 Col 7 (-8 mths) x 2	17 Col 7 (-9 mths) x 1	18 Sum Col 8-17	19 Divide Col 18 by 10
30/11/2005	2,741																	
31/12/2005	2,847																	
31/01/2006	2,928																	
28/02/2006	2,956																	
31/03/206	3,048																	
30/04/2006	3,074																	
31/05/2006	2,917																	
30/06/2006	2,968																	
31/07/2006	3,004																	
31/08/2006	3,008																	
30/09/2006	3,050																	
31/10/2006	3,140			2,741	14.6	14.6	145.6											
31/11/2006	3,119			2,847	9.6	9.6	95.5	131.0										
31/12/2006	3,221			2,928	10.0	10.0	100.1	86.0	116.5									
31/01/2007	3,251	2,741	18.6	2,956	10.0	28.6	285.9	90.1	76.4	101.9								
28/02/2007	3,169	2,847	11.3	3,048	4.0	15.3	152.8	257.3	80.1	66.9	87.3							
31/03/2007	3,289	2,928	12.3	3,074	7.0	19.3	193.2	137.5	228.7	70.0	57.3	72.8						
30/04/2007	3,342	2,956	13.1	2,917	14.6	27.6	276.3	173.9	122.2	200.1	60.0	47.8	58.2					

1	2	3	4	5	6	7	8	9	10	11	12	13	14	15	16	17	18	19
		14 mths	% change	11 mths	% change	Add 2 +4	Col 7 x 10	Col 7 (-1 mth) x 9	Col 7 (-2 mths) x 8	Col 7 (-3 mths) x 7	Col 7 (-4 mths) x 6	Col 7 (-5 mths) x 5	Col 7 (-6 mths) x 4	Col 7 (-7 mths) x 3	Col 7 (-8 mths) x 2	Col 7 (-9 mths) x 1	Sum Col 8-17	Divide Col 18 by 10
31/05/2007	3,466	3,048	13.7	2,968	16.8	30.5	304.9	248.7	154.6	107.0	171.5	50.0	38.2	43.7				
30/06/2007	3,397	3,074	10.5	3,004	13.1	23.6	235.9	274.4	221.0	135.3	91.7	142.9	40.0	28.7	29.1			
31/07/2007	3,235	2,917	10.9	3,008	7.5	18.4	184.5	212.3	243.9	193.4	115.9	76.4	114.3	30.0	19.1	14.6	1,204	120.4
31/08/2007	3,268	2,968	10.1	3,050	7.1	17.3	172.6	166.0	188.7	213.5	165.8	96.6	61.1	85.8	20.0	9.6	1,180	118.0
30/09/2007	3,335	3,004	11.0	3,140	6.2	17.2	172.3	155.3	147.6	165.1	183.0	138.1	77.3	45.8	57.2	10.0	1,152	115.2
31/10/2007	3,389	3,008	12.7	3,119	8.7	21.3	213.2	155.1	138.0	129.1	141.5	152.5	110.5	58.0	30.6	28.6	1,157	115.7
30/11/2007	3,281	3,050	7.6	3,221	1.9	9.4	94.4	191.9	137.8	120.8	110.7	118.0	122.0	82.9	38.6	15.3	1,032	103.2
31/12/2007	3,287	3,140	4.7	3,251	1.1	5.8	57.9	84.9	170.6	120.6	103.5	92.2	94.4	91.5	55.3	19.3	890	89.0
31/01/2008	3,001	3,119	-3.8	3,169	-5.3	-9.1	-90.8	52.1	75.5	149.3	103.4	86.3	73.8	70.8	61.0	27.6	609	60.9
29/02/2008	3,013	3,221	-6.5	3,289	-8.4	-14.8	-148.5	-81.8	46.3	66.1	127.9	86.1	69.0	55.3	47.2	30.5	298	29.8
31/03/2008	2,927	3,251	-10.0	3,342	-12.4	-22.4	-223.8	-133.6	-72.7	40.5	56.6	106.6	68.9	51.8	36.9	23.6	-45	-4.5
30/04/2008	3,100	3,169	-2.2	3,466	-10.6	-12.7	-127.4	-201.5	-118.8	-63.6	34.7	47.2	85.3	51.7	34.5	18.4	-239	-23.9
31/05/2008	3,082	3,289	-6.3	3,397	-9.3	-15.6	-155.7	-114.6	-179.1	-103.9	-54.5	28.9	37.7	64.0	34.5	17.3	-425	-42.5
30/06/2008	2,855	3,342	-14.6	3,235	-11.7	-26.3	-263.2	-140.1	-101.9	-156.7	-89.1	-45.4	23.2	28.3	42.6	17.2	-685	-68.5
31/07/2008	2,749	3,466	-20.7	3,268	-15.9	-36.6	-365.7	-236.9	-124.5	-89.2	-134.3	-74.2	-36.3	17.4	18.9	21.3	-1,004	-100.4
31/08/2008	2,869	3,397	-15.5	3,335	-14.0	-29.5	-295.2	-329.1	-210.5	-109.0	-76.4	-111.9	-59.4	-27.3	11.6	9.4	-1,198	-119.8
30/09/2008	2,484	3,235	-23.2	3,389	-26.7	-49.9	-499.2	-265.6	-292.5	-184.2	-93.4	-63.7	-89.5	-44.5	-18.2	5.8	-1,545	-154.5
31/10/2008	2,183	3,268	-33.2	3,281	-33.5	-66.7	-666.7	-449.3	-236.1	-256.0	-157.9	-77.8	-50.9	-67.2	-29.7	-9.1	-2,001	-200.1
30/11/2008	2,133	3,335	-36.0	3,287	-35.1	-71.1	-711.5	-600.0	-399.4	-206.6	-219.4	-131.6	-62.3	-38.2	-44.8	-14.8	-2,429	-242.9
31/12/2008	2,209	3,389	-34.8	3,001	-26.4	-61.2	-612.1	-640.3	-533.3	-349.4	-177.1	-182.8	-105.3	-46.7	-25.5	-22.4	-2,695	-269.5

1	2	3	4	5	6	7	8	9	10	11	12	13	14	15	16	17	18	19
		14 mths	% change	11 mths	% change	Add 2 +4	Col 7 x 10	Col 7 (-1 mth) x 9	Col 7 (-2 mths) x 8	Col 7 (-3 mths) x 7	Col 7 (-4 mths) x 6	Col 7 (-5 mths) x 5	Col 7 (-6 mths) x 4	Col 7 (-7 mths) x 3	Col 7 (-8 mths) x 2	Col 7 (-9 mths) x 1	Sum Col 8-17	Divide Col 18 by 10
31/01/2009	2,079	3,281	-36.6	3,013	-31.0	-67.6	-676.3	-550.9	-569.2	-466.7	-299.5	-147.6	-146.3	-79.0	-31.1	-12.7	-2,979	-297.9
27/02/2009	1,930	3,287	-41.3	2,927	-34.0	-75.3	-753.5	-608.7	-489.7	-498.0	-400.0	-249.6	-118.1	-109.7	-52.6	-15.6	-3,295	-329.5
31/03/2009	1,984	3,001	-33.9	3,100	-36.0	-69.9	-698.9	-678.1	-541.1	-428.5	-426.9	-333.3	-199.7	-88.5	-73.1	-26.3	-3,494	-349.4
30/04/2009	2,173	3,013	-27.9	3,082	-29.5	-57.4	-573.7	-629.0	-602.8	-473.4	-367.3	-355.7	-266.7	-149.8	-59.0	-36.6	-3,514	-351.4
31/05/2009	2,253	2,927	-23.0	2,855	-21.1	-44.1	-641.1	-516.4	-559.1	-527.4	-405.8	-306.0	-284.6	-200.0	-99.8	-29.5	-3,370	-337.0

BUY SIGNAL

A less negative reading

APPENDIX 5
RECOMMENDED READING

VALUE INVESTING

Dreman, D. (1998). *Contrarian Investment Strategies: The Next Generation*, Parsipanny, NJ: Simon & Schuster.

Graham, B. (1973). *The Intelligent Investor*, 4th edition, New York: Harper Row.

Greenblatt, J. (2010). *The Little Book That Still Beats the Markets*, revised edition (original, 2006), Hoboken, NJ: John Wiley & Son.

Lee, K. (1998). *Trouncing The DOW*, New York: McGraw-Hill.

Montier J. (2009). *Value Investing: Tools and Techniques for Intelligent Investors*, Hoboken, NJ: John Wiley & Son.

O'Higgins, M. (2000). *Dogs of the Dow*, 2nd edition, New York: HarperCollins.

Wright, K. (2010). *Dividends Still Don't Lie*, Hoboken, NJ: John Wiley & Son.

GROWTH STOCK INVESTING

Fisher, P.A. (1984). *Common Stocks and Uncommon Profits*, revised edition, Seattle, WA: Pacific Publishing Company Ltd.

Hagstrom, R. (1995). *The Warren Buffett Way*, Hoboken, NJ: John Wiley & Son.

Slater, J. (1996). *Beyond The Zulu Principle*, London: Orion.

Slater, J. (2008). *The Zulu Principle*, revised edition (original, 1992: Orion), Petersfield, Hamps.: Harriman House.

TRADING / SPECULATING

Faith, C. (2007). *Way Of The Turtle*, New York: McGraw-Hill.

Lefevre, E. (1993). *Reminiscences of a Stock Operator*, revised edition (original 1923), Hoboken, NJ: John Wiley & Son.

TECHNICAL ANALYSIS

Marber, B. (2007). *Marber on Markets*, London: Harriman House.

Schannep, J. (2008). *Dow Theory for the 21st Century*, Hoboken, NJ: John Wiley & Son.

Shipman, M. (2008). *Big Money, Little Effort*, London: Kogan Page Ltd.

HEDGE FUND INDUSTRY

Einhorn, D. (2008). *Fooling Some of the Investors All of the Time*, Hoboken, NJ: John Wiley & Sons.

Lack, S. (2012). *The Hedge Fund Mirage*, Hoboken, NJ: John Wiley & Sons.

OTHERS

Marks, H. (2011). *The Most Important Thing*, New York: Columbia University Press.

O'Shaughnessy, J.P. (1994). *Invest Like The Best*, New York: McGraw-Hill.

O'Shaughnessy, J.P. (1997). *What Works on Wall Street*, New York: McGraw-Hill.

CHARTS

FIGURES

TABLES

INDEX

ABOUT THE AUTHOR

RORY GILLEN is the founder of GillenMarkets, a website that provides vital information and insights for people who wish to manage their own investments. He was a co-founder of Dublin-based stockbroking, corporate finance and funds management group, Merrion Capital, where he was head of institutional research. He left Merrion Capital in 2009 to establish GillenMarkets. He is a Chartered Accountant and lives in Greystones, County Wicklow in Ireland with his wife and three children.

OAK TREE PRESS

Oak Tree Press develops and delivers information, advice and resources for entrepreneurs and managers. It is Ireland's leading business book publisher, with an unrivalled reputation for quality titles across business, management, HR, law, marketing and enterprise topics.

NuBooks is its recently-launched imprint, publishing short, focused ebooks for busy entrepreneurs and managers.

In addition, through its founder and managing director, Brian O'Kane, Oak Tree Press occupies a unique position in start-up and small business support in Ireland through its standard-setting titles, as well as training courses, mentoring and advisory services.

Oak Tree Press is comfortable across a range of communication media – print, web and training, focusing always on the effective communication of business information.

Oak Tree Press, 19 Rutland Street, Cork, Ireland.

T: + 353 21 4313855 F: + 353 21 4313496.

E: info@oaktreepress.com W: www.oaktreepress.com.